PELAGIUS

AMS PRESS

NEW YORK

PELAGIUS

A Historical and Theological Study

By

JOHN FERGUSON, M.A.(Cantab.), B.D.(London)

Professor of Classics, University College, Ibadan.

Awarded the Kaye Prize in the
University of Cambridge, 1952

CAMBRIDGE:
W. HEFFER & SONS LTD.
1956

Library of Congress Cataloging in Publication Data

Ferguson, John, 1921-
    Pelagius: a historical and theological study.

    Reprint of the 1956 ed. published by W. Heffer,
Cambridge, Eng.
    "The writings of Pelagius": p.
    Bibliography: p.
    Includes indexes.
    1. Pelagius. 2. Pelagianism.
[BT1450.F4   1978]   273'.5   77-84700
ISBN 0-404-16107-3

From the edition of 1956, Cambridge, England
First AMS edition published in 1978

Manufactured in the United States of America

AMS PRESS, INC.
NEW YORK, N.Y.

IN
PIAM
MEMORIAM
A.F.

PREFACE

This dissertation was awarded the Kaye Prize in the University of Cambridge in 1952 and by the conditions of that award is here published as it was then presented, except that one chapter has, on the recommendation of the adjudicators, been omitted. I would like to express my gratitude to Dr. Newton Flew and Prof. G. B. A. Fletcher for their encouragement in various ways, to my wife for the meticulous care she has extended to the index, to Miss Norah Saxelby for undertaking the typing and Miss Barbara Cooper for helping with the proof-reading, and to Messrs. W. Heffer and Sons Ltd. for the skill and accuracy with which they have prepared the book for production.

J. F.

CONTENTS

I

THE SITUATION OF THE STATE

THE fourth century of our era saw the Roman Empire battered. The imposing edifice which Augustus had constructed out of two generations of civil strife was tottering to its fall. Already in the third century the writing was appearing on the wall. In 240 the barbarians, who had been kept back during the reign of Caracalla by a costly system of bribes and subsidies, broke through the defences on all sides. In the West they crossed the Rhine and poured into France and Switzerland, and the coast of Spain suffered from their raids. In the North East the Goths swept down the river valleys to the Black Sea, routed the Roman armies, and killed the emperor Decius. In the East the Persian power was resurgent, and Sapor I in 260 captured alive the emperor Valerian. In Britain came raids from the Saxons and Irish. Cities were sacked. Athens was driven to the hurried rebuilding of her defences. Coin-hoards tell the story of hasty flight without return.

Meantime rival emperors arose. There was murder and civil strife for the imperial honour. The year 238 shows the tragic position at its clearest. In March, 235, the tough Thracian peasant Maximinus was proclaimed emperor by the German legions: Alexander, his predecessor, was promptly done to death. Maximinus was a brilliant and courageous soldier who momentarily secured the frontiers on the Rhine and Danube, but he had no administrative ability or experience, and "represented nothing but the tyranny of a brutal and licentious soldiery."[1] Exorbitant taxation fanned the flame of resentment into open revolt. In 238 Marcus Antonius Gordianus and his son were driven to assume the purple. Vitalianus, Maximinus' praetorian prefect, was treacherously assassinated, and in the exaltation of the moment there ensued a wholesale slaughter of Maximinus' real or supposed adherents. But one of the Thracian's supporters, Capellianus, commander of the third legion, marched against Gordianus' headquarters

[1] H. S. Jones, *The Roman Empire*, p. 279.

1

at Carthage, and won an overwhelming victory. The son died in battle; the father committed suicide.

But the senate were not yet done, and had in any event gone too far to draw back. They now called to the purple a commander of proved ability named Pupienus and an experienced administrator named Balbinus. Balbinus was one of those of whom it might justly be said "capax imperii nisi imperasset." He had a long record of important offices, but proved impotent to deal with the situation in Rome. There were riots, murder and conflagration. Pupienus went out to meet Maximinus. However the battle never came, for Maximinus' army, being short of food and fearful of his indiscriminate wrath, turned upon him, and murdered him, together with his son and Caesar Maximus. Meanwhile there was trouble in the East where the Persians and Goths were breaking through the frontiers. Pupienus and Balbinus were preparing to take command out there, when in an attitude of mutual and general suspicion they came into collision with one another, and were both cruelly murdered by the praetorian guard.

Such a situation could not long continue, and the soldier-emperors Claudius, Aurelian, Tacitus and Probus fought back the invading barbarians and restored confidence in the principate, and the accession of Diocletian in 284 marked the beginning of an era of consolidation, a new system of administration, measures to meet the economic dangers of the time, and the remoulding of the defence strategy of the Empire. His abdication in 305, and the proclamation of Constantine by the army at York on 25th July of that year, spelt a new series of civil wars, out of which Constantine emerged victorious in 324 and ruled for thirteen years as sole emperor.

This was the testing-time for the empire. Out of the civil wars which brought an end to the republic, had come the strong and stable system of Augustus. Shaken during the year of the four emperors, it had achieved new strength under the Flavians, and shown itself capable of withstanding the excesses of a Caligula, a Nero or a Domitian. Under Trajan, Hadrian and the first two Antonines the Pax Romana stood through most of the civilized world and enshrined standards of culture, justice and prosperity in which provinces and capital alike rejoiced. The new settlement was consequent upon more than a century of disturbance, much of which was morally and materially disastrous. In Diocletian and Constantine the Empire found two statesmen of first-class ability who knew what they were about. "What he aimed at," wrote M. P. Charlesworth of Constantine, "and what he strove for with all the resources at his command, was to stabilize and buttress in every way the fabric of the Roman Commonwealth, and to preserve it from those dangers that the third century had so painfully revealed."[1] "Every Roman citizen knew that the first object of an Emperor was the peace, unity and safety of the Roman realm."[2] Political, economic and military reforms were directed to that end. It was now to be seen whether the result would last.

THE ENEMY FROM WITHIN

Constantine died on Whitsunday, 337, and the answer to the question was not far to seek. Indeed it was visible even before his death. For though Constantine had seen that the unification of the Empire was impossible under the quadripartite system of Diocletian, and hence rejected the latter when once it had played its part in restoring order to the local administration, when it came to the succession he was not so clear. In 335 he distributed the territories under his dominion to his three sons, Constantine II, Constantius and Constans, and his two nephews, Delmatius, who joined the other three with the rank of Caesar, and Hannibalianus, who was given the territory of Pontus with the extraordinary title of "King of Kings." The seeds of strife here sown were not slow to flower. Within a week or two of the emperor's death the troops stationed in Constantinople declared that they owed no allegiance except to the children of Constantine, and promptly murdered his brothers and all their descendants except Gallus and Julian. Discord and disorder lasted till 3rd September, when the three brothers finally agreed upon the apportionment of the Empire. Three years later Constantine the younger attacked his brother Constans, but was himself killed at Aquileia. For ten years the two remaining brothers

[1] M. P. Charlesworth, *The Roman Empire*, p. 191.   [2] *Ib.*, p. 181.

B

had their hands too full with existing problems of government
to encroach upon one another. But the year 350 is almost as
confused and confusing as 238. In this year Constans was
forced to suicide by Magnentius, who assumed the purple, and
was accepted in Italy and the West. On the Danube the
commander-in-chief, Vetranio, himself became emperor to
prevent the secession of those provinces to the usurper. The
situation was complicated by the entry of Nepotianus, a relative
of the imperial house, who seized Rome and held it against
Magnentius for some weeks. Eventually Constantius turned
westwards and Vetranio, who had earlier given in to Magnentius, made way for him. There followed some jockeying for
position, Magnentius giving the rank of Caesar to his brother
Decentius, and Constantius the like authority to his cousin
Gallus. In 351 a bloody battle was fought at Mursa in which
some 50,000 men are reputed to have fallen, and two years
later Constantius secured final victory at Mons Seleuci in the
Alps, and Magnentius and his brother committed suicide.

But the troubles were not yet over. Gallus in the east had
made himself unpopular by his odious tyrannies, and like the
tenants of the vineyard in the famous parable, maltreated
Constantius' deputies who were sent to investigate. In the
last years of 354, however, he allowed himself to be lured into
the power of his cousin and was beheaded. A fresh usurper
arose at Cologne only to fall, and with the raising of Julian to
the rank of Caesar the succession was secured. In 361 Constantius died, and two years later Julian was killed in the East.
His successor Jovian was short-lived, and was in turn succeeded
by Valentinian. There followed a period of strong though
cruel rule: the pretenders Procopius and Firmus were ruth-
lessly suppressed, and after the weak interlude of Gratian, the
rising of Maximus in Britain, and the establishment of Eugenius
by Arbogast as puppet emperor, Theodosius was established as
master of the Roman world. Had he lived, the story might
have been different, for his rule was firm, and, apart from the
massacre at Thessalonica, not unenlightened. But the power
passed into the weak hands of Honorius and Arcadius, and
there was another wave of usurpers and pretenders—Constantine, Attalus, Jovinus, Constantius and Boniface.

THE ENEMY FROM WITHOUT

Amidst all this sedition and uncertainty it is not surprising that the defences of the realm were breached. Already in the last days of Constantine's reign the first growlings of the storm were to be heard. In 332 the Goths were threatening the Danube, but on 20th April, were resoundingly defeated and for the moment fell back. Three years later rebellion broke out in Cyprus. In 337, only six weeks before the Emperor's death, Sapor II of Persia declared war on Rome, and Mesopotamia and Armenia were overrun. A protracted war, and the heroic defence of Nisibis through three sieges, led to an uneasy peace in 350. Nine years later Sapor attacked again, and captured Amida, Singara and Bezabde. Julian, now emperor, counter-attacked, but missed his opportunity of besieging the enemy capital of Ctesiphon and died of a wound received in guerrilla warfare east of the Tigris. His successor, the popular but incompetent Jovian, was forced to the humiliation of giving up five provinces and several fortresses to the Persians, as well as abandoning Armenia, as the condition of peace. War continued spasmodically for the rest of the century.

But more serious was the danger from the north. In the mid-350s the Sarmatians and Quadi were pressing upon the line of the Danube, the Alamanni almost captured Autun, Cologne fell into the hands of the Franks and the disaster reverberated around the frontiers of the Empire, the Germans swept through Alsace. For the time being the campaigns of Julian provided security, but it could at best be temporary. In 366 the Alamanni were again in Eastern Gaul, and two years later they captured Mainz. In the following year Valentinian won a great victory in the Black Forest. But he saw the tide was rising : it was vain to try to push it back : the one chance was to build up a strong sea-wall. He repaired the Rhine defences, and built the new fortress of Basle : in 370 a temporary peace was patched up.

In the east the Goths were building up their strength. In southern Russia the Ostrogoths under Hermanric had established a mighty power. On the Danube Athanaric pressed upon the frontier. The rebellion of Procopius gave them their chance and for three years war dragged on which ended in their repulse. But now a new menace appeared and the Mongolian Huns began to sweep south-westward from the plains of Asia. They crushed the Alans, broke the power of Hermanric and the Ostrogoths, and threatened the Visigoths. The Quadi and Sarmatians pressed across the Danube before them. Athanaric and Fritigern sought refuge within the *limes*, ravaged Thrace, and annihilated the emperor Valens and his legions at Adrianople on 9th August, 378, and the echoes of the disaster again thundered round the empire. But the fortresses stood firm, the Frankish generals, Bauto and Arbogast, checked the incursion, and for the moment Athanaric and the Visigoths were assimilated into the body of the *imperium*.

Nearly fifteen years passed without major disaster. The firmness of Theodosius and the skill of his general Stilicho enjoyed their reward. Eugenius and Arbogast were defeated, a serious rising in Africa by Gildo, which threatened the corn-supply, was crushed, for a year or two Alaric and the Visigoths devastated North Greece, and in the East Gainas enjoyed a brief triumph. But these were all internal disturbances, and none long-lasting. With the new century the tide broke through. Valentinian had tried to strengthen the dams. Theodosius had opened a sluice-gate to let through some of the swirling flood in comparative harmlessness. But the mountain of water outside was ceaselessly piling up, and the waves were breaking upon the walls with an increasing fury. The Huns turned south-east and swept through the Caspian Gates across the Caucasus and Mesopotamia, Syria and Asia Minor, pillaging and devastating as they went. As the century advanced they were to bleed Constantinople white with tribute, ravage Illyria and Thrace, and press their frontiers across the Rhine towards the south of Gaul. On 31st December, 406, the Vandals, Alans and Suevi were forced across the Rhine in face of this expansion, and Gaul was lost to the Empire. The invaders even reached Spain. Radagaisus and the Germans broke through into Italy with 200,000 men at the most conservative estimate.[1] The legions abandoned Britain, and in the

---

[1] Oros, *Hist.*, vii, 37, 13, secundum eos qui parcissime referunt, ducenta milia hominum.

confused period that follows St. Patrick was carried off by raiders to Ireland. In 401 Alaric rose again and invaded Italy. He was checked at Pollentia in 402, but the violent death of Stilicho in 408 removed the only major obstacle in his path, and in 410 he sacked Rome. A third thunderclap rang around the world, and the genius of Augustine turned to contrast the transitoriness and mutability of human fortune, even at its highest, with the enduring treasure of the City of God.

Moral Degeneracy

The moral atmosphere of the times may be seen through the eyes of Ammianus Marcellinus. Sir Samuel Dill, in his great work on this period, culls from the historian the picture that follows: "The Roman noble has changed little in three hundred years. It does not surprise us to hear that the masters of the world are possessed of vast domains in every province, from the rising to the setting sun. Although they have no longer the political power of their ancestors, they have the vanity of a pampered caste, and they wish to prolong an inglorious name by gilded statues which commemorate nothing. They ride through the streets in lofty carriages, adorned with a vulgar splendour of dress, which is not redeemed even by its ingenuity. In their progresses they are attended or preceded by an army of slaves, clients and eunuchs. Their choicest pleasures are in swift horses, hurrying through the streets with the speed of the post on the great roads; or in long and elaborate banquets, at which the size and weight of fish or game are recorded, as in Juvenal's day, as a matter of historical interest. Their libraries are opened as seldom as their funeral vaults, but they rave about music and theatrical performances. Hydraulic organs, and lyres as large as carriages, minister to a degraded taste in music. In a time of famine, when all foreigners, including the professors of the liberal arts, were expelled from Rome, three thousand dancing girls with their teachers were allowed to remain. If the great man visited the public baths, he would salute effusively some slave of his vices, whom all decent people would avoid. His only friendships are those of the gaming-table. If a respectable man from provincial parts ventures to call on the great personage, he is received at first with effusive civility. If the visit is repeated in all honest confidence, he will find that his very name and existence have been forgotten. The effeminate noble who takes a journey to visit a distant estate will plume himself on the effort as if he had performed the marches of an Alexander or a Caesar. He will order a slave to receive three hundred lashes for bringing him his hot water late. These men, who have not a particle of religious belief, are the slaves of anile superstition. They will not bathe or breakfast or start on a journey till they have consulted a calendar to find the position of a planet."[1]

Much of this, unpleasant and undesirable as it is, is the triviality of vice. It can be matched and surpassed by the vices of aristocratic society in many other periods. As Dill remarks, there is nothing here that did not attract the lash of Juvenal. But if we allow for the morbidity of the journalist at any period and the lack of balance which moralists like Jerome and Salvianus habitually display, three facts about this age stand out.

In the first place there was no longer the dedication to service which had once been the peculiar glory of the Roman aristocracy. "Si deus annuit cum ad eam negotii partem accesserimus, ut de veteribus Romanis aliqua dicantur, evidenter divino munere adprobabimus tam iustum tunc erga illos fuisse domini favorem quam nunc erga nos iustam severitatem."[2] This may easily be accounted for alike in the increasingly autocratic tendencies inherent in the system of empire, in the peril which high office carried with it, and in the transfer of effective power, as may be seen as early as 69, to the military. By the end of the fourth century it was the generals who exercised real authority, and they were almost without exception barbarian. The senatorial class was left with the pomp and ceremony of traditional office, but it was a facade concealing the emptiness which lay behind, an *imago sine re.* Arbogast the Frank, Stilicho the Vandal, Gainas the Goth—these were the inheritors of the years when Maximinus or Galerius became one of the masters of the worlds on the score of personal prowess. Even the seat of government was

[1] S. Dill, *Roman Society in the Last Century of the Western Empire*, pp. 121-2.
[2] Salvianus, *De Gub. Dei*, vii, 2.

no longer in Rome, and even when the west enjoyed its own sovereign it was at Milan or Ravenna that the affairs of state were concluded. "Agnoscisne tuos, princeps venerande, Penates?" asks Claudian,[1] but the greatest response was a rare despatch and a still rarer consultation.[2] The society of Symmachus and Praetextatus, though it was raised above the morality of the majority of their contemporaries, was fundamentally escapist, and the letters of Symmachus, unless indeed they enclosed bulletins which are lost to us,[3] contain little notice of the tides that were tossing outside the study in which he discussed Vergil and Aristotle with his friends.

Secondly it was an age of extraordinary cruelty. Years of warfare commonly result in a rise in crimes of violence and an indifference to human life. None the less, the cruelty of Valentinian must appear almost incredible. Yet we have it on the authority of Ammianus that he kept two bears which he fed on human flesh. In a passionate outburst he commanded that a stable-lad should lose his right hand for clumsiness in helping him to mount; that a huntsman should be flogged to death for releasing a hound before due time. The savagery became a part of his nature, and at times appears almost calculating, as in the execution of local government officials for a trivial misdemeanour, or of debtors who lacked property on which to distrain. Massacres were not uncommon, and Ambrose excommunicated the great Theodosius for his wanton slaughter of the citizens of Thessalonica.[4] And something of the same spirit is discernible even in the refined and cultured Symmachus. He was preparing a lavish entertainment on the occasion of his son's elevation to the praetorship. But many of the animals died en route; the Spanish steeds were disabled; the crocodiles would not eat and had to be killed; and, worst blow of all, the prized Saxon gladiators perished in a mutual suicide-pact rather than face the humiliation of the arena. Symmachus in narrating this has none of the compassion of Cicero and Seneca, but only aggrieved disappointment and contempt.[5]

---

[1] *De Sexto Cons.*, 53.   [2] Symmachus, *Ep.*, i, 13; iv, 5.   [3] Cf. ii, 25.
[4] Cf. the massacre of the Goths in Constantinople in 400.
[5] *Ep.*, ii, 46; v, 56.

Thirdly, another feature commonly found in the wake of wars and armies, it was an age of loose sexual morality. When all allowance has been made for the prudish pruriency of Jerome and Salvianus this seems indisputable. Salvianus in the fifth century writes of the aristocracy of Southern Gaul: "Quis potentum ac divitum non in luto libidinis vixit? paene unum lupanar omnium vita."[1] He describes Africa as a "civitas scaturiens vitiis"[2] and asks "Quis in illo numero tam innumero castus fuit?"[3] Spain comes in for the same castigation.[4] In Rome, Jerome warns his female disciples against the dangers of high society. "Difficile inter epulas servatur pudicitia."[5] Further the system of domestic slavery led easily to illicit relationships between master and maid, and the revelations of the Kinsey report within our own generation will prevent us from viewing with too much surprise or judging with too much Pharisaism the condonation of such intrigues within Christian households.[6] The principle of sacerdotal celibacy led, as so often, to clerical concubinage.[7] Jerome's letters rank with the sixth satire of Juvenal as a "legend of bad women."

Lastly a word should be said about the lower orders. Here the authorities unite in their condemnation, and when allowance has been made for class prejudice we cannot doubt the justification of much that they say. Slaves are treated with the utmost scorn.[8] As for the city mob, they became increasingly pampered as the centuries passed. Magnificent and spacious baths were erected for them by successive emperors. The dole of corn was extended in the third century to include wine, oil and even pork. Their chief delights were the pantomime, the gladiatorial displays, and the chariot-races; their resorts the low tavern and the brothel. It is easy to wax indignant from a distance, forgetful that much of this was as innocent, if idle, as our own music-halls, "pubs" and "dogs." But the

---

[1] De Gub. Dei, vii, 16.   [2] Ib., vii, 70.   [3] Ib., vii, 75.
[4] Ib., vii, 27.   [5] Ep., 117, 6, cf. Ep., 54, 107, 108, 127, 130.
[6] Paul. Pell., Euch., 166; Jer., Ep., 54, 107.
[7] Jer., Ep., 22, 117; cf. Sulp. Sev., Dial., i, 8, 4; i, 9, 4.
[8] Jer., Ep., 54; Salv., De Gub. Dei, iv, 26; Symm., Ep., vi, 8.   It is fair to say that when Evangelus shows these sentiments he is severely taken to task by Praetextatus, v. Macr., Sat., i, 11.

obscenities of the pantomime far outweighed the risqué humour of our own day, the sadistic enjoyments of the arena both induced and satisfied a taste for blood from which we are happily freed—all honour to the martyr who flung himself to his death in the arena among the execrations of the crowd whose cruel pleasures he had dared to interrupt. The theatre and the circus stand to Salvianus[1] as a greater danger than the irruptions of the barbarians. Further they were not the recreations of an honourable toil, but the occupations of indolent degenerates.

THE RICH AND THE POOR

Wars cannot be fought without money, and they form a severe drain upon resources and manpower alike. Military operations have increased taxation as their inevitable concomitant. In times of aristocratic government the result is to widen the gulf between rich and poor, for those in power ensure that the heaviest burden falls upon the peasants and upon the middle-class. We know something of the income of a senator. It might well amount to fifteen million sesterces or more, and even Symmachus received five million. Further, the landed estates they might own were enormous in extent. Ammianus speaks of Sextus Petronius Probus as "opum amplitudine cognitus orbi Romano, per quem universum paene patrimonia sparsa possedit."[2] Symmachus possessed at least three town houses and fifteen retreats in the country, including large estates in Apulia, Mauretania and Samnium. At least two of the sites of Ausonius' mansions in Gaul have been tracked down and identified;[3] we know them to have been furnished with sumptuous baths and extravagant libraries. The renunciation of wealth by some converts to Christianity, Paula[4] or Paulinus[5] or some disciples of St. Martin, gives a further indication. But on the whole the Christians failed to reform the world, but themselves were corrupted by it. The privileges accorded to the *clerici* by Constantine were the thin end of the wedge, and Jerome writes scathingly of the luxury of the higher clergy.[6]

---

[1] *De Gub. Dei*, vi, 49. [2] Amm. Marc., xxvii, 11, 1.
[3] Pauliacus: *Ep.*, v, 16; Lucaniacus: *Ep.*, xxii, 13. [4] Jer., *Ep.*, 108, 5.
[5] Greg. Tur., *De Glor. Conf.*, 107; cf. Aus., *Ep.*, xxiv, 115. [6] *Ep.*, 52.

"They hold their hands out, as if to give a blessing, in fact to receive a reward for their dutiful attentions."[1] Seduction and captation became so serious as to require suppression by law.[2] The weight of taxation fell on the middle-class, or curiales. They were the "nervi reipublicae ac viscera civitatum."[3] And, though Salvianus in the fifth century might complain of their tyranny,[4] it is clear that during this period they were steadily depressed. Enormous disabilities were placed on them to prevent them from escaping the ever-increasing, grinding weight of taxation. "The curial's personal freedom was curtailed on every side. If he travelled abroad, that was an injury to his city; and if he absented himself for five years, his property was confiscated. Even for a limited time, and for a public object, as for example to present himself before the Emperor, he could not go from home without the formal permission of the governor of the province. He was forbidden absolutely to reside in the country. It is almost needless to say he had no power to dispose of his property as he pleased, since the State regarded his property as security for the full discharge of all his financial obligations. He could not enter into any contract or business relation which might conceivably weaken the hold of the State upon his possessions. He was forbidden, for example, to accept the agency of an estate, or to rent public lands, or to farm the taxes. The curial who had no children could dispose only of one-fourth of his estate by will, the remainder being taken by the municipal treasury. The municipality became the sole heir of an intestate curial. If his natural heirs were not citizens of the place, or if his daughter or widow married a stranger, they had to resign one-fourth of the property to the curia. He could not take Holy Orders without leaving his curial property in the hands of a proper substitute, or absolutely abandoning it to the service of the community. We have not by any means exhausted the melancholy list of the disabilities and hardships which were heaped upon the wretched class, but enough has been said to show the causes of its depletion."[5]

[1] *Ep.*, 22, 16.   [2] *Cod. Th.*, xvi, 2, 20.   [3] *Nov. Maj.*, 1.
[4] *De Gub. Dei*, v, 18.
[5] S. Dill, *op. cit.*, 257–8, where full references will be found.

The burden of taxes steadily increased, and the curials, despite their ever-diminishing numbers were absolutely responsible for any deficit within their own district. The upper classes who already succeeded by intrigue in obtaining assessments favourable to themselves,[1] inexorably swallowed up the smaller land-holders. The middle-class disappeared, and the feudal system emerged. Hence it is that Salvianus, who tends to see in the love of money the root of all evil, and like the Cynics to equate the love of pleasure with the love of lucre, contrasts the days of the Republic, when the citizens eschewed wealth and espoused poverty in their own lives, that they might direct all their energies to the commonwealth, with his own time when the public coffers were empty, and the rich lived in rapacious luxury.[2]

> Then none was for a party;
> Then all were for the state;
> Then the great man helped the poor,
>   And the poor man loved the great:
> Then lands were fairly portioned;
>   Then spoils were fairly sold:
> The Romans were like brothers
>   In the brave days of old.
>
> Now Roman is to Roman
>   More hateful than a foe,
> And the Tribunes beard the high,
>   And the Fathers grind the low.[3]

Hence it is that Paulinus of Nola issues his condemnation of the rich in the words of prophet or evangelist.[4]

ACHIEVEMENT

In modification of this justly gloomy picture four things deserve to be said.

The first is that despite the rapacity of the tax-gatherers and the incursions of the barbarians we have an extraordinarily tranquil picture of life in the Gallic countryside, not only in the fourth century from Ausonius, but also in the fifth from Sidonius Apollinaris. Occasionally we read of "fures tota regione vagantes"[5] or of starvation when the land is unfaithful

---

[1] Cf. the complaints from Africa. *Cod. Th.*, xii, 1, 166.
[2] *De Gub. Dei*, i, 10, ff.   [3] Macaulay, *Lays of Ancient Rome*.
[4] *Ep.*, xxv, 2.   [5] Aus., *Ep.*, iv, 23.

and fails in fertility.[1] But in general there is peace and
contentment. And Sidonius has left us what must rank among
the more memorable word-pictures of natural scenery in Latin
literature.[2] We are apt to forget the resilience of the countryside. Its permanence may be scarred but rarely broken.
Secondly, the age had a culture of its own, limited though
real. The circle of Symmachus combined a magniloquent
exaltation of one another's achievements with a genuine
appreciation of Vergil and the classical authors. Ausonius
can quote Catullus, Horace, Afranius, Varro, Pliny, Annianus,
Laevius, Plautus, Menander and Plato, and compose a cento,
and a somewhat immodest one at that, of Vergilian lines.
None the less Ausonius, Prudentius, Claudian and Sidonius are
not unworthy representatives of Latin literature in its sunset.
So too in thought. Jerome complains that his contemporaries
do not even know the titles of Plato's books, and that you rarely
even find dotards conning them in corners.[3] But at Athens
the school of Plato continued to the time of Justinian, and in
the person of Julian a Platonic philosopher became for
some troubled months βασιλεύς. Neo-Platonism produced
Iamblichus at the beginning of the fourth century, Plutarch
and Syrianus at the end, and Proclus in the fifth, though, apart
from Julian's debt to Iamblichus, these probably had little
effect in Rome and the West.[4] But Aristotle was translated by
Praetextatus and taught by Eusebius at Lyons.[5] Plato was
among the most precious studies of Augustine, even if he could
not find in those pages the Word made flesh. And a vague
tradition of Stoicism or a degenerate Epicurean indifference
seems to have passed as the heritage of the contemporary
Roman aristocracy.[6]

Thirdly something should be said of the immense powers of
Rome to assimilate new citizens. It was the much-abused
Caracalla who in 212 conferred the citizenship upon almost all
the free inhabitants of the empire. We have already seen how
Goths and Vandals and Franks were absorbed, and achieved
positions of high responsibility. The words of the Gothic

[1] Ib., xxii, 21, 42.   [2] Sid. Ap., Ep., ii, 2.
[3] Ep., Gal., iii, 5.   [4] But cf. Sid. Ap., Ep., i, 6; iii, 6.   [5] Ib., iv, 1.
[6] For the Epicureanism see [Prosp.] De Prov. Div., 25–85. For the Stoicism
see Ausonius' picture of his father. Idyll, ii, Parentalia, i.

chieftain Athaulf show the magic of Rome. "At first I longed to destroy and beat down the Roman Empire, but after I had learnt from experience that the Goths, because of their unbridled savagery, could not obey laws, I chose instead to seek the glory of restoring completely the Roman name and of buttressing it by using the strength of the Goths, in the hope that later ages might know of me as the restorer of Rome." By the year 400 the flow of the tide was too swift and too strong. But the achievement of Rome did not perish. To some extent, at least, it was absorbed, and passed down through the Dark Ages to the modern world.

Lastly the Christianization of the Empire was not merely the secularization of the Church. Even that was not altogether loss, for it meant that some of the higher traditions of law and culture passed into hands from which they could not be extirpated by the sword. But the reaction of Christian ideas upon the legislature can be suggested by a brief examination of Constantine's enactments. Some of the humanitarianism is superficial. Thus branding on the face is forbidden because it is the "imago dei," but branding is not forbidden. Seduction and rape are rigorously punished—so rigorously that a slave who abets such crimes is to have boiling lead poured down his throat. None the less there is genuine philanthropy in these laws. The condition of slaves is ameliorated; a peasant in debt is not to have his plough-oxen seized by distraint; prison life is alleviated; debtors are not to be scourged; precautionary measures are taken for famine relief. The same spirit breathes through the Codex Theodosii and the laws of Majorian. There is a genuine concern for equitable dealing and a patent sympathy for the oppressed masses. And the Christianizing of the Goths by Ulfilas was a major factor in facilitating their peaceable assimilation.

Principal Sources

Primary : Jerome, Augustine, Orosius, Sulpicius Severus, Salvianus, Ammianus Marcellinus, Claudian, Prudentius, Ausonius, Symmachus, Sidonius Apollinaris.

Secondary : Camb. Anc. Hist.; Camb. Med. Hist.; Gibbon, *Decline and Fall of the Roman Empire*; H. S. Jones, *The Roman Empire*; M. P. Charlesworth, *The Roman Empire*; F. W. Walbank, *The Decline of the Roman Empire in the West*; S. Dill, *Roman Society in the Last Century of the Western Empire*.

II

THE CONDITION OF THE CHURCH

THE CHURCH AND THE WORLD

The embracing of Christianity by Constantine, and its steady acceptance during the fourth century, except for the brief reign of Julian, as the State religion was at once its greatest victory and its greatest defeat. Its Founder had taught with zealous passion the peril that attends worldly power[1] and the lesson of humility.[2] He had Himself renounced all pretensions to temporal authority,[3] and in doing so no doubt lost the support of those who had other plans and aspirations for the Messiah, perhaps, on a plausible hypothesis, that of Judas Iscariot himself. In the last act of His life He showed that victory is the reward of an uncompromising love which humbles itself into apparent defeat. He laid upon His disciples the way of the Cross.[4] So too the early Church avoided the accumulation of individual possessions,[5] seeing in the love of money the root of all evil,[6] and for one reason or another followed the Epicureans in the abrogation of temporal power.[7]

Such quietism could not last in a missionary religion. It was all very well for Tatian writing in about 160 to reject political power, wealth, military command, and loose living as all alike unacceptable to the Christian,[8] but severe problems arose with the conversion of those already in authority. The early Christians pronounce with singular unanimity the incompatibility of the Christian profession with participation in war.[9] But were they to impose the certainty of martyrdom

[1] Luke xxii. 24–7; Mark ix. 33–7.   [2] John xiii. 1–16.

[3] Matt. iv. 8–10; Luke iv. 5–8; John xviii. 36.

[4] Matt. x. 38; Mark viii. 34, x. 21.   [5] Acts iv. 32.

[6] 1 Tim. vi. 10.   [7] See C. J. Cadoux, *The Early Church and the World*.

[8] *Discourse to the Greeks*, xi.

[9] *Egyptian Church Order*; *Canons of Hippolytus*; *Testament of our Lord*; Athenagoras, *Apol.*, 35; Minucius, *Octavius*, 30, 6; Justin, 1 *Apol.*, xiv, 3; Irenaeus, *Contr. Haer.*, iv, 34, 4; Origen, *Contr. Cels.*, iii, 7; v, 33; viii, 69; Tertullian, *De Corona*, 11; *De Idol.*, 19; *De Pat.*, 3; Cyprian, *Ep.*, 1, 6; 56, 2; Arnobius, 1, 6; Lactantius, *Inst. Div.*, vi, 20, 15 etc.

upon every soldier-convert by forcing him to abjure his military service, more especially during the long period of the Pax Romana when his duties would be largely police-work? Clearly if idolatry or the renunciation of faith were involved the Christian must say "no." But this apart, the Church tended to temporize. By the time of Diocletian, there are sufficient Christians in the army to demand a purge in the interests of national security, but not enough for such a purge itself to endanger the safety of the realm. The fourth century saw a great change and in 418 it is the pagans who are purged from the ranks by Theodosius II.

What was true of the attitude to military service was true in general. The events of the fourth century were a quickening and intensification of processes already under way. The establishment of Christianity as the state religion was the logical culmination of the process of three centuries. It sprang from the sense of the universality of the Church. "Wheresoever Jesus Christ is, there is the Universal Church" wrote Ignatius to the Smyrnaeans, and the words occur three times in the "Martyrdom of Polycarp." Already Pliny finds every age and rank among the Christians of Bithynia: Irenaeus and Clement claim the diffusion of the Church throughout the whole world: Tertullian makes his proud and famous boast "Britannorum inaccessa Romanis loca, Christo vero subdita." Two and a half centuries of spasmodic persecution served to show the impossibility of domination of the Church by the State. It remained to assert the supremacy of the Church. For the time paganism was tolerated, and in 331 Constantine restored the temple of Concord. First Lactantius and then Hilary knew well the virtues of toleration: "Religio cogi non potest: nihil est tam voluntarium quam religio." "Let them have, if they please, their temples of lies: we have the glorious edifice of the truth." The end of the century saw a violent change. The paganism which was virtually intact in 380 was virtually extinct in 400. Valentinian and Valens had been tolerant. Gratian confiscated the pagan revenues and deprived the priests and vestals of "victum modicum iustaque privilegia." The altar and statue of Victory in the senate had been maintained by Constantine, removed by Constantius, and restored by Julian. It was now removed again by Gratian. A great verbal battle was fought on these grounds between the staunch friends but champions of rival faiths, Ambrose and Symmachus. The authority of the Church won. Theodosius formally proposed in the senate "whether the worship of Jupiter or that of Christ should be the religion of the Romans" but by that time the proposal was a formality and the result assured. There was an absolute prohibition of sacrifice and the approach to temples, and in the countryside and provinces some wanton violence, not discouraged by the iconoclasm of a Martin or the fanaticism of a Cyril. Meantime in Ambrose at least the significance of the victory was clear, for he had uncompromisingly confronted the Arian Empress Justina with the standards of orthodoxy, and won penitence from Theodosius for the massacre of Thessalonica. The State must bow the knee to the Church.

THE CORRUPTION OF THE CHURCH

None the less it is clear that all was not healthy in the body ecclesiastic. Times of adversity may breed fanaticism, but they ensure sincerity. Times of prosperity tend to produce the time-server and the nominal adherent. Arthur Hugh Clough rewrote the fourth commandment for such an age

> At Church on Sunday to attend
> Will serve to keep the world thy friend.[1]

There is no doubt that the acceptance of Christianity at court brought into the Church great numbers of such nominal adherents. Neither is there any doubt that the opening of the doors of high society to those already within the Church had the effect a similar operation is reputed to have had on some members of the 1929 Labour government. The magnificence and luxury dazzled them, obliterated from their minds their Master's warnings, and swept them along in its train. Their high purpose was blunted: they lost the strait path they had been following, attracted by the busy prosperity of the broad highway. As a current epigram has it, instead of keeping straight, they preferred to move in the best circles. What

[1] A. H. Clough, *The Latest Decalogue.*

delicacy of taste, sneers Jerome, do these clerical gourmands show, who once were content with black bread in a hovel.[1] Something of this apostasy has already been indicated but a more detailed analysis will not come amiss. In the first place the great pomp attending the hierarchy is a noteworthy sign of the times. When Constantine moved his capital to Byzantium he took over and developed the court-ceremonial of Persia and the East. Clad in robes of purple or embroidered silk, with a diadem or tiara on his head and jewel-studded shoes on his feet, he was saluted with an almost religious veneration. It is small wonder that the Goth Athanaric, visiting Theodosius in Constantinople in 381, felt that he was paying homage to a God on earth. Something of this seeped through to the lords of the Church. After all they were asserting the primacy of the spiritual arm to the secular. Further, the lords spiritual were rapidly becoming lords temporal as well: the ecclesiastic politician was born.[2] The bishopric of Rome was a prize to be won. The pagan Praetextatus used to remark jokingly to Pope Damasus: "Make me bishop of the Church of Rome, and I will become a Christian without delay."[3] The year 367 saw the unedifying spectacle of civil war for the coveted office between the partisans of Damasus and Ursinus, so that one day brought 137 deaths. Damasus won, and the prize was an extended judicial authority in addition to the bishopric. But Ammianus Marcellinus in recording the incident thinks it natural that men should thus compete for the chance of being enriched by the offerings of the ladies of Rome, of riding in sumptuous raiment through the streets, and giving banquets of more than regal munificence.[4]

But further, the passion for riches attacked the clergy of all ranks. We read of monks who amass greater fortunes in the spiritual profession than the secular,[5] of one in the Nitrian desert who accumulates by weaving no less than one hundred solidi;[6] of clerics who engage in business to win wealth and repute,[7] "non victum et vestitum quod Apostolus praecipit, sed maiora quam saeculi homines emolumenta sectantes."[8]

---

[1] *Ep.*, 52, 6.   [2] Zos., v, 41.   [3] Jer., *Contr. Ioann. Hier.*, 8.
[4] Amm. Marc., xxvii, 3, 12.   [5] Jer., *Ep.*, 60, 11.   [6] *Ib.*, 22, 33.
[7] *Ib.*, 52, 5.   [8] *Ib.*, 125, 16.

Captation and seduction become so rife that Valentinian has
to forbid monks and ecclesiastics from entering the houses of
widows or orphans.[1] With this grasping spirit went meanness.
Clergy would amass secret hoards of wealth, don consciously
ascetic clothes, and plead that their sacred office exempted
them from giving to the poor.[2] And with both, especially
among the higher clergy, went living of unbelievable luxury.[3]

With the taste for luxury went a moral degeneracy—the
contrast between the pretence of fasting and the reality of
feasting,[4] the pretence of poverty and the reality of luxury,[5]
the pretence of chastity and the reality of concubinage.[6]
Salvianus contrasts unfavourably the debauchery and immorality of the Catholic Christians of Aquitaine with the heretic
Goths and Vandals.[7] "Nostris peccatis barbari fortes sunt :
nostris vitiis Romanus superatur exercitus," Jerome says.[8] It
is needless to elaborate this, but it accounts for much of the
moral fervour of the reformers.

Fourthly, the Church itself was factious and divided. We
shall have occasion presently to discuss the controversies from
a theological standpoint. Here it remains to note that whereas
once the pagan world had stood in amazement with the cry
"See! How these Christians love one another!" now they
turned aside in scorn from the spectacle of dissension and
mutual hatred. "Nullas infestas hominibus bestias ut sunt
sibi ferales plerique Christianorum expertus."[9] A glance at a
page or two of the Arian controversy will suffice. Ischyras,
compelled by three Meletian bishops with blows to circulate
the tale of Athanasius' sacrilege;[10] the accusation of murder
levelled against the bishop;[11] the brutal campaigns of Philagrius
and Gregory, including the death of Potammon as a result of
beating;[12] the invasion of the vigil service on 8th February, 356,
by soldiers brandishing swords and discharging arrows with the
sort of casualty list one would expect;[13] the stripping and beating

---

[1] *Cod. Th.*, xvi, 2, 20; cf. Jer., *Ep.*, 52, 6.   [2] Salv., *Ad Eccl.*, iv, 22.
[3] Sulp. Sev., *Dial.*, 1, 21, 3; Jer., *Ep.*, 52, 11.
[4] Jer. *Ep.* 22, 28.   [5] Salv., *Ad Eccl.*, iv, 22.
[6] Jer., *Ep.*, 22, 14; Sulp. Sev., *Dial.*, i, 8, 4; i, 9, 4.
[7] Salv., *De Gub. Dei*, vii, 14.   [8] *Ep.*, 60, 17.   [9] Amm. Marc., xxii, 5.
[10] Ath., *Ap.*, 64.   [11] Theod., i, 30; Soc., i, 27.
[12] Ath., *Hist. Ar.*, 12–14; Fest., *Ep.*, 13.   [13] Ath., *De Fuga*, 24.

of virgins, some to the death, by the Manichaean Sebastian.[1] There was continual rioting: Alexandria was notorious for it. At Nyssa riots drove out Gregory; at Doara they drove out the Arian bishop and enabled Gregory to take his place. Basil depicts the Church in notable imagery as two fleets fighting in a storm.[2] We have already seen the disgraceful incidents in Rome which preceded the elevation of Damasus to the papacy. It was perhaps at Pollentia in 402 that Christian for the first time engaged in warfare with Christian. The body of Christ was sorely divided.

One more count in the indictment must be made. It relates to the loss of any effective belief in the Holy Spirit. There are few more painful occupations than that of contrasting the book of Acts with St. Basil's work on the Holy Spirit. In the former the Holy Ghost appears more than fifty times as a living reality, working in and through the Church; the latter is a sterile grammatical exegesis of the apposite preposition to a particular context, redeemed only by its magnificent conclusion. It is dogmatic and fundamentalist, and it deals not with the living but the dead. It is academic in the worst sense. Bishops and deacons took the place of apostles and prophets. The Montanists tried to revive the exaltation of early Christianity. They first called the Holy Spirit God, and insisted that He had never ceased to work wonders in the Church, and their fervent faith enabled them to work wonders anew. They were the instruments of the Spirit: He was the plectrum which struck music from them. The Spirit again held the place He held in the Apostolic Church, as the source of lively inspiration. "Let those look to it," writes Tertullian, "who judge of the Holy Spirit according to the successive ages of time; whereas they ought to regard what is new, indeed what is newest, as most full of power, inasmuch as it participates in that exuberance of grace which is promised for the latter days . . . Men of weak faith might suppose that the grace of God worked only in the past to produce constancy in suffering or wonderful revelation, but He is always working as He promised." Montanism produced a great martyr in Perpetua, and won a great writer in Tertullian. But it suffered from being an overstatement.

[1] *Ib.*, 6; *Hist. Ar.*, 72; *Ap.*, 27.   [2] *De Spiritu Sancto*, xxx, 76.

The Montanists claimed for their revelation a validity which surpassed the authority of the apostles. Further, they fell on the one side into an ardent extremism, and in the effort to avoid this tried to reduce the ministry of the Spirit to a mechanical precision. From this the Church reacted and rejected their testimony. It was long before it was to be recovered.

THEOLOGICAL CONTROVERSY

The divisions of the Church were by no means only struggles for power. From the first Paul had to warn the churches to which he ministered against those who sought to lead them away from the true Faith. The problem remained to define that true Faith. The first apostles had not worked by creed and definition, but from the central certainties which they had experienced. These were threefold—the power of God revealed in the life of Jesus, the miracle of His resurrection, and the continuance of His grace in their lives by the power of the Holy Spirit. They demanded personal adherence not intellectual conviction, πίστις εἰς not πίστις ὅτι. But later generations who had not enjoyed the direct experience of the first two, even if they might know the third, were inevitably involved in the intellectual attempt to understand what underlay the witness of their fathers in the faith.

It follows that the major question which faced the Church was the nature of the person of Jesus. To the Ebionites, as to Theodotus, Christ was a mere man, ψιλὸν ἄνθρωπον εἶναι τὸν Χριστόν, though endowed with divine wisdom and power to an unique degree. Even this last the younger Theodotus denied, setting the heavenly Melchisedek above the earthly Christ, as the Platonic Idea is above its visible translation into material form. Paul of Samosata stressed the human achievement of Jesus as the basis for his recognition as the Son by the Father. He achieves divinity by His obedience, an idea we may perhaps derive from the letter to the Hebrews—ἐκ προκοπῆς τεθεοποιῆσθαι. To the Docetists on the other hand there was never any human Christ at all—that was all illusion —only the divine reality. And Praxeas, Noëtus, Beryllus and Sabellius, though they never went to the length of denying the genuine human life of Jesus, maintained the perfect identity of God the Father and God the Son. God became the Son by the assumption of a human life. The incarnation is one πρόσωπον or rôle played by the absolute monadic unity of God. The Subordinationism of the first group the Church rightly rejected, even in its "dynamic" form, as doing insufficient justice to the quality in Jesus which wrung from Thomas the great confession "My Lord and my God." But they also, and perhaps with less justification, rejected the Monarchianism of the others, which in its clearest and fairest expression did not fail to do justice to the humanity of Christ. Indeed it was the Patripassianism of the second group which failed to win adherence from a generation increasingly imbued with Greek speculation, and less with Jesus' revelation of God, not as an abstract philosophical entity, but a living and loving Father who suffers with His erring children and yearns for them when they go astray.

Orthodoxy found its expression in Hypostasianism. The Son is a hypostasis of the Father. Tertullian assumes three stages in the process of *filiatio*, the eternal immanent state of being of the Son of the Father, the forthcoming of the Son alongside the Father for the process of creating the world, and the incarnation of the Son in the world. Origen makes a brilliant contribution in removing the process of hypostasis outside the sphere of time : the Son is begotten from eternity : He is a necessary hypostasis of the Father, as rays are necessary to light. And at Nicaea orthodoxy won its triumph in the familiar words ἐκ τῆς οὐσίας τοῦ πατρός, γεννηθεὶς οὐ ποιηθείς, ὁμοούσιος τῷ πάτρι.

Yet this topic still remained the central theme of controversy in the fourth and fifth centuries. It appeared to the orthodox, with some justification, that the theology of Arius led to an effective denial of the true Godhead of Christ, while that of Apollinaris and the Monophysites led to disbelief in His full manhood. The first controversy occupied most of the fourth century; the second most of the fifth. We need not follow the story of the Tritheists, Cononites, Jacobites and Monothelites of the two centuries that followed. Enough has been said to make it clear that here is the single question of foremost importance, and the continual ground of controversy and dispute.

But if it is important to realize the domination of theological controversy by the problem of finding a faith which might do justice alike to the humanity and divinity of our Lord, to the fulness, so to say, of the name Jesus Christ, it is also important to notice briefly two other persistent grounds of discord, heresy and schism. The first is an extreme ascetic dualism, which tended to identify evil with matter, and to renounce all carnal intercourse therefore as inherently wrong. This type of system appears notably in some of the Gnostics, the Manicheans, Encratites, and at the end of the fourth century in the Priscillianists. The Church, finally, though somewhat grudgingly, rejected the extremer implications of views of this sort, though they are not wholly absent from Paul in the first century, nor from Augustine and Jerome at the beginning of the fifth. The Church is only to-day beginning to throw off the idea that sexuality and sinfulness are synonymous, and the earlier orthodoxy allowed marriage as a concession to human frailty and to avoid the graver sin of fornication, but regarded celibacy as a higher vocation.

The other major ground of schism was a matter of church discipline which reflected a more fundamental theological cleavage. It arose in Africa in the third century, and its direct occasion was the discontent felt with the easy way in which those who had escaped martyrdom during time of persecution by denying their faith were readmitted to the full communion of the Church. The wide and firm statesmanship of Cyprian in no way condoned the failure of the *Lapsi*, but by politic mildness guided them back into active faith. The Καθαροί or Puritans, represented first by the Novatianists and later by the Donatists, showing a moral earnestness which at times bordered on fanaticism, disavowed the justification of the Church in receiving back those who had broken their baptismal vows by grave sin. God in His infinite mercy might indeed grant forgiveness to the backslider who turned again to Him in penitence, but to the Novatianists at least the Church had no right to pronounce such absolution. Problems of sin and grace were already before the Church.

MONASTICISM

It is not to be imagined that the story of the Church is merely one of sin and schism. Difficulty and disaster always attract the attention more blatantly than unobtrusive fidelity of service. But it is true that the Christian of the fourth century found it increasingly difficult to maintain an absolute loyalty to his Master in a society permeated with easy-going sensuality and greed of gain.[1] Hence there was a continual impulse to withdraw,[2] and the greatest glory of the age is the number of those who surrender all prospect of wealth and worldly advancement, and dedicate themselves wholly to serve God by a life of poverty and service to man.

The origins of Christian monasticism are obscure. It may well be that St. Anthony gave the major impulse to the movement, though we can no longer take the details of the extant biography as either historical or intended to be. Certainly we can date the first beginnings with a fair degree of accuracy. The legendary date of Anthony's renunciation of the world was 285, and we can safely say that the movement dates to the latter years of the third century, but only became extensive in the fourth. Lactantius does not know of it, and it achieves no place either in Eusebius' history or his life of Constantine. But his commentary on the Psalms indicates the existence of a Christian monasticism,[3] and by 356 the movement is sufficiently organized and widely known for Athanasius to take refuge with the monks of the Thebaid; four years later he writes of monasticism as spread throughout the τόποι of Egypt.

The tale is not wholly one of gain. The early anchorites, living in solitary and isolated λαῦραι, might give way to an unhealthy morbidity. The ideal life of Anthony himself represents him as spending a long period in a horrible tomb. Fanatical asceticism, though rare, was another danger, and pillar-saints like Simeon and Daniel appeared from time to time. Furthermore, men did not enter the monasteries solely from spiritual motives. They withdraw not merely from the temptations and allurements of the world outside, but from taxes and imposts and the more unpleasant responsibilities

[1] Paul Nol., *Carm.*, x, 33, 316.   [2] *Id., Ep.*, xxv.
[3] Eus., *in Ps.*, 68, 7; 84, 4.

of citizenship, and in 365 the Emperor Valens was compelled to legislate in order to prevent such evasion. Nor were
they free from temptation when within, and we have already
seen the accusations of avarice and sensuality which Jerome
levels against some of his monastic brethren. And they were
by no means always popular with the man in the street.
Jerome tells how in 384, on the death of a young girl ascetic
named Blasilla, as some supposed from excessive fasting, the
populace of Rome raised the cry: "Quousque genus detestabile
monachorum non urbe pellitur? Non lapidibus obruitur?
Non praecipitatur in fluctus?" and Salvianus speaks of the
monks of his day as being mocked, cursed, persecuted and
hated, and treated with all the abomination which was heaped
upon Jesus Himself.

But this was on the whole exceptional, and monasticism is
one of the great movements in religious history. It received
wise inspiration. Pachomius turned the devotees from the
danger of solitary extravagances to the spiritual richness of the
κοινὸς βίος, and enunciated the vital principle that in the
spiritual life work and prayer go hand in hand.

> Work shall be prayer, if all be wrought
> As Thou wouldst have it done,
> And prayer, by Thee inspired and taught
> Itself with work be one.[1]

Basil wisely and sensibly governed the monasteries in his
diocese, set them on the essential tasks of Christ's representatives, to tend the sick and care for the needy, and brought them
back into contact with city life. In Gaul Martin established a
monasticism based upon a sincere renunciation of the world
and fidelity to the New Testament. In Palestine Jerome turned
his retirement to scholarship and supported the foundation of
nunneries by his friend and pupil Paula. "Quod prius
ignominiae fuerat, iam erat portea gloriae."

Principal Sources

Primary: Eusebius, Socrates, Sozomen, Athanasius, Jerome,
Augustine, Sulpicius Severus, Basil, Salvianus, Zosimus.

Secondary: S. Dill, *Roman Society in the Last Century of the Western
Empire*; L. Duchesne, *Histoire de l'Eglise*; F. J. Foakes-Jackson,
History of the Christian Church.

[1] John Ellerton, *Behold us, Lord*.

III

BRITAIN

Britain was occupied by Claudius in A.D. 43. We know something of the motives which prompted him. He needed a military victory to offset his physical defects and demonstrate his fitness for the principate. (Similar motives hastened the fall of Jerusalem in A.D. 70). He had to do something to make good the foolish boasting of his predecessor Caligula. He saw that an independent island on the outskirts of the Empire was bound to be a refuge for political malcontents and a constant spur to disaffection : indeed at that very time British ships were harrying the coast of Gaul. He sought to establish a strong chain of imperial defence, by the occupation of Britain and Ireland, which he imagined lay between Britain and Spain, and could thus form a link in a system uniting the latter country with Gaul. He sought to fulfil the work which the great Julius had begun. And he was no doubt attracted by the prospect of the island's wealth, in part known through trade, and in part hinted at, and no doubt exaggerated, by rumour. By about A.D. 50 possession of the South East was consolidated, and legions were settled at Gloucester and Lincoln. 61 saw a setback in the revolt of Boudicca, and the sacking of London, St. Albans and Colchester, but the ground was recovered, and twenty years later Agricola was able to secure North Wales, and advance far into Scotland. Meantime he encouraged Romanization, building and town-planning, and education after the Roman manner. These advances were consolidated under Hadrian and Antoninus, but at the end of the second century the pretensions of Albinus stripped the island of legions, and a wave of destruction swept over the two walls as far south as York and Chester. Septimius Severus restored the situation, and for most of the third century there was an era of peace and growing prosperity, and the countryside is besprinkled with farms and houses. But the troubles on the mainland reacted upon the inhabitants of the island. Stone walls are added for greater security to Caerwent and Silchester, and there is some indication of Saxon raids on the coast near Eastbourne.

The closing years of the century form a remarkable episode, when first Carausius and then Allectus take advantage of the difficulties elsewhere to split off from the Empire and become independent rulers of Britain. This situation lasted for perhaps ten years before Constantius Chlorus was able to re-establish Roman suzerainty and pose as the "redditor lucis aeternae."

THE PROSPERITY OF BRITAIN

The years that followed, and the reign of Constantine, who was first proclaimed emperor at York, showed the province at its greatest prosperity. There was untroubled peace, so that it was no longer necessary to occupy the milecastles on Hadrian's Wall, though the forts were still held. Coins of Constantine are more abundant than those of any other emperor. Archaeological evidence shows a large number of country-houses, towns and villages in occupation. It is worth pausing a moment to consider the nature of this prosperity.

Strabo, writing in the first century, gives us an indication by his list of the goods exported from Britain before the occupation. They comprise skins, slaves and hunting dogs, corn and cattle, iron, silver and gold. This picture is confirmed by later investigations. Air photography has revealed the systematic division of the country into fields for intensive cultivation. The flocks and general wealth of Britain are vividly portrayed on the Capheaton patera; a statuette from the North of England shows a sturdy ploughman with his team of oxen. Horse-breeding is indicated by the bones of native ponies discovered at Newstead, the chariot-race depicted on a tessellated pavement at Horkstow in Lincolnshire, or the sculptured charioteer in Lincoln itself. Hides were used for boots and shoes, shields and tents for the army. By the fourth century an imperial weaving establishment was situated at Winchester, and the cloaks and wraps emanating from it were in high demand in the export trade; this indicates an interest in sheep-breeding as well as in craftsmanship. The fenland was extensively cultivated and corn was produced for the troops in Germany as well as those at home. Further under the Romans an impulse was given to fruit and vegetable farming. We know that they introduced the cherry, and almost certainly the vine, the walnut and sweet chestnut; probably also some varieties of apple, plum and damson, among trees the box, plane and laurel, among vegetables the cabbage and broad bean. Bede's description of the island's natural resources merits full quotation :

"Opima frugibus atque arboribus insula, et alendis apta pecoribus ac iumentis; vineas etiam quibusdam in locis germinans : sed et avium ferax terra marique generis diversi. Fluviis quoque multum piscosis, ac fontibus praeclara copiosis, et quidem praecipue issicio abundat et anguilla. Capiuntur autem saepissime et vituli marini, et delphines, necnon et ballenae : exceptis variorum generibus conchyliorum; in quibus sunt et musculae, quibus inclusam saepe margaritam, omnis quidem coloris optimam inveniunt, id est, et rubicundi, et purpurei, et iacintini et prasini, sed maxime candidi. Sunt et cochleae satis superque abundantes, quibus tinctura coccinei coloris conficitur, cuius rubor pulcherrimus nullo umquam solis ardore, nulla valet pluviarum iniuria pallescere; sed quo vetustior est, eo solet esse venustior. Habet fontes salinarum, habet et fontes calidos, et ex eis fluvios balnearum calidarum, omni aetate et sexui per distincta loca, iuxta suum cuique modum accommodos. Aqua enim (ut sanctus Basilius dicit) fervidam qualitatem recipit, quum per certa quaedam metalla transcurrit, et fit non solum calida, sed et ardens. Quae etiam venis metallorum, aeris, ferri, et plumbi et argenti faecunda, gignit et lapidem gagatem plurimum optimumque : est autem nigrogemmeus et ardens igni admotus, incensus serpentes fugat, adtritu calefactus adplicita detinet aeque ut succinum."[1] The prosperity can hardly have been less in the fourth century.

The mineral resources are at first sight more surprising than the agricultural and pastoral development, but they were in fact considerable, though not as considerable as travellers' tales had led to be expected, and their later lack has been in part due to the heavy workings of the Roman period. Coal was known in its outcrops, and used, but it never became a commercial asset before the time of deep-mining. Gold was found in the remarkable mine at Dolaucothy in South Wales,

[1] Bede, *H. E.*, i, 1.

with its pithead baths, pit props, elaborate drainage system and seven-mile-long canal. Silver was obtained by lead from cupellation, and of lead there was such abundance that other interests imposed restrictions on output.[1] Copper was mined in Wales, and smelted at Silchester, but this was probably earlier. On the other hand the tin mines of Cornwall came to a new prosperity with the exhaustion of the Spanish mines in the latter part of the third century, and pewter dishes are found. Lastly, iron was produced from the Forest of Weald throughout the period of occupation; the fourth century saw development of the resources of Herefordshire; and traces of iron-working are found in many other countries.

The Romans exploited these resources as never before, and they brought in addition new standards of industry and craftsmanship. The development of textiles has been mentioned. Building construction in wood, brick or stone thrived, and Constantius in the fourth century, to rebuild Autun, sent to Britain for stonemasons "quibus illae provinciae redundabant."[2] Pottery was made and exported : the ancient skill in enamel-work was developed. Water-mills were introduced, and legend tells of an Irish king, Cormac mac Airt, who sent to England when he wanted water-mills constructed. Painting and mosaic work were taught in the Roman fashion, on the whole with artistic loss, though the pavements at Cirencester have a majesty of their own, and the chariot-race at Horkstow is thrilling in its liveliness.

But the prosperity was more than material : it left its mark upon the whole culture. The cities Rome founded have lasted, where tribal capitals like Silchester and Caister have decayed. The great trunk roads linked the country in one single system. Agricola encouraged the introduction of Roman dress and Roman meals, and by tactful flattery even the study of Latin, so that already a teacher of rhetoric named Demetrius is found in York, and Martial can boast that his poems are recited in Britain. Perhaps Gildas, in a later age, shows the process of Romanization most clearly : he is steeped in Vergil and the classical authors, and still thinks of Latin as "nostra lingua."[3]

---

[1] Plin., *N. H.*, xxxiv, 49.   [2] *Paneg. Lat.* (Baehrens), viii, 21.
[3] Gildas, 23.

THE EVENTS OF THE FOURTH CENTURY

This prosperity remained unbroken till 342, but in the next twenty-five years the frontier was continually threatened by incursions of the Picts and Scots from the North and West, who probably at this time burnt Corbridge. Further trouble came from Irish tribes called the Attacotti, and the Saxons began again to harass the south-east coast. No doubt the effect was little felt beyond the frontiers, but it was a straw in the wind, and some country-houses near the coast, such as Wiggonholt in Sussex, were destroyed by the raiders. Constans was obliged to come over in 343 to make a demonstration: "Insperatam imperatoris faciem Britannus expavit."[1] In 367 came disaster. In a vast "barbarica conspiratio"[2] Picts and Scots, Irish and Saxons swept across the country. The farmers fled to the towns, the slaves who provided so much of the manpower escaped. Ruined houses and hastily hidden coin-hoards testify to the terror and the disaster. Theodosius restored the military situation, but the *villae* were steadily abandoned, their productive capacity was gone, and the economic prosperity of the island was ruined.

The other significant series of episodes in the fourth century was the emulation of Carausius by a succession of usurpers, but these, instead of being content with Britain, laid claim to the whole Western Empire. Their excursions to the Continent in search of a throne drained the island of skilled troops, and though the *foederati* were left to protect the frontier—and there is no more eloquent testimony to the degree of achieved Romanization than the confidence in her local allies thus displayed—this withdrawal must have increased the danger of invasion immeasurably. The attempt of Magnentius in 350 was easily suppressed, and it would be unwise to generalize without evidence upon the results of his essay, though the activity of the Picts and Scots at this time is to be noted. Magnus Maximus won recognition as Augustus by Theodosius and exercised his rule for five years from 383 to 388. He is familiar in literature both in Rudyard Kipling's "Puck of Pook's Hill" and as Maxen Wledig of the Mabinogion. He

---

[1] Firmicus Maternus, *De Errore Prof. Rel.*, 28, 6.

[2] Amm. Marc., xxvii, 8.

stripped the Wall of troops, and no Roman coins from there can be dated later than 383, though the coastal forts of Yorkshire and the south-east were still manned. But the attempt of Constantine III in 409 removed the last prop of Roman power in Britain, and after 410 Roman coins are no longer to be found, save in isolation, though Britain still appears hopefully as a province in documents of the fifth century.

THE CHURCH IN BRITAIN

The original inhabitants of the island were a non-Aryan people called the Ivernians. They had been conquered and absorbed by an invasion of Goidelic Celts, probably from the Rhineland; these in their turn were driven westward by the Britons. The religion of these last was a simple polytheism, such as is common to many peoples at their stage of development. That of the Goidels however was more abstruse and more interesting. It is generally known as Druidism; it was pantheistic in flavour, and had acquired a certain integument of philosophy. It was a ritualistic religion with its own holy places. Human sacrifice was practised, and the link with nature-worship can be seen alike in the astronomical lore and the hallowed moment which brought about the famous midsummer morn sacrifice at Stonehenge. It was from the philosophy of Druidism that Willis Bund sought ultimately to derive Pelagian Christianity.[1] It is not proved, but it is not impossible.

The Romans naturally brought with them their own religion, or rather religions. Officially the worship of the Emperor Claudius was established at Colchester, and dedications are found to the Discipline of the Emperor, or the Fortune of the Roman People. Worship of Jupiter was inevitably widespread. Otherwise the Olympian pantheon is surprisingly ill-represented. Mars, the god of war, and Hercules are worshipped by the soldiers; Minerva, the goddess of learning, by the civil servants. The Roman genius for assimilation is seen in the identification of local deities with the familiar pantheon. Thus Sulis-Minerva comes from Bath, Mars Belatucader from Carlisle, Mars Cocidius from the country where Cumberland and

[1] *The Celtic Church in Wales*, p. 108.

Northumberland join. Foreign soldiers bring in their own gods, Garmangabis, Ricagambeda, Setlocenia, Mars Thincsus, Jupiter Dolichenus or Dea Syria. Above all there was Mithras, and the recent discoveries at Carrawburgh have thrown new light upon his worship. But none of this penetrated very deeply into the life of the people.

About the introduction of Christianity we are frankly ignorant, but stories of its foundation by Paul, Aristobulus, or Joseph of Arimathea, have no sufficient evidence in their support, and Bede's story of the appeal from a local chief named Lucius to Eleutherus, bishop of Rome,[1] is not traceable beyond the fifth century. None the less the representation of its introduction in the latter part of the second century must be chronologically accurate. It may have come from the soldiers; we are first aware of soldier-converts in the reign of Marcus Aurelius. But more likely it entered from Gaul, possibly by way of trading-contacts. There is no early evidence of Christianity among the legions, whereas the connection of the British and Gallic churches is well attested. However it came about, at the beginning of the third century Tertullian can speak with triumphant if exaggerated rhetoric of "Britannorum inaccessa Romanis loca, Christo vero subdita."[2] and later in the century Origen knows of British converts and can even speak of the conversion of Britain, though he admits elsewhere that so far only a minority have heard the Gospel.[3] With this background we need not doubt the martyrdom of St. Alban, which was believed at Verulamium in 429, though in view of Sozomen's comment that Constantius allowed the Britions to practise Christianity,[4] we may prefer to date it with the Saxon Chronicle to 283, rather than with Bede and Gildas to 303. With him died Aaron and Julius, and, shortly after, Augulus, a bishop. The persecution was neither severe nor lasting, and the Council of Arles in 314 saw the presence of three British bishops, Eborius of Eboracum (York), Restitutus of London, and Adelphius of Coloniae Londinensium, together with a presbyter Sacerdos and a deacon Arminius. The names need not here delay us, though they offer some pretty

[1] Bede, *H. E.*, i, 4. [2] Tert., *Adv. Jud.*, 7.
[3] *Hom. in Luc.*, 6; *Hom. in Ezech.*, 4; *Comm. in Mt.*, 39. [4] Soz., i, 6.

puzzles: Eborius probably represents a local name, perhaps Ivor. There were no British bishops at Nicaea, but Constantine includes the Britons among those who accepted his ruling as to the date of Easter.[1] Gildas and Bede both speak of Arian influence in the island,[2] but this, as we shall see, was exaggerated. Three bishops attended the Council of Ariminium in 359; they had to claim their travelling expenses from Constantius.[3] Archaeology throws some light upon the diffusion of the Gospel, though the relics are disappointingly few. There is a tiny church at Silchester, and another at Caerwent. The wooden "vetusta ecclesia" at Glastonbury probably dates from this period, and there was certainly an early church at Canterbury.[4] It has been plausibly suggested that underneath St. Peter's, Cornhill, in London, lie the remains of the official chapel of the government buildings, which will thus have become the first officially recognized church. Fonts found in London and Brecon have been assigned to the Roman period. There appears, despite Haverfield, to be Roman work *in situ* in the churches in Lyminge and Brixworth. The curious word-square found at Cirencester seems to be Christian. The chi-rho monogram, representing the name of Christ, has been found in a villa at Frampton (strangely associated with scenes from pagan mythology), engraved on a silver cup of foreign extraction at Corbridge, carved on a stone at Chedworth, on a number of lamps, and on fourth century coins. On an ingot of tin found at Battersea it is associated with the words "Spes in Deo." A silver pin found in London depicts Constantine gazing at the vision of the heavenly Cross. Tombstones marked "hic iacet" or in which the age of the deceased is carelessly recorded are probably Christian. There are a few such, though some must belong to the fifth century. During the troubled period in the middle of the fourth century a governor of Cirencester sets up again a statue and column "of the old religion" which had been knocked down by zealots who may reasonably be supposed Christian.

The evidence is real but it is scanty, and this scantiness led

---

[1] Eus., *Vit. Con.*, iii, 19.   [2] Gild., *Hist.*, 9; Bede, *H. E.*, i, 8.
[3] Sulp. Sev., ii, 41.   [4] Bede, *H. E.*, i, 26.

Haddan to a scornful and eloquent indictment: "Up to the time of the departure of the Romans, such Christianity as existed among us, weak at best, and scantily spread, appears to have been confined mainly, if not exclusively, to Roman settlements and Romanized natives, and to have struck, in consequence, but feeble roots in the land. It was foreign, not native; it was confined to the Roman provinces of Britain itself; it had no strength or character of its own, but was a feeble reflection of its Gallic sister across the Channel, from which almost certainly it was derived. Its history is confined almost to the mere fact of its existence, or is, at best, a skeleton of dates, filled up almost by negatives. It was a Church up to this period, which had produced no known writer except Pelagius and the semi-Pelagian Fastidius; and of these the first certainly, and almost certainly the second, lived and wrote abroad; a Church which had contributed nothing beyond a silent vote to any ecclesiastical movement whatever, and had lain open to the subtle machinations of the metaphysical Easterns, through the simplicity of her ignorance; a Church, the first utterance of whose voice, when she found one, was in the form of the fiercest possible denunciations of her own short-comings and of those of her people in the well-known complaint of Gildas; a Church that had hitherto sent no missions; for even Palladius, Patrick, Ninian, who date also at the very close of the period, were sent by St. Martin of Tours, and by the Bishop of Rome; a Church, which when assailed by heresy, was compelled to send to her neighbours for a fit champion of the truth; a Church that looked to Gaul for the saints whom she should follow and reverence, and by whose names she should call her sacred buildings, Hilary, Martin, Germanus, and whose own almost single saint was only a convert and a martyr in the same day, if his story, indeed, can be trusted at all; a Church that has left a trace indeed . . . but the very faintest trace of her two centuries and a half of existence, in brick or stone, in sculpture or in inscription; a Church too poor to endow even her own bishops; a Church which, so far (it was different afterwards), had no traceable customs or ritual peculiar to herself; a Church which, in a perhaps happy obscurity, on the one hand, escaped persecutions with but one probably small exception; but on the other (omitting, indeed, the heretic Pelagius), formed no school, threw no new light on the truth, supplied no commentaries on Scripture, devised no religious or charitable institute, added nothing of any kind to the common stock; such is the view which a reasonable criticism gives us of the Church of Britain up to the Saxon invasion of her shores."[1]

This is forceful criticism, but it really will not stand. No one would pretend that the British church was as strong as some others, but the wholesale condemnation of the above passage is unwarranted. In the first place it is factually inaccurate. The monuments are not numerous, but they are not insignificant. We cannot assert so dogmatically the confinement of Christianity to the Roman provinces. Nemthur, where Patrick's father Calpurnius was a deacon, and his grandfather Potitus a presbyter, hardly comes into that category, even if we discount, as we probably should, the allegation that Pelagius and Caelestius were Scoti. Kirkmadrine in Wigtonshire has provided us with two Christian inscriptions in stone. Chrysostom speaks of the conversion of the British Isles, and the plural is meaningful.[2] Willis Bund's examination of Goidel Christianity has shown a peculiar and characteristic ascetic zeal, and a mission was even in the troubled course of the sixth century sent from Wales to Ireland. It is, to say the least of it, contradictory, to complain of the obscurity of the British church, and then to assert dogmatically that it devised no charitable institute. Indeed the complaint of poverty may contradict this very assertion, for Sulpicius considers the poverty of the bishops praiseworthy, which implies that it was deliberately assumed.[3] In the second place the figures whom we may take as in any way representative of British Christianity are decidedly forceful. Britain gave to the Gallic Church Mello of Rouen (though he was a late convert) and Faustus of Riez. Pelagius and Fastidius are not trivial figures. Patrick, protest his "rusticitas" as he may, combines a patent singleness of heart with a pellucid clarity of exposition.

[1] Haddan, *Remains*, pp. 216–8.

[2] Chr., *Quod Christus sit Deus*, 12.

[3] Sulp. Sev., ii, 41.

Thirdly we have in the pages of Bede the picture of a thriving and vigorous church at the beginning of the fourth century : "At ubi turbo persecutionis quievit, progressi in publicum fideles Christi qui se tempore discriminis silvis ac desertis abditisve speluncis occulerant, renovant ecclesias ad solum usque destructas, basilicas sanctorum martyrum fundant, construunt, perficiunt, ac veluti victricia signa passim pro-palant, dies festos celebrant, sacra mundo corde atque ore conficiunt: mansitque haec in ecclesiis Christi quae erant in Britannia pax usque ad tempora Arrianae vesaniae."[1] And fourthly, and most important of all, the evidence of the fourth century, apart from the mysterious visit of Victricius right at the end, shows a church firm in orthodoxy and respected by the ecumenical leaders. Only Ariminium stands against them, and they were not alone in succumbing to the persuasion of the Arians on that occasion. We have seen them at Arles, and subscribing to the decisions of Nicaea. Athanasius testifies to their support of him and his faith after the Council of Sardis.[2] Hilary in 358 felicitates them on being free from all contagion of the detestable heresy.[3] Athanasius again speaks of their orthodoxy in 363.[4] Chrysostom tells how churches and altars have been constructed in Britain, and men discuss the interpretation of Scripture "with differing voices, but not with differing belief."[5] Jerome remarks on their enthusiasm for pilgrimages. "The road to the heavenly hall stood open from Britain as well as from Jerusalem." "They worship the same Christ and observe the same rule of truth as the rest of the Christian world."[6] The picture is not one of weakness, blown about by every wind of false doctrine, but of a stable orthodoxy.

Principal Sources

Primary : Bede, Gildas, Caesar, Tacitus.

Secondary : R. G. Collingwood and J. L. Myres, *Roman Britain*; M. P. Charlesworth, *The Lost Province*; I. A. Richmond, *Roman Britain*; S. E. Winbolt, *Britain under the Romans*; F. Haverfield, *The*

[1] Bede, *H. E.*, i, 8. [2] Ath., *Apol.*, 1; *Hist. Ar.*, 28.
[3] Hil., *De Synodis*. [4] Ath., *Ep. ad Jov.*, 2.
[5] Chr. *Quod Christus sit Deus*, 12; *in princip. Act.*, 3, 1.
[6] Jer., *Ep.*, 46, 10; 58, 3; 146, 1.

Romanisation of Roman Britain; R. G. Collingwood, *Roman Britain*; J. Collingwood Bruce and I. A. Richmond, *Handbook to the Roman Wall*.

W. Bright, *Early English Church History*; Willis Bund, *Celtic Church in Wales*; A. W. Haddan, *Remains*; Bp. Browne, *Church in these Islands before Augustine*; W. E. Collins, *The Beginnings of English Christianity*; H. Williams, *Christianity in Early Britain*.

IV

PELAGIUS—THE FIRST PERIOD

It was into this atmosphere and from this background that Pelagius came. But before studying the influence which extrinsic circumstances and contemporary events had upon his thinking, it will be well to make clear the facts of his life.

EARLY DAYS

It cannot be too strongly emphasised that the one certain fact about Pelagius' life prior to his arrival in Rome is that he came from the British Isles. This is strongly attested from a multiplicity of sources. Bede describes him as "Pelagius Bretto";[1] Augustine says he was known as "Brito" to distinguish him from Pelagius of Tarentum.[2] To Prosper he is "Pelagius Brito,"[3] to Orosius "Britanicus noster,"[4] and Mercator and Gennadius speak in similar terms.[5] Prosper also in verse describes him as a snake from Britain :

> "Dogma quod antique satiatum felle draconis
> Pestifero vomuit coluber sermone Britannus."[6]

and again :

> "Contra Augustinum narratur serpere quidam
> Scriptor, quem dudum livor adurit edax.
> Quis caput obscuris contectum utcunque cavernis
> Tollere humo miserum propulit anguiculum ?
> Aut hunc fruge sua aequorei pavere Britanni,
> Aut hic Campano gramine corda tumet."[7]

Jerome, after likening him to a great mountain-dog, through whom the devil barks, writes an obscure sentence : "Habet progeniem Scoticae gentis, de Britannorum vicinia,"[8] which might appear to imply that he was an Irishman, but may only mean that anyone would expect him to be a barbarous Irishman rather than a civilized Briton. Similarly when he is described as "Scotorum pultibus praegravatus"[9] it need be no

---

[1] Bede, *H. E.*, i, 10.   [2] *Ep.*, 186, 1.
[3] *Chr.*, A.D. 413, cf. *C. Collatorem*, 58.   [4] *Apol.*, 12.
[5] Mercator, *Lib. subnot. in Verba Iul.*; Gennadius *De Vir. Ill.*, 43.
[6] *De Ingratis*, i, 13.   [7] Bede, *H. E.*, i, 10.
[8] Jer., *Pref. Lib. 3 in Jerem.* The old reading "Albinum" for "Alpinum," though attractive, is wrong.   [9] *Id.*, *Prolog. in Jerem.*

39

more than a term of abuse; "Scotus" is almost synonymous with "barbarous."[1] At the same time, though there can be no certainty or even probability, it is not impossible that he might have come from north of the wall. We have seen in the last chapter that there were Christian settlements there; there were probably Scoti in Galloway by the fourth century, and it would add a certain point to Prosper's repeated likening of him to a snake, in that Procopius, who knows the island only by hearsay believes that the wall divides an area of civilization and plenty from an area of "poisonous snakes and other terrors."[2] Another tradition would claim him as Welsh. This rests upon three strands of evidence. One is the name Pelagius, which may represent the Latin Marigena and the Welsh Morgan.[3] The fact of the names Pelagius and Pelagia being found elsewhere does not, as some have suggested,[4] rule this out; if anything, it makes it more probable, for if, by a happy chance it is possible to translate a "barbaric" name into one already accepted and familiar, it is more likely to be done. Secondly, a late tradition on which very little, if any, reliance can be placed, associates him with the famous monastery of Bangor Yscoed near Caerleon.[5] This may be put on a par with the stories which make of him a bishop or a Professor of Cambridge University. Thirdly, we have seen Willis Bund's attempt to derive Pelagianism from Goidelic religion. "The faith of the Goidelic Celts," he wrote, ". . . is usually called, from its great exponent, Pelagianism."[6] Chevalier is of the same view: "Les doctrines fondamentales du druidisme . . . ne furent sans doute pas étrangères à la naissance de l'hérésie pélagienne et au succès qu'elle obtint dans son pays d'origine, particulière-ment dans les régions de population gaëlique."[7] But the connection has not been proved, and modern scholarship seems to be turning away from it. Neither of these theories of Pelagius' origin is impossible; other hypotheses claim him for

---

[1] Claudian, De Bello Gothico, 417. Cf. Jer., Ep., 69, 3; Adv. Jovin., ii, 7.

[2] Procop., Bell. Goth., iv, 20.

[3] Ussher, Antiquitates, c, 8; Bury, Hermathena, xxx, 1904, p. 35, note; Bright, Early English Church History, p. 14.

[4] Souter, p. 2.   [5] J. Bale, Centuriae.   [6] The Celtic Church in Wales, p. 108.

[7] Essai sur les reveils réligieux du pays de Galles, p. 391; cf. Wörter, Der Pelagianismus, p. 36.

Ireland,[1] or an Irish settlement in south-west Britain.[2] If later tradition however is to be taken into account, there is also the statement of Polydorus Virgil that he was "homo Britannus, natus in Britannia citeriore."[3] It will be plain how soon we are driven into the realm of conjecture.

If there is uncertainty here, where we have direct statements to go on, we shall be unwise to attach too much certainty to mere inferences, however ingenious, particularly when we find them conflicting, and the one or two statements we have from early authorities are highly questionable. Thus we know nothing for sure about his date of birth, except that it can hardly have been before 350 or after 380, and that the tradition which gave him and Augustine the same year of birth is a patent and typical fiction. We know nothing certain of his family. De Plinval[4] argues, with some reason, that if he belonged to the aristocracy he would have had a hereditary cognomen, and therefore his parents could not have been of any great standing, and tentatively suggests on the basis of medical references in Pelagius' writings,[5] that his father may have been a Greek doctor who came over to Britain in 343 with Constans. Souter, on the other hand, writes "It is perfectly clear that he had received a first-class education and it may thus be presumed that he was of wealthy family."[6] Certainly we must take Orosius' aspersions upon his education as merely polemical, and without any ground in fact.[7] Souter's careful analysis of the sources of the commentary on St. Paul's epistles shows a sound and exhaustive knowledge of the Bible, some reading and assimiliation of classical authors, including direct reminiscence of Lucretius, Vergil, Horace and Juvenal, and knowledge of Christian writers alike in Greek and Latin, including Ambrosiaster, Jerome, Augustine, Rufinus, Chrysostom and almost certainly Theodore of Mopsuestia.[8] To these classical authors we can certainly add Terence, Cicero and

---

[1] Zimmer, *Pelagius in Irland*. He points out the respect with which Pelagius was treated in Ireland.

[2] *Ib.*; also Bury, *Life of St. Patrick*, p. 296.

[3] *Angliae historiarum*, lib., xxiii.   [4] De Plinval, p. 60, ff.

[5] E.g. "cancer" *in 2 Tim.*, ii. 18.   [6] Souter, p. 3–4.   [7] Oros., *Apol.*, 29.

[8] Souter, ch. v. Cf. also H. Williams, *Christianity in Early Britain*, p. 181.

Sallust, perhaps also Ovid.[1] Certainly in one passage he lists Vergil, Sallust, Cicero and Terence as authors of damnable folly and a waste of time to read.[2] But he had read them, at least in part. It is curious that his verbatim citation of Vergil, as well as the two references which Souter gleans from the commentaries should be from the fourth book of the Aeneid.[3] We cannot feel that he warmed to Dido as Augustine did, and it looks as if he had read it at some time as a set book for special study. But he has some genuine knowledge of classical philosophy. He knows something of Socrates;[4] it is hard to say from what source, and he never mentions him by name. He may be acquainted with Plato's Theory of Forms.[5] He certainly is familiar with Aristotle's doctrine of substance,[6] whose acceptance into the body of orthodox Catholicism lay far in the future, though Augustine himself made use of it. He may too know Aristotle's mean, and appears to refer to σωφροσύνη.[7] And his moralizing has affinities with the Stoics, and at more than one point he expresses his understanding of the law of nature in sheerly Stoic terms.[8] Neither is there any doubt that he was a man of trained ability in exposition. "Acute quippe videntur haec dici, sed in sapientia verbi" is a typical comment of Augustine's,[9] and Jerome described him, despite his provincial origin, as "homo latinissimus."[10] It was this very clarity and persuasiveness which made him so dangerous an enemy to the orthodox faith. Now we have already seen some evidence that the leaders of the British Church espoused a voluntary poverty. A natural concomitant of this would be that the same educational opportunities should be open to all who joined in the fellowship of the Church. In this way we can reconcile the undoubted width and depth of his education with the indications of his comparatively humble origin.

We do not know why he left Britain. Souter has suggested,

---

[1] De Plinval, p. 73. [2] Pel., *Humanae*, 2.

[3] *De Cast.* iv, 5; *Comm.*, in 1 Thess. i. 8; in 1 Cor. xvi. 13; Verg., *Aen.*, iv, 174, 188, 569–70.

[4] Pel., *Humanae*, 1. This particular story is to be found in Apuleius *Florida*, i, 2.

[5] See p. 134. [6] Aug., *De Nat. et Grat.*, xix, 21.

[7] Pel., *De Div*, v, 1. [8] *Comm.*, in Rom. vii. 22; in Eph. vi. 5.

[9] *De Nat. et Grat.*, vi. [10] *Ep.*, 50.

on the basis of a number of passages in his writings, that there is evidence of a serious quarrel with his father, and a legacy of bitterness unusual in Pelagius.[1] De Plinval thinks that he was being trained for a secular career and reacted away from it.[2] Certainly the commentary on Ephesians vi. 4 is interesting. The verse runs "Et vos, patres, nolite ad iracundiam provocare filios vestros, sed edocete illos in disciplina et in correptione domini." Pelagius' exposition reads "Ne eos ad saecularia studia provocantes, iracundiam discere faciatis, sed divinae legis eos instituite disciplinis, talibus ergo parentibus filios praecepit oboedire." It looks as if his impulse was to a religious calling, while his father tried to direct him into some secular profession. We shall see later how he finally resolved this conflict. The immediate outcome is uncertain. It is unlikely that he undertook the monastic life; if he did, he subsequently renounced it, but he is never found authentically associated with any monastic institution. Augustine and Mercator indeed refer to him as "monachus"[3] and he is so addressed throughout the proceedings at Diospolis[4] but this probably only refers generally to his ascetic tendencies and to the fact that he was not practising a secular occupation. Zosimus at Rome speaks of him as "laicum virum."[5] On the other hand there is no evidence of his secular employment, and though his skill in controversy may indicate some legal training, he is not referred to as a lawyer like his associate Caelestius, and we get an impression of barristerial slickness from the latter wholly absent from his more ponderous companion. De Plinval[6] sees some suggestion of legal training in his detailed knowledge of the processes of Roman punishment,[7] in his emphasis upon equity, especially in the justice and equity of God,[8] and in his meditation upon the idea of possibility, which might have been occasioned in part by legal maxims of the type "impossibilium nulla obligatio."[9] If so, his revolt from the brutalities of legal

---

[1] *Pelagius' Doctrine in relation to his early life* in *Expositor* for 1915, pp. 180, ff.

[2] De Plinval, p. 64.

[3] Aug., *De Gest. Pel.*, xiv, 36; *De Haeresibus*, 88; Mercator, *Lib. subnot. in verba Iul.*, ii, 2.

[4] E.g. Aug., *De Gest. Pel.*, xx, 44.

[5] Zos., *Ep., Postquam a nobis.*, cf. Oros. *De Arb. Lib.*, 4.   [6] De Plinval, pp. 65, ff.

[7] *De Div.*, 6.   [8] *De Div.*, 8; *Qualiter*, p. 115.   [9] Celsus, *Dig.*, 4, 17.

execution[1] will have been an additional factor in turning him from the career. It is quite likely that the intended purpose of his departure was to further his education, perhaps in Gaul, perhaps in Rome.

He is certainly to be found in Rome in 405, when the great controversy first stirs. Of the period intervening there were two theories. One, following a late tradition, regarded the time as spent in the lands of the East. "Peragratis Gallis in Aegyptum et Syriam aliasque Orientis regiones tandem pervenit."[2] In support of this may be adduced his knowledge of the commentaries of the Greek fathers, and the apparent derivation of his later theological views from Origen : Jerome describes his doctrine as "Origenis ramusculus."[3] There also appears to be a debt to Chrysostom, which is most easily explained by a visit to the east, and some have even identified him with the monk Pelagius whose defection that saint, writing in 405 to Olympias, so bitterly bewails.[4] Others consider that the time was spent in Rome, and we have an explicit statement from Mercator that he imbibed his heretical opinions from Rufinus during the papacy of Anastasius (398–402).[5] The association with Rufinus, and later with Theodore of Mopsuestia, with whom he corresponded would amply account both for his Origenist views, and for such knowledge of the Greek fathers as he shows, which, though real, is not wide, and in view of his explicit renunciation of the profession it is not easy to identify him with Chrysostom's monk. Further, during his later visit to Palestine there is no indication of any earlier visit to the neighbourhood. De Plinval's meticulous scholarship has now unearthed two weighty arguments in support of this second view.[6] The first is that Augustine speaks of Pelagius as having long lived in Rome;[7] the second that Jerome writes of their "veterem necessitudinem" in 414.[8] The second

---

[1] *De Vita Christ.*, 3.   [2] J. Bale, *Centuriae.*

[3] *Ep.*, 133, 3.   But cf. Aug., *De Gest. Pel.*, iii, 10.   [4] *Ep.*, 4.

[5] Merc., *Lib. Subn.*, 2–3.   Kidd, *History of the Church to A.D.* 461, III, 57, denies that this is the Rufinus associated with Jerome.   But Jerome's linking of Rufinus and Pelagius, however vituperative, is explicit.   Whoever it was, he provided a bridge with the East.

[6] Page 64, note 5.   [7] *Ep.*, 177, 2; *De Gr. Chr.*, ii, 24.

[8] *Comm. in Jerem.*, iv, 1, 6.

presupposes that they met in Rome, when Jerome was there between 382 and 385. Unless Pelagius did indeed visit Palestine, or unless we are to assume that a mutual friendship with Pammachius is sufficient to establish such a "necessitudo," that seems conclusive evidence of his whereabouts at that time, and the evidence of Augustine and Mercator, while not ruling out of court the possibility of a brief visit to the east, makes it impossible that Pelagius can be the monk of Chrysostom's letter.

PELAGIUS' PERSON AND CHARACTER

We get some idea of what he looked like in later life through the vituperative pens of Orosius and Jerome. The overwhelming impression is one of size. He is a veritable Goliath,[1] broad-shouldered like a wrestler,[2] bull-necked.[3] Jerome compares him to a great hound from the Alps:[4] we inevitably think of a St. Bernard. By about 415 he was given to corpulence, "grandem et corpulentem,"[5] and his step was slow, like a tortoise.[6] He was weighted down with porridge, Jerome suggests,[7] and the very jibe is enough to refute the cheap and coarse insinuations of Orosius about his luxurious living.[8] He was full of face,[9] and liked to have his head bare.[10] His brow was stern[11]; his enemies spoke of him as butting with his horns.[12]

The malicious and unscrupulous insinuations against his morals are not for a moment supportable. Indeed he displayed a temper in controversy which his opponents might well have emulated. Augustine never descended to cheap abuse, as did Jerome and Orosius. On the contrary he speaks of him in terms of marked respect—"non parvo provectu Christianus" and "vir ille tam egregie Christianus."[13] He heard at Rome of his "high renown,"[14] and knew him as a highly esteemed friend of the worthy Paulinus of Nola.[15] He

---

[1] Oros., *Apol.*, 2. [2] *Ib.*, 31; Jer., *Dial. adv. Pelag.*, i. [3] Oros., *Apol.*, 31.
[4] *Comm. in Jerem.*, iii, 1. [5] *Ib.*, cf. Oros., *Apol.*, 31.
[6] Id., *Dial. adv. Pelag.*, iii, 16. [7] Id., *Comm. in Jerem.*, Prolog. 4.
[8] *Apol.*, 31. [9] *Ib.* [10] *Ib.*, 16.
[11] Jer., *Dial. adv. Pelag.*, ii, 10. [12] *Ib.*, i, 29. Cf. id., *Ep.*, 50, 4.
[13] *De Pecc. Mer.*, iii, 1; iii, 6. [14] *De Gest. Pel.*, xxii, 46.
[15] *Ep.*, 186, 1.

appraised his zeal—"hominem zelo ardentissimo accensum"[1]
—his zeal indeed for God,[2] and applauded his noble character
and pure living.[3]   Here was a good man, one who should be
spoken of on all sides.[4]   Even when the controversy is well
under way, and he is seeking with all his powers to refute
Pelagius' views he speaks of him "familiore affectu,"[5] and
addresses him as "dominus dilectissimus et desideratissimus
frater."[6]   We must remember too that Jerome had once
thought him worthy of his friendship,[7] and for all his abuse,
does not fail to recognize his high qualities.[8]   His asceticism
was widely famed and admired, and his personal influence
upon Timasius and James in inducing them to renounce worldly
riches and adopt the ascetic life would have been unthinkable
unless he himself had been an exemplar of the sort of life
which he was advocating.   They indeed, after they had come
to criticize his views, retained a deep and earnest love for him
personally.[9]   If he had a moral fault it lay in a real or apparent
lack of humility.   His enemies accuse him of the sin of pride.[10]
Yet it is an accusation too easily levelled against those who are
loyal to the truth as they see it in defiance of numbers or
authority.   He indeed claims, and Augustine agrees, that real
humility and loyalty to the truth go together.[11]   Pelagius was
certainly aware, and could warn others, of the danger of that
false pride which masks itself under a sanctimonious counter-
feit of true humility.[12]   But his repeated assertion that pride is
the gravest sin has something in it of a man conscious of his
own most pressing temptation.[13]   He himself stresses that there
is no virtue in a title without the actuality.   A Christian is not
one who bears the name of Christian, but one who follows and
imitates Christ in all things.[14]   Augustine thought him inclined
to shuffle and conceal his true opinion.[15]   We shall see that this
is explicable in terms of a genuine conviction of orthodoxy and
desire to avoid any other imputation.

[1] *De Nat. et Grat.*, i, 1.   [2] *De Dono Pers.*, 53.   [3] *De Pecc. Mer.*, ii, 25.
[4] *Ib.*, iii, 5.   [5] *De Nat. et Grat.*, lxi, 71.   [6] *De Gest. Pel.*, xxvii–xxviii, 52.
[7] *Comm. in Jer.*, iv, 1, 6.   [8] *Ep.*, 50, 5; 133, 11.
[9] Aug., *De Gest. Pel.*, x, 22.   [10] Oros., *Apol.*, 2; Jer., *Dial. adv. Pelag.*, i.
[11] Aug., *De Nat. et Grat.*, xxxiv, 38.   [12] *Ep. ad Demetr.*, 20.
[13] Aug., *De Nat. et Grat.*, xxvii–xxxiv, 30–39.   [14] *De Vita Christ.*, 6.
[15] *De Pecc. Orig.*, xii, 13.   Cf. *De Gest. Pel.*, x, 22, "verborum eius ambiguitate"; *De Grat. Chr.*, xli, 45, "verborum ambiguitate."

PELAGIUS AT ROME

We may then assume that Pelagius spent the greater part of twenty-five years in Rome, from about 384 till he left the city in 409. How he lived during this period we do not know. But we may certainly regard this as the creative and formative period of his life. His British background, his education, his response to the life of the world around, his clear and sure grasp of the gospel, and now the influence of Rufinus, whom he probably met at the house of Pammachius,[1] perhaps even at the introduction of Jerome, who was a friend of Rufinus[2] were steadily and firmly moulding his thoughts. During this period he must have composed his most substantial works, a treatise in three books on the Trinity, a collection of Scriptural passages relating to Christian practice, called by Augustine and Orosius "Testimoniorum liber" or "Capitulorum liber" and by Gennadius "Eulogiarum liber," and modelled on an early work by Cyprian,[3] and his monumental commentary on St. Paul. It was during this period too that he made the closest though perhaps not the happiest friendship of his life, that with Caelestius. Besides his writing, the moral laxity of the time shocked him into calling his contemporaries to a stricter ascetism and a deeper loyalty to the Gospel.

The first certain event of his life took place in 405, and is recorded by Augustine[4] himself. A bishop quoted with approbation to Pelagius the famous prayer from Augustine's Confessions.[5] "Da quod iubes et iube quod vis." The prayer was in any event over-epigrammatical. It seemed to Pelagius to turn the individual into a mere marionette, impotent before the leading-strings of God, and to destroy the very foundation of that moral effort he had set himself to inculcate in himself and others. He was deeply shocked and violently indignant to such a point that altercation nearly broke out between himself and the bishop. His own thought was moving in quite another direction, and it must have been about this same time that he wrote a letter to Paulinus, which Augustine had read.[6] Pelagius claimed that the letter was filled with the

---

[1] Aug., *De Pecc. Orig.*, iii, 3.   [2] Jer., *Ep.*, 81, 2.
[3] Aug., *C. Duas Ep. Pel.*, iv, 8, 21.
[4] *De Dono Pers.*, 53.   [5] Aug., *Conf.* x, 40.   [6] *De Grat. Chr.*, xxxv, 38.

grace of God, and its theme that we can do nothing without God. But as Augustine read it, its theme seemed to be the powers of human nature, and that the grace of God was there manifested; whether he meant by grace the forgiveness of sins, the teaching and example of Christ, or the power of a blazing love kindled by God in our hearts, was nowhere specified.

We hear no more for four years, but in 409, with Alaric at the gates of Rome, Pelagius and Caelestius withdrew, first to Sicily, and then to North Africa.

CAELESTIUS

Caelestius is now to join Pelagius on the centre of the stage, and we may pause to see what is known about him. He was a young man of aristocratic lineage, born, apparently, an eunuch, who had been trained and practised as an advocate, "auditori-alis scholasticus."[1] But even before he met Pelagius his attention was turning towards the religious life, and he wrote three letters "De monasterio incitamentum."[2] The influence of Pelagius converted him to forsake his legal career for a stricter form of the religious life. Whether it was at the house of Pammachius and under the tutelage of Rufinus that he first met Pelagius is uncertain, but from the fact that he is described as a pupil of Pelagius not of Rufinus, and that Pelagius' views must have been forming before he met Rufinus it might seem more likely that they had met before. On the other hand Caelestius combined a certain impetuosity with his ability, and it does not seem probable that if he held these views in the 390s nothing would have been heard of him for so long. All he tells us is that he heard Rufinus deny original sin, and that is perfectly compatible with a subsequent acceptation through Pelagius' influence and teaching.

Once won over he threw his considerable abilities into the task of propagating Pelagius' views. Indeed it is doubtful whether a major controversy would ever have burst out but for his outspoken advocacy. Pelagius does not in general appear as one who regards his views on sin and grace as a Gospel to be blazoned from the housetops. He is concerned rather with the practical issue of moral effort versus moral indifference. It is

---

[1] Mercator, *Lib. Subn. in Verba Iul.*, 2. [2] *Gennadius, De Vir. Ill.*, 45.

in this light that we may regard Augustine's contrast of Pelagius and his disciple : "Ille apertior, iste occultior fuit; ille pertinacior, iste mendacior; vel certe ille liberior, hic astutior."[1] Caelestius was a publicist and a systematizer, as Pelagius was not, and rapidly became the "magister et totius ductor exercitus."[2]

He was a man of real ability—"prodigiosus" Vincent calls him.[3] His eloquence was copious and ready to hand—"incredibili loquacitate."[4] There was no doubt of his skill in dialectic.[5] Augustine, himself already practised in controversy, admired his technique, and felt that with Caelestius he knew where he was. The modern reader too can admire Caelestius' keenly analytical mind, his probing intellect, but finds it hard to see in him that moral fervour and solidity whose combination is the most attractive feature of Pelagius' personality. Pelagius seems to have eschewed controversy so far as he could, Caelestius to have espoused it, and there is a continual impression that the latter is "making points," arguing for victory rather than for truth, enjoying the interplay of wit for itself. This is not to doubt his sincerity; it is to say that his emphasis was different from his master's, more intellectual, less moralistic.

At the time they went to Africa Caelestius, again unlike his master, was contemplating entering the priesthood. The events of 412 put an end to that at Carthage, but his wishes seem later to have been fulfilled at Ephesus.

PELAGIUS AND CAELESTIUS AT CARTHAGE

Pelagius and Caelestius probably stayed in Sicily until the news came of the fall of Rome. Return being then plainly out of the question, they crossed to Africa. The dominant figure of the African church, Augustine, was fully occupied with the Donatists, and was absent from Hippo. Pelagius spent a short while there, before moving on to Carthage. Augustine, who would have liked to meet him, was disappointed to find him gone sooner than he expected, but relieved to find no trace of the teaching later to be termed "Pelagian." Nothing could

[1] *De Pecc. Orig.*, xii, 13.   [2] Jer., *Ep.*, 133, 5.
[3] Vinc. Ler., *Comm.*, xxiv, 63.   [4] Mercator, *Lib. Subn. in Verba Iul.*, 2.
[5] Cf. Aug. *De Perf. Iust.*, ad init.

more clearly indicate how Pelagius' prime concern was with men's living, and how he felt no missionary zeal about his intellectual views for their own sake; at the same time we may easily understand how Augustine felt that there was concealment and tergiversation involved.

In 411 Augustine was still deeply involved in the Donatist controversy, and though he and Pelagius passed one another at a distance on two or three occasions they had no opportunity of a formal meeting. But he learned in casual conversation with some Christians that the novel view was being spread abroad that what children gained from baptism was not remission of sins but a higher sanctification through union with Christ.[1] This was a new and somewhat startling idea to him, new, as he constantly asserted the whole Pelagian position to be,[2] startling, because it appeared to deny the necessity of baptism to cleanse the infant from the inherited taint of original sin. However, he had neither the leisure nor the opportunity to deal with the question then, and he did not feel Pelagius and Caelestius to be of sufficient standing for any serious heresy to be involved. It is interesting to speculate what would have happened if the great protagonist and antagonist, both men of considerably more transigence and charity than their associates, had met in peace to discuss their differences amicably and constructively. But it was not to be, and Pelagius sailed for Palestine, leaving behind Caelestius, full of evangelical zeal and freed from his moderating influence.

Caelestius threw himself with vigour into his self-appointed task. He talked and wrote,[3] and the result was that he won to his viewpoint quite a large number of the Christian community, and caused a considerable flutter in the pigeon-cotes of those who were unconvinced.[4] At this point he was hoping to take orders as a presbyter,[5] when he was accused of heresy before bishop Aurelius. The accusation was in the hands of a deacon from Milan named Paulinus, who was visiting Africa to collect

---

[1] *De Pecc. Mer.*, iii, 12. Cf. *Contr. Duas Ep. Pel.*, iv, 2.

[2] Cf. *De Pecc. Mer.*, iii, 6, 11, 12; *Contr. duas Ep. Pel.*, iv, 29, 32; *Contr. Iul.*, i, 4, ff.

[3] Aug., *De Pecc. Mer.*, i, 64.

[4] Id., *De Gest. Pel.*, 62.   [5] Id., *Ep.*, 157, 22.

material for his biography of Ambrose.[1] A short charge ("libellus minor"[2]) was drawn up on seven counts, probably in the order and terms that follow. He was accused of himself teaching, and employing others to teach[3] (a significant touch, showing Caelestius as an organizer) :

1. That Adam was created mortal and would have died even if he had not sinned.

2. That the sin of Adam injured himself alone and not the human race.

3. That infants at the moment of birth are in the same condition as Adam was before the Fall.

4. That infants, even though they are not baptized, have eternal life.[4]

5. That the race of man as a whole does not die by the death or fall of Adam, nor does the race of man as a whole rise again by the resurrection of Christ.

6. That the Law has the same effect as the Gospel in introducing men into the kingdom of Heaven.

7. That even before the coming of Christ there were men without sin.[5]

Caelestius faced the charges with legal acumen.[6] He countered question with question, avoided direct answers wherever possible, responded with "perhaps" when Paulinus demanded a plain "yes" or "no," stood on the authority of others, though when challenged he could or would mention only Rufinus by name, and claimed when pressed on the subject of Infant Baptism that he stood by the practice of the Church; the theory was a matter on which Christians were in fact, and might legitimately be, divided. "Iam de traduce peccati dixi, quia intra Catholicam constitutos plures audivi destruere, necnon et alios astruere : licet quaestionis res sit ista,

---

[1] Paul, *Vit. Ambr.*, 1; Mercator, *Lib. Subn. in Verba Iul.*, i, 1.

[2] Aug., *De Pecc. Orig.*, 3.   [3] Mercator, *op. cit.*

[4] Omitted, no doubt by accident, in Mercator, *op. cit.* and *De Gest. Pel.*, xi, 23; in *De Pecc. Orig.*, xi, 12, attributed not to Caelestius but Sicilian Pelagians.

[5] Nos. 6 and 7 placed after no. 2, in Aug., *De Gest. Pel.*, xi, 23, *De Pecc. Orig.*, xi, 12, but not in the official record. *De Pecc. Orig.*, ii–iii. No. 7 paraphrased in *Mercator, op. cit.*, ii, 5.

[6] Aug., *De Pecc. Orig.*, iii–iv.

non haeresis. Infantes semper dixi egere Baptismo, ac debere baptizari : quid quaerit aliud ?" It seems that the prosecution concentrated upon this question of Infant Baptism, perhaps because it least admitted ultimate evasion, and brought the issues into a clearer light. Caelestius was either invited, or voluntarily decided, to submit a written statement on the topic at some later stage in the investigation.[1] In it he went further, and professed that the purpose of baptism was to enable the infant to share in the common redemption of mankind. This remained ambiguous : it might not mean redemption from sin but admission to a higher sanctification. Later still, though not in the course of this trial, he was to acknowledge baptism for the remission of sins; but he meant thereby that from birth infants were capable of sin.[2] In fact the moment of baptism was not the moment in question. The real question was "Do you believe in an inherited taint?" To that question Caelestius could not answer "Yes," and at this stage he could not or would not answer "No," but he never concealed his doubts. He steadfastly refused to disavow the propositions imputed to him, and was excommunicated. For a moment he thought of appealing to Rome, but when he finally departed it was for Ephesus and the East.[3]

Principal Sources

Primary : Pelagius, Mercator, Augustine, Jerome, Orosius, Prosper.
Secondary : G. de Plinval, *Pélage*; A. Souter, *Texts and Studies IX*; Arts in Smith's *Dictionary of Christian Biography*; W. Bright, *Select Anti-Pelagian treatises of St. Augustine*, Introduction; L. Duchesne, *Histoire de l'Eglise*. See bibliography at end.

[1] Aug., *De Pecc. Orig.*, xix, 21.
[2] Id. *De Pecc. Mer.*, i, 64.
[3] Mercator, *op. cit.*, i, 1, 2.

V

AUGUSTINE

The dominating figure in the Church at this time was Augustine. He was born at Tagaste in Numidia on 13th November, 354, and was now approaching the age of sixty, and at the height alike of his powers and his reputation. His father Patricius was a man of some violence and coarseness; Augustine freed himself from the latter, but his heritage is seen in the depth of his emotional conflicts, and the vigour of his polemic. His mother, Monnica, is rightly revered as one of the great exemplars of Christian womanhood; she was destined to win first her husband and then her son for Christ.

Augustine's youth was free and loose; to-day we may feel that he exaggerated its sinfulness, so that an expedition to scrump pears takes on the aspect of mortal sin, but his psychological reaction from it was real and bitter. He tried, like so many of his contemporaries, to escape into the circus or the games, but found his passions there the more inflamed. It was from himself that he was flying and he could not escape. He passed from Tagaste to Carthage, back and forth, and in 383 went to Rome, and thence to Milan.

As his intellectual and spiritual life developed three groups of influences may be discerned. The first came from the pagan philosophers, Cicero's "Hortensius," Plato and Plotinus. They gave him a vision and an aspiration, a vision of God, immortality, truth, beauty and absolute reality. But it remained an aspiration. Communion was not yet for him. Secondly for nine years he was profoundly influenced by Manichean dualism. Its radical contrast of good with evil responded to his own psychological experiences; for that reason it deepened his conviction of evil as something endemic, and, perhaps less happily, left him with a morbid attitude towards concupiscence and sexual intercourse. Thirdly he had before him the example of two radiantly Christian lives in his mother Monnica and his spiritual father Ambrose. The spiritual leaven was working in him, slowly but inexorably. There was a moment of crisis, and, broken before the Cross, he found his true strength. His restlessness was over; he found his rest in God.

On 25th April, 387, he was baptized. Presently he returned to Africa, and there after a short period of communal life with some friends he was ordained priest by the bishop of Hippo, Valerius, whose coadjutor and successor in office he was to become. His career in the church was marked by his zeal for orthodoxy and catholicity, even to the enunciation of the dangerous principle of coercion, as may be evidenced in his conduct of the Donatist controversy, by the sweep and authority of his learning, which made him one of the great doctors of the Church, and by his personal humility and simplicity of life even in high office. His controversial engagements are marked by his passion for the truth, and his personal forbearance towards his opponents.[1]

AUGUSTINE AND PELAGIANISM

Caelestius had departed, but his views remained behind. Augustine, with somewhat more leisure at his command, entered the lists. He first primed himself with a more thorough knowledge of the theology which underlay the disputable propositions which the bishop's court had condemned,[2] and discovered, for example, the distinction between salvation and the higher sanctification alluded to above, and expressed in terms of a distinction between "eternal life" and "the kingdom of heaven."[3] He discovered too that the Pelagians maintained the relationship of the sins of mankind to the sin of Adam not to be organic, but the result of imitation.[4] This is the doctrine anathematized in the famous words of the 9th Article of the Church of England : "Original sin standeth not in the following" (i.e. the imitation) "of Adam (as the Pelagians do vainly talk)." Here discussion turned to the interpretation of Romans v. 12. The Greek words ἐφ' ᾧ πάντες ἥμαρτον were erroneously rendered in the Latin version Augustine used as "in quo omnes peccaverunt." The Pelagians more accurately

[1] E.g. *Epp.*, 133, 134, 139.   [2] *De Pecc. Mer.*, i, 64.
[3] *De Pecc. Mer.*, i, 23, 58; ii, 41; *Contra duas Ep. Pel.*, i, 40; *Serm.*, 294, 2; *Ep.*, 194, 32.
[4] *De Pecc. Mer.*, i, 9.

rendered it as "quia" or "propter quod." Further Augustine came upon a number of verbal dilemmas posed by the Pelagians, such as Pelagius' own "If baptism effaces original sin, can the child of baptised parents be born in sin?"[1]

He set himself to eradicate these views alike by his personal influence, by writing books and tracts,[3] and by his preaching.[3] In sermons at this time he spoke of the universal domain of sin; infants as well as adults needed Christ as their Saviour, and it was for this reason that they received Baptism and Holy Communion, according to the practice of those days. From the universality of sin he turned to the grace of God. We need God's "co-operating grace" indeed, but we need His "prevenient grace" as well. The two phrases are Augustine's own; the first comes from the "domino cooperante" of Mark xvi. 20 the second from Psalm lix. 10 "Deus meus misericordia eius praeveniet me." The first represents the need for the continual help and guidance of God; the second explains Paul's conviction that even his will to good is implanted by God,[4] and is justified by Jesus' own words "No man can come to me, except the Father which sent me draw him."[5] In none of these sermons does he mention Pelagius or Caelestius by name.

MARCELLINUS

About this time his friend Flavius Marcellinus, tribune and notary, indeed according to Cassiodorus "primicerius notariorum," whose brother Apringius became proconsul of Africa, wrote to Augustine to say that he was harried by Pelagians of a missionary turn of mind, and to ask Augustine's judgment upon the views they were propounding. These views correspond closely to those which Caelestius was called on to recant at Carthage, but especially the first three, relating to the mortality of Adam, the relation of our sin to his, and the principle underlying infant baptism. Augustine undertook his answer in three books. The first concentrates upon the position of Caelestius : it is based upon a treatise whose author he does not name.[6] Here he takes as his theme the Pauline antithesis between the first Adam and the second Adam.

---

[1] *De Pecc. Mer.*, iii, 16.   [2] *De Gest. Pel.*, 25.   [3] *Serm.*, 170, 174, 175.
[4] Phil., ii. 13.   [5] John, vi. 44.   [6] *De Pecc. Mer.*, i, 64.

Death is not just an accident of sinful man, nor is it a natural
attendant of his existence; it is the punishment for the sin of
Adam, and it has affected his whole progeny. The practice
of infant baptism points as its justification to the existence of an
inherited trait from which the infant needs redemption; in
baptism he is incorporated into the body of Christ, and finds
his salvation. This book alone shows the majesty of Augustine's
thoughts, and the power which found an answering echo alike
in Luther and those against whom Luther was rebelling. It is
Catholic in its unquestioning acceptance of the institutions of
the Church, Protestant in its rich insistence upon fidelity to the
New Testament. There is however here nothing of natural
philosophy. In the second book he allowed himself a greater
freedom of speculation. Here he treats of the wider issues of
Pelagianism, but he is still unwilling to impugn either Pelagius
or Caelestius by name. He is willing to admit the abstract
possibility of sinlessness in this life, a position to which he long
clung[1] though he finally rejected it.[2] But in fact no man is
wholly without sin, save only the one Mediator, the God-man,
Christ. At this point he had concluded the argument he
wished to present when he came upon Pelagius' commentary
upon the Epistles, and felt constrained to rebut further the
arguments upon original sin which he there found. If
Christian discipleship demands that we shall hate the sin but
love the sinner, Augustine shows his in hating the heresy while
loving the heretic. "Hominem non odi" he might well say,
"sed eius vitia." He has no mercy for the Pelagian view of
original sin which he combats with all the considerable
armoury at his command. But for Pelagius himself, who is
now for the first time specifically named, he has nothing but
the highest respect, and speaks of him, to use a hackneyed
phrase, more in sorrow than in anger.[3]

Even with this additional book he was not done. Marcellinus was disturbed at Augustine's assertion of even the
abstractest of possibilities that a man could live without sin,
and questions him further.[4] The result was the treatise "De

---

[1] *De Gest. Pel.*, xxx, 55; cf. *De Spir. et Litt.*, ii, 3.

[2] *Contra duas Ep. Pel.*, iv, 27.

[3] *De Pecc. Mer.*, iii, 1; iii, 6.   [4] *De Spir. et Litt.*, i, 1.

Spiritu et Littera." He begins by arguing that the impossibility of an event is not disproved by the absence of actual examples. Those who say that man can live or has lived without sin are comparatively harmless, but those who deny the necessity of grace must be vigorously withstood. "Atrociter" (or "acriter") "disputavi" he wrote later "contra inimicos gratiae Dei."[1] The rest of the work is an exaltation of God's grace, mediated by the Holy Spirit, a contrast between the Law and the Gospel, bringing out clearly the inadequacy of the former by itself, and a beautiful exposition of 2 Cor. iii, 6, the verse from which the treatise takes its name. The passage with the greatest direct bearing upon the controversy is the discussion of the will to believe.[2] Freewill is the natural gift of God. Of itself it is a "via media" which may turn to faith or faithlessness. The will to faith is a gift of God's grace through His Spirit. "Nam illud quod dictum est, Deus est enim qui operatur in nobis et velle et operari, pro bona voluntate : iam gratiae est, quam fides impetrat, ut possint esse hominis opera bona, quae operatur fides, per dilectionem, quae diffunditur in corde per Spiritum Sanctum qui datus est nobis."[3] The law might give the individual the knowledge of his duty; it cannot give him the power to fulfil it : that enabling love comes from the Spirit.

Augustine in the Pulpit

This was only the beginning. Finding that the views of Pelagius and Caelestius, so far from being exterminated by the decision at Carthage, were actually spreading, Augustine set himself the more vigorously to preach against the heresy, and sought with all his eloquence and authority to controvert it in three notable sermons.[4] The third of these, preached at Carthage on 27th June, 413, will illustrate the current stage of the dispute. The Gospel for the day consisted of the conversation between Jesus and Nicodemus. Taking this as his starting-point Augustine addressed himself to the whole question of infant baptism, and faced the Pelagian position that infants are baptized not for remission of sins but for a higher sanctification, and that Adam's sin affected his descendents only by

[1] *Retract*, ii, 37.   [2] *De Spir. et Litt.*, xxxiii–xxxiv, 57–60.
[3] *Ib.*, xxxiii, 57.   [4] *Serm.*, 115, 293, 294.

example. He met too the dilemmas they posed, that the children of baptized parents should be free from inherited taint, and that, if Adam's sin injured those who had not themselves sinned, the saving work of Christ should be equally efficacious for good even in the lives of those who have not believed. But he laid greatest stress, preaching to a Carthaginian congregation, upon the words of Cyprian, their great martyr-bishop,[1] and read from one of his letters a passage which he interpreted as a clear assertion that the object of infant baptism was the remission of sin contracted in the fact of their birth. Augustine's temper and spirit is well shown in his closing words. He is governed by an absolute loyalty to what he believed to be the truth. But precisely because of that loyalty and within that loyalty he is governed also by the spirit of Christian love towards those whom he believes to be in error. He is passionately anxious for their sakes that "error iste nefarius"[2] shall be removed from their minds, and that they should not by persisting therein cut themselves off from communion with the Church. It appears that the result of his campaign was to win over some of those who had accepted Pelagius' views, and to discourage the others from public activity. But he was well aware that the battle was not won; resistance was only driven underground. "Occulte mussitant" he said.[3] For the rest of the year however controversy was quiescent, and Augustine and Pelagius corresponded in terms of deep affection. Pelagius is "dominus dilectissimus," "desideratissimus frater," "tua benignitas."[4] Curiously, there is no mention at all of their theological differences; Augustine was later to complain that Pelagius unfairly misinterpreted this.[5]

DEMETRIAS

The following year saw new occasions of division. The noble Demetrias, daughter of Juliana and grand-daughter of Proba, resolved to take the vow of virginity; her only bridegroom should be Christ. She had come to Africa with her mother at much the same time as Pelagius, leaving Rome because of the danger from Alaric, only to fall in with equal danger at the

---

[1] *De Gest. Pel.*, xi, 25.   [2] *Ib.*   [3] *Ep.*, 157, 22.
[4] *Ep.*, 146   [5] *De Gest. Pel.*, xxvii–xxviii, 52.

hands of the rapacious Count Heraclian. Her Christian
education had been under the guidance of Augustine and
Alypius,[1] but she must also have known Pelagius with some
degree of intimacy. Her parents had planned marriage for her
but acceded willingly to her purpose, which, we are told,
gladdened all the churches of Africa.[2] Letters were addressed
to her both by Jerome[3] and Pelagius.[4] Jerome directed her
to a life of study and fasting, labour and good works through
her wealth, warned her to be careful in her choice of companions, and not to worry her head over difficult theological
problems which might be raised by followers of Origen. It
looks as if he were suspicious of the influence of Pelagius,
whose teaching was to him "Origenis ramusculus." Newman
describes the letter as "sage and sobering." Pelagius' moral
exhortations to her are equally strongly felt, but more generally
expressed. He draws out a contrast between the life she would
have lived in the secular world, and that which she was to live
in the convent. The care she would have taken to surpass her
neighbours in splendour of dress and ornament must now be
directed to surpassing them in moral probity and excellence
of living. She would have had the eyes of the world upon her;
now she had the eyes not only of the world, but of God and his
angels. Christ her Bridegroom did not care less than an
earthly husband that she should rightly deck her person for
Him. She must be blameless and harmless, a veritable child
of God, shining as a beacon amidst a crooked and perverse
generation.[5] All this shows Pelagius' high concern for moral
rectitude; it shows also a sound psychology, in seeking to
transfer to a higher object the passions and ambitions of the
world, to "sublimate" them, using the word as it is used in the
loose jargon of popular psychology. More specifically he
directs her to Bible study and to prayer, and warns her against
the sin of sloth. At the same time he uses Demetrias as an
example of the power of the human will. It is God indeed
who arms us with the spiritual weapons of understanding and
right thinking when we stand unarmed before the world, but
only in order that we may be free and unconstrained executants

[1] Aug., *Ep.*, 150, 188.   [2] Jer., *Ep.*, 130, 6.
[3] Jer., *Ep.*, 130.   [4] Pel., *Ep. ad Demetr.*   [5] Phil. ii. 15.

of His justice, "voluntarium, non coactum." He has given us
a capacity for right or wrong action; he wants us to choose the
right, but gives us the possibility of wrong choice in order that
our fulfilment of His will may come from our own wills, not
from His. Thus there is what we may call a kind of natural
holiness in our hearts. "Est enim, inquam, in animis nostris
naturalis quaedam (ut ita dixerim) sanctitas." It may be
seen in the noble and righteous lives of many of the pagan
philosophers, whose virtues he eloquently extols "castos,
patientes, modestos, liberales, abstinentes, benignos, et honores
mundi simul et delicias respuentes, et amatores iustitiae non
minus quam scientiae." It may be seen too in the perfect
righteousness of the patriarchs even before the Mosaic Law,
Abel, Enoch, Noah, Melchisedek, Joseph, Job. Such
righteousness seems alien to us because our wills are wrongly
orientated, and we are oppressed by a weight of evil habit.
But that which evil habit has done, the force of good habit
can undo. Our salvation is in our own hands. "Spiritales
vero divitias nullus tibi praeter te conferre poterit."[1]
Augustine was to reply to this in a letter to Juliana,[2] in which
he protested that the virtues of Demetrias, great and outstanding as they were, did not come from her own strength,
but were the gift of God; she must be humble and honour the
Saviour to whom alone she owed her high merits. His immediate response however to Demetrias' acceptance of the veil
was the treatise "De bono viduitatis," directed to Juliana and
Proba. It is evident that he, like Jerome, was anxious about
the influence of Pelagius. He warns them against those who,
in their exaltation of the power and freedom of the human will,
deny the need for prayer, saying "Why should I ask God for
that which He has set in my own power?" He asserts with
pressing vigour that free will has no power apart from God's
grace, and calls on them to remember, and to remind others,
that

> Every virtue we possess
> And every victory won
> And every thought of holiness
> Are His alone.[3]

---

[1] *Ep. ad Dem.*, 11.   [2] *Ep.*, 188.   [3] Harriet Auber, *Hymn on the Holy Spirit*.

The very fervency of his advocacy offended Juliana, and failed to convince Pelagius.

HILARY

The next occasion for intervention was a letter from one Hilary in Sicily. This indicated that Pelagianism was rife in the island, and especially at Syracuse. We cannot now tell whether this was the product of Pelagius' brief stay there on his way to Africa, or whether the ideas were reimported from there later, or whether, as Augustine half-suspected, Caelestius was at work, seeking fresh converts. Hilary raised five points which he found to be popularly held in Sicily; the very method of their formulation shows a failure to discriminate between essentials and inessentials, while it may serve as a reminder that Pelagius had a wider message to give than the mere denial of original sin, which has been obscured in the concentration upon the foremost issue. The five points Hilary presented were as follows :[1] that man can live without sin, and without difficulty fulfil the commandments of God, if he will; that an infant on whom death descends before baptism is given does not deserve to perish, being born without sin; that the rich man who retains his riches instead of giving them up cannot enter the Kingdom of God even if he uses his riches to fulfil God's commandments; that swearing is absolutely forbidden; and that the nature of the Church is to be completely free from spot or blemish. Augustine replied in a long and elaborate letter,[2] which might, as de Plinval suggests,[3] be almost accounted a fourth volume to the treatise "De Peccatorum Meritis." In this letter he does three things. In the first section he draws out the theological implications of the practical problems which Hilary has raised, implications about which the latter was largely unaware or at the very least unconcerned. Neither the Law nor free will have of themselves any adequacy; we are at every point driven back upon our need for the free grace of God; hence the centrality in the Christian life of the prayer of repentance. Secondly he tackled afresh, and with far more assurance and authority, the theory of original sin, returning to the scriptural centre of controversy, the "in quo omnes peccaverunt" of

[1] Aug., *Ep.*, 156. [2] *Ep.*, 157. [3] G. de Plinval, *Pélage*, p. 267.

Romans v. 12 and arguing for a physical inheritance of original sin. Thirdly he discussed at length the place of riches in the Church. He did not want in any way to derogate from the injunction to renounce worldly wealth. But the Church was a great net containing all manner of fishes; the big fish had his place as well as the little fish, and there was work to be done within and in the name of the Church by the resources of the wealthy. The events in Africa and Sicily were leading Augustine to develop his theological position, but they show too a growing practical anxiety over the spread of Pelagian teaching.

EUTROPIUS AND PAUL

Augustine was not yet done with trouble in Sicily. Later in this same year, or possibly at the beginning of the following year, two bishops named Eutropius and Paul[1] forwarded to him a document which was circulating among the Christians of Sicily, and which attempted to reduce to absurdity, by a series of sixteen arguments, the orthodox position. The document was anonymous, but was attributed to Caelestius.[2] Augustine accepts the attribution, seeing that he has come upon similar arguments in a work undoubtedly by Caelestius.[3] Jerome too combats much the same position in a writing which he regards as by Caelestius, though he does not mention him by name.[4] And indeed we may see the keen and shrewd brain of the lawyer in the formulation of these sharp intellectual dilemmas.

1. If sin cannot be avoided it is not sin (neither philosophy nor justice would allow the name of sin, which implies moral responsibility, to that which is absolutely inevitable). If it can be avoided, man can live without sin.

2. If sin comes from necessity, it is not sin; if from free will it can be avoided.

3. If sin is an essential part of human nature, it ceases to be sin; if an accidental, it can be avoided.

[1] Cf. Oros., Comm., i. Bright calls him Eulogius (p. xxiv), but this is a confusion with the bishop of Caesarea who presided at Diospolis.
[2] De Perf. Iust., i.   [3] Ib.   [4] Jer., Ep., 133; Dial., 21.

4. If sin is a substance,[1] it must be created by God. Such a statement is blasphemous. Sin therefore is not a substance existing of itself but something which men do. But if so it is something which they might not do, that is, it can be avoided.

5. An "ought" implies a "can." A man ought to live without sin : therefore he can.

6. The injunction to live without sin implies its possibility.

7. God wills us to live without sin : the will of God must be capable of fulfilment.

8. God does not will us to live with sin : it is blasphemous to suppose then that he would create man incapable of living without sin.

9. If sin comes from natural necessity, it is not blameworthy; if from our free decision it can be avoided, for God would not give us a will inclined to evil rather than good.

10. God made man good and commanded him to be good. It is blasphemous to say that man is evil and incapable of good.

11. Sin consists in "leaving undone those things which ought to be done and in doing those things which ought not to be done." The very statement makes clear that it is possible to do the former and refrain from the latter.

12. If man's alleged inability to be free from sin comes from nature, it is not sin. If from will, will may be changed by will.

13. If the inability comes from outside, he is not responsible; if from inside he is not responsible for a failure to be what his very nature prohibits him from being.

14. It is heretical to deny the goodness of human nature. (The mention of the Manicheans at this point is significantly directed against Augustine). But to say that human nature cannot be free from the evil of sin is to do precisely that.

15. God would not be just if He held against any man as a sin something which that man could not avoid.

---

[1] The word "substance" is here used loosely, not technically, to render the Latin "res". But Pelagius himself, with some Aristotelian training, does actually use "substantia" in a parallel passage. v. Aug., *De Nat. et Grat.*, xix, 21.

16. Each of us can be without sin, though we are not. But if we examine why, we freely admit that the fault is ours.[1]

From these philosophical and theological considerations Caelestius proceeded to a full and careful examination of their scriptural basis. We are reminded, and it is perhaps salutary, that controversy was never allowed to soar far off on the wings of abstract speculation, but was continually brought back to the touchstone of the revealed Word of God. He cites a series of texts to show the injunction of sinlessness, which certainly in making the injunction appear to assume the possibility of its fulfilment.[2] Typical, though the only quotation from the Gospels, are the words from the Sermon on the Mount "Be ye therefore perfect, even as your Father in Heaven is perfect." A further series of texts shows that the will of God is not only not impossible, but not even difficult, of fulfilment.[3] The yoke of Jesus is easy and His burden light; His commandments are not grievous. There follows a particularly interesting passage in which Caelestius collects the texts which are commonly used in criticism of his contentions.[4] These are fairly and fully quoted with no attempt at misrepresentation, and their collective testimony is as weighty in disavowing the possibility of a life of perfect virtue as the earlier passages were in supporting it. Caelestius makes no attempt to explain, or to explain away the texts, as indeed Augustine with some triumph points out. Instead he counters each of them, without any effort at reconciliation with a large number of other texts which contradict and controvert their implication of the impossibility of sinlessness. With a rare sense of context these answers are chosen where possible from the same work as the original text. Thus the passage from Job, "Who is pure from sin?" is countered by

---

[1] *De Perf. Iust.*, ii–vii, 1–16, summarized.

[2] *De Perf. Iust.*, ix, 20. The texts are Deut. xviii. 13; xxiii. 18; Lev. xix. 2; Ps. xv. 1–2; xviii. 24; cxix. 1; Prov. xi. 20; Matt. v. 48; 1 Cor. xv. 34; 2 Cor. xiii. 11; Eph. i. 3–4; v. 27; Phil. ii. 14–15; Col. i. 21–2, 28; 1 Pet. i. 13–16. The warning should be given that the English Bible is not always a reliable guide to Caelestius' reading.

[3] *De Perf. Iust.*, x, 22. The texts are Deut. xxx. 9–14; Matt. xi. 28–30; 1 John v. 3.

[4] *De Perf. Iust.*, xi–xix, 23–42. The texts are Job xiv. 4; Ps. xiv. 1, 3; cxvi. 11; cxliii. 2; Prov. xx. 9; Eccles. vii. 21; Mark x. 18 or Luke xviii. 19; Rom. iv. 16; 1 John i. 8.

"I am a just man," "I know that I shall be found just," "My prayer is pure," "He inflicts many wounds upon me without cause," "I have kept his ways, and have not departed and will not depart from his commandments," "Throughout my life my heart has not reproached me." "I was clothed with justice."[1] Similarly the quotation from the Gospels "Why callest thou me good? There is none good, save only God," is met by references to the good man from the lips of Jesus.[2] Caelestius ends his work by returning to his initial theme. He asks if there can exist a completely sinless man, and replies that if God wills it, there can; God does will it; therefore there can.[3]

We need not follow Augustine's answer in all its details. His reply to the document is to be found in the treatise "De Perfectione Iustitiae Hominis" from which Caelestius' case has been already quoted. The treatise is not precisely datable. It must be before 418, because at the very end he says that he does not venture to criticize, though he cannot defend those who declare that there have been, besides Christ, men either without sin, or whose sin was not imputed to them, and this position was in fact condemned at the Council of Carthage in that year. It seems best to date it early in 415: the communication from the bishops came within a year of his correspondence with Hilary, and it is unlikely that with his mind full of the problems involved, and his concern for the spiritual well-being of the Sicilian churches he would have delayed in answer. The dilemmas posed by Caelestius, though each is worded concisely and cogently, are as a whole somewhat repetitive. Augustine does not fully answer his fundamental assertion, which is that the word "sin" implies moral responsibility, that is to say the free action of the will, and not an inherited and inevitable taint. He does successfully meet Caelestius' difficulty about whether human nature is naturally good or evil in the orthodox conception of human nature as naturally good, but corrupted. Above all he again and again reiterates that the means to a life without sin, which is indeed possible, is the grace of God

---

[1] Job xiv. 4 as against xii. 4; xiii. 18; xvi. 17; ix. 17; xxiii. 11; xxvii. 6; xxix. 14.

[2] Mark x. 18 = Luke xviii. 19, as against Matt. v. 45; xii. 33.

[3] *De Perf. Iust.*, xx, 43.

mediated through Jesus Christ our Lord. In the second part of his answer he reasserts the validity of the texts which Caelestius has sought to counter, noticing that he has only contradicted them without explaining them, and buttresses them further from his wide and deep knowledge of the scriptures. But he also explains Caelestius' texts in such a way that they may cohere with his own teaching, principally through a subtle distinction between perfection of desire and perfection of attainment, perfection in seeking and the perfection of finding, and through his admission of the possibility of sinless living by the grace of God. He ends with the solemn words that if any man denies the necessity of the prayer "Lead us not into temptation"—and to say that human will without the grace of God suffices to avoid sin is tantamount to this—he is to be anathema.[1]

TIMASIUS AND JAMES

A third occasion which turned Augustine to write against Pelagius was his encounter with Timasius and James. These have already been mentioned as young men of noble parentage and good education who had been induced by the personal influence of Pelagius to renounce secular ambition for the service of God.[2] With his exhortations to the spiritual life they had naturally imbibed many of his theological views. Augustine, however, had made a considerable impression upon them by the manner in which he extolled and expounded the grace of God. They now sent to him the "De Natura" of Pelagius, and asked him for a point by point reply to it.[3] In this they were governed, as much as anything, by the very deep affection in which they held Pelagius himself.[4]

The contents of this work may be deduced from Augustine's quotations and criticisms. In later life he summarized it as defending human nature against God's grace by a very full exposition of the available arguments.[5] Pelagius began by a distinction between the possible and the actual. He was not

---

[1] *Ib.*, xxi, 44.   [2] Aug., *Ep.*, 179, 2.
[3] *De Gest. Pel.*, xxiv, 48.   [4] *Ib.*, x, 22.
[5] *Retract.*, i, 42. "Argumentatio" which Augustine here uses is defined by Cicero *Part. Or.*, 13 as "explicatio argumenti" and *De Inv.*, i, 40 as "inventi artificiosa expolitio."

maintaining that any sinless man actually existed, but that it was possible for him to do so. "De posse et non posse, non de esse et non esse contendimus."[1] To those who admit the possibility, but only by the grace of God, he replies that the important point is then established of the possibility : the means by which that possibility may be realized are secondary.[2] He goes on to argue that man has this possibility by his natural endowment, and hence does not need the aid of special grace.[3] Sin is not a substantial entity, it is to be found in action, and, not being a substantial entity, is incapable of warping human nature.[4] When man has actually sinned then he stands in need of help; here we must pray for God's pardon; God enters the scene as a doctor to heal the wound.[5] But this sin comes from ourselves, and it is basically the sin of pride. "Tam peccare superbire est quam superbire peccare."[6] Pride is an exaltation of self by self, and it is thus avoidable. But the possibility, or indeed the actuality, of not sinning does not put us on a level with God : the angels are not God's equals.[7] In fact he claims sinlessness and righteous living for many of those mentioned in the Old and New Testaments,[8] but reiterates that he is dealing in possibilities not actualities.[9] God does not command impossibilities[10]; if our nature made it impossible for us to be free from sin, our wills would be constrained and not truly free[11]; in the endowment of our human nature God has granted us the power of not sinning, and this power, coming from God, may rightly be called ours by God's grace, or we shall be introducing a totally illegitimate division in God.[12] The argument at times lacks Pelagius' usual clarity, and indeed Augustine at one point terms it tortuous and somewhat obscure. This is the place where negative piles on negative till we arrive at the conclusion "si voluerimus non posse non peccare, non possumus non posse non peccare."[13] The work was interspersed

---

[1] *De Nat. et Grat.*, vii, 8.   [2] *Ib.*, x, 11.   [3] *Ib.*, xi, 12.

[4] *Ib.*, xix, 21. Bright, *Anti-Pelagian Treatises of St. Augustine*, xxiii, terms this the "theory that evil was a privation of good," but surely wrongly. Pelagius' point is that sin is not an Aristotelian substance with a certain permanence attaching to it, but is to be discovered in a series of actions, each of which is "sinful."

[5] *Ib.*, xviii, 20; xxvi, 29.   [6] *Ib.*, xxix, 33.   [7] *Ib.*, xxxiii, 37.
[8] *Ib.*, xxxvi, 42.   [9] *Ib.*, xlii, 49.   [10] *Ib.*, xliii, 50.
[11] *Ib.*, xlvi, 54.   [12] *Ib.*, li, 59.   [13] *Ib.*, xlix, 57.

F

with more detailed discussion of some passages of scripture, and
Pelagius adduced in his support a number of quotations from
the Fathers of the Church, including one from Augustine,[1]
and one in which by a rare failure in accurate scholarship he
quoted some words of the Pythagorean philosopher Sextus
under the impression that they were written by a bishop of
Rome named Xystus.[2] Incidental (and the fact that they are
incidental is significant) but of great interest are two references
to the person of Jesus. In one he makes the point that in
Christ death was not the punishment of sin.[3] In the whole of
the controversy surprisingly little is made of this point, to which
we shall have to recur later. In the second passage unfortunately there is no direct citation of Pelagius, and we cannot
be sure that Augustine is interpreting him fairly. Augustine
suggests that to Pelagius Christ was necessary (the exact
phrase is, a little strangely, "Christi nomen") in order that
we might learn from His example the nature of right living, not
in order that we might be helped by His grace to live rightly.[4]
Certainly the characteristic theme of the work was its defence
of human nature.[5] Augustine speaks, with a touch of irony,
of "multum ab isto laudata potentia naturae et voluntas
hominis,"[6] and read the conclusion as being that the grace of
God consists in "naturam cum libero arbitrio conditam."[7]

Augustine in his reply, which must be dated to early in 415,
is respectful to Pelagius, though not to his views, and deliberately refrains from mentioning him by name.[8] He speaks
with approbation of his moral earnestness,[9] and with rather less
approbation of his intellectual acumen, which is considerable,
but savours too much of the wisdom of the world.[10] Once or
twice his rejection of Pelagius' views leads him to a certain
petulance,[11] but in general he calls for reconciliation[12] and an
end of dispute,[13] stands on the ground of personal friendship,
and wants no more than that his friend should walk in the
way of truth.[14] Once again it is not needful to follow Augustine's refutation of Pelagius detail by detail. His general

[1] *Ib.*, lxvii, 80. [2] *Retract.*, i, 42. [3] *De Nat. et Grat.*, xxiv, 26.
[4] *Ib.*, xl, 47. [5] *Ib.*, xxxiv, 39. [6] *Ib.*, xviii, 20.
[7] *De Gest. Pel.*, xxiii, 47. [8] *Ib.*
[9] *De Nat. et Grat.*, i, 1. Cf. lxviii, 82. [10] *Ib.*, vi, 6.
[11] E.g. *Ib.*, lv, 65. [12] *Ib.*, xliv, 52. [13] *Ib.*, liv, 63. [14] *Ib.*, vi, 6.

position is asserted in the opening section of his reply.[1] The righteousness of God is not to be found in the Law but in the saving work of Christ. All have sinned and are saved only by His free grace through His blood. Those who say that man can live righteously by nature make the Cross of Christ of no effect. The truth is that human nature was created without blemish; it was corrupted by the sin of Adam. All have sinned either in Adam or in themselves. Redemption comes of Christ, freely, not according to merit. "Universa igitur massa poenas debet :" the phrase is important in view of later teaching that mankind is a "massa peccatrix" or even a "massa perditionis."[2] But we are saved through the mercy of God who sent Jesus Christ into the world to save those sinners "quos praescivit, et praedestinavit, et vocavit, et iustificavit, et glorificavit;" in the majesty of the conception the sonorous prose soars on wings of eloquence, and the rhythms and assonances of Fronto, Apuleius and the "elocutio novella" leap from the page. Augustine's fundamental criticism of Pelagius in this work is that the logical conclusion of his arguments is to put righteousness and salvation outside Christ and His Church, whereas Augustine knows himself to be in complete dependence upon Christ, and all his powers to come from Him. This contention is repeated again and again. At the very outset he argues that if human nature can assure itself of eternal life unaided, then faith in Christ is needless.[3] Further on he calls Pelagius back to his Christian profession : "O frater, bonum est ut memineris te esse Christianum."[4] Again, as we have seen, he suggests that Pelagius' Christianity means following Christ's example, not dependence on His grace.[5] Towards the end, in a discussion of baptism, he remarks with quiet sarcasm that Pelagius cannot completely forget that he is a Christian, although his memory of the fact is insubstantial ("licet tenuiter recordatus est"), and at that point, stands aside from his defence of human nature.[6] There is much of

---

[1] *Ib.*, i–v, 1–5.

[2] *De Dono Pers.*, 35; *Contra duas Ep. Pel.*, II, vii, 13; *De Pecc. Or.*, xxxi, 36; *Ep.*, 186, 19; 194, 4; *De Div. Quaest.*, I, ii, 16; *De Corr. et Grat.*, 16; *Contra Iul.*, v, 14.

[3] *De Nat. et Grat.*, ii, 2.   [4] *Ib.*, xx, 22.   [5] *Ib.*, xl, 47.

[6] *Ib.*, lii, 60 and cf. liv, 64.

detailed interest.   One point to which we shall recur is that
though he does not allow sinlessness to the patriarchy and
prophets of the Old Testament, he will not refuse to allow it to
Mary the Mother of Jesus.[1]   The broad sweep of his knowledge
of the Bible, and his extraordinary powers of assimilation are
again made clear; to this is added a careful understanding of
the Fathers, a plea for the reading of text in context, and a
pleasant echo of days in Milan with Ambrose.[2]   His own belief
and temper are clearly shown.   Pelagius asserts that man can
live without sin otherwise than by the grace of God.   This,
says Augustine, is what Christian hearts find it impossible to
bear.   But he must hear what Pelagius has to say, hear it, and
set it right.[3]

The above summary will make clear three things.   First
that Pelagianism, from being a series of deductions occasioned
by the needs of moral exhortation and incidental to them, is
being rapidly systematized and is on the way to becoming an
ordered and coherent intellectual faith.   We may be justified
in seeing here the influence of Caelestius.   At Carthage and
in Sicily we find him making a systematic presentation of the
case earlier than Pelagius, and feel that he is excited by the
intellectual argument for its own sake, whereas with Pelagius
it remains subservient to the need for righteous living.
Secondly, under the impact of criticism Pelagius' views are
undergoing some modification.   Thus the emphasis upon the
possibility rather than the actuality of sinless living is a new
emphasis, brought about by denial of the actual sinlessness of
the patriarchs he is fond of exampling.   Similarly the conception of the grace of God as including His initial endowment
of human nature is a new development necessitated by
accusations that he denied the grace of God.   And the focus
of attention has moved from the subsidiary question of baptism
to the more fundamental question of grace and sinlessness.
Thirdly, Augustine's answers, while retaining charity and
affection towards Pelagius personally, show a gradual hardening against his views.   Augustine was once perhaps ready to
concede that there may have been sinless men in the past, and
was certainly not prepared to anathematize the statement out

---

[1] *Ib.*, xxxvi, 42.   [2] *Ib.*, lxi–lxvii, 71–81.   [3] *Ib.*, xliv–xlv, 52–3.

of hand. Now he exempts Mary from consideration, but will
not allow any other possible candidate.

Timasius and James thanked Augustine warmly for the
amazingly diligent and detailed ventilation of the subject.
They said that his words mediated to them the grace of God,
which refreshed and renewed them.[1]

[1] *De Gest. Pel.*, xxiv, 48; *Ep.*, 168.

Principal sources—See Chapter IV.

VI

EVENTS IN PALESTINE

THE scene now shifts to the Holy Land. Pelagius had been living there since his departure from Carthage. Of his life we can only surmise. It is interesting in view of his express and repeated condemnation of riches that he did not lack wealthy and influential friends. Such were Ctesiphon, the learned Anianus, and John, bishop of Jerusalem, himself, whom Orosius seems to attack under the pseudonym "Phineus."[1] This was not a new departure; at Rome he had had access to the homes of Marcella, Pammachius and Oceanus; in Africa Demetrias was a person of standing and substance; he had long been intimate with Paulinus of Nola; Augustine and Jerome speak of him as a friend; and we have evidence of his close association with other bishops.[2] Orosius puts the worst interpretation upon this as clear witness of unscrupulous secular ambition masking itself under the guise of religion.[3] But the spectacle of close personal friendship combined with radical political, religious, philosophical or intellectual differences is not so unfamiliar that we need put it down to insincerity. Indeed his very concern for the souls of the rich would make him bound to walk with them; it is the sick who need the physician, and it was thus he healed and won Timasius and James. Despite the vituperations of Orosius it is unlikely that he committed himself to the baths and banquets of a life of luxury.

He must have continued his mission, though he apparently did not exercise a public ministry as he had done at Rome. But his influence spread by personal contact and by writing, and Jerome says with a rhetorical flourish that his letters wing their way even over the rivers of Ethiopia.[4] Pelagius wrote personally to Jerome through his friend Ctesiphon.[5] The result was only that Jerome came in to the attack.

[1] Oros., *Apol.*, 29, cf. 31; Aug., *De Gest. Pel.*, xxv, 50; *Ep.*, 179, 1.

[2] Oros., *Apol.*, 31; Aug., *De Gest. Pel.*, xxv, 50.

[3] Oros., *Apol.*, 31.   [4] Jer., *Dial.*, ii, 12.   [5] Jer., *Ep.*, 133, 1.

JEROME

Jerome stands with Augustine and Chrysostom as one of the three great Church leaders of the age. He must be frankly written down as one of the most scholarly but least attractive of the Fathers. We do not know much of his early life. Prosper says that he was born in 330,[1] but this is not possible, seeing that he was at school in 363,[2] speaks of himself as little more than a boy in 374,[3] and only began his unending literary labours after 370. He would therefore at this stage be probably nearing seventy. He was born at the small town of Stridon near Aquileia, and, though his parents were Christians, was not in fact baptized in infancy. He describes himself as a slacker at school,[4] but his whole life was spent in an intellectual atmosphere. He went to Rome to complete his education, and under Aelius Donatus worked hard at the study of rhetoric.[5] At first he lived loosely,[6] but the Christian Church reclaimed him, and some time before 366 he was baptized, though his serious devotion to the Christian life did not come till after his education was completed.[7] He became a serious scholar, acquired a large library, which he used to take around with him,[8] and spent the next eight years in learning Greek, and in wide reading among the classical Greek authors.[9]

He now travelled first to Gaul, then to Aquileia, and then after a "subitus turbo"[10] of the type he was unhappily prone to occasion, via Thrace, Pontus, Bithynia, Galatia, Cappadocia and Cilicia to Antioch. There a serious illness, in which his life was despaired of, turned him to a renewed emphasis on spiritual rather than secular studies, Christianity rather than Cicero, and to a devotion to asceticism and the solitary life.[11] He spent five bitterly formative years in the desert. He describes his spiritual conflict vividly in writing to Eustochium : "I sat alone; I was filled with bitterness; my limbs were ugly and rough with sackcloth; my skin was filthy and took on the

---

[1] Prosp., *Chron.*, 420.　　[2] *Jer. Comm. in Hab.*, i, 10.　　[3] *Ep.*, 52.
[4] *Contr. Ruf.*, i, 30.
[5] *Contr. Ruf.*, i, 16; i, 30; *Comm. in Eccles.*, i; *in Gal.*, ii, 13; *Ep.*, 50, 1.
[6] *Ep.*, 6, 4; 14, 6; 48, 20.　　[7] *Ep.*, 3, 5.　　[8] *Ep.*, 22, 30.
[9] *Ep.*, 22, cf. 9, 5; 50, 1; Ruf., *Apol.*, ii, 9.
[10] *Ep.*, 3, 3.　　[11] *Ep.*, 22, 30.

black colour of an Ethiopian's. Every day I passed in tears and groaning; and, if ever the sleep which hung upon my eyelids overpowered my resistance to it, I banged my bare bones, which were hardly able to stick together, upon the ground."[1] He remained in this condition till he succeeded in arousing against himself the opposition of the other solitaries,[2] and was compelled to leave.

He now returned to Antioch, thence to Constantinople, and thence to Rome, where he stayed from 382 to 385. It was during this period that he probably, as we have seen, first met Pelagius. He had now two great concerns. One was with Biblical scholarship, in which he professed himself a follower of Origen. The other, which concerns us more directly, lay in the encouragement of that asceticism to which he had tuned his own life. Around him there grew up a circle of aristocratic ladies, devoted to the practices of asceticism, Christian living and good works. There was Paula, and her daughters Blesilla, Eustochium and Paulina; Marcella and her sister Asella and friend Principia; Titiana and her daughter Furia; Lea and Fabiola, Marcellina and Felicitas. Their emphasis was upon withdrawal from the irremediable corruption of contemporary society, and devotion to holy learning and practical charity. Jerome had a remarkable capacity for winning the enduring devotion of some while he provoked the furious enmity of others. His relationships with these ladies occasioned a good deal of slanderous gossip; there was some opposition to the practices of monastic asceticism, which broke out into an ugly incident when it was rumoured that they had caused the death of Blesilla. His respect for Origen's intellectual genius, though it was not uncritical, led to suspicion of his orthodoxy; his knowledge of the pagan classics was held against his very Christianity. In addition his temper in controversy was bitter and violent. He did not hesitate to retort the slanders of immorality against those who made them,[3] to describe the opponents of Origen as "mad dogs,"[4] and to descend to the cheapest scurrility in his abuse of Onasus.[5] When Damasus died, Jerome, who had once been

[1] *Ep.*, 22, 7.   [2] *Ep.*, 15; 16; 17.   [3] *Ep.*, 50.
[4] *Ep.*, 33, 4.   [5] *Ep.*, 40.

spoken of as his successor in the papacy,[1] was put aside, and it is hardly to be wondered at. With his brother Paulinian, his friend Vincentius, and his devoted disciples Paula and Eustochium he left for Palestine.

Once there they settled at Bethlehem, which was to be his home for the last thirty-four years of his life. They built a monastery and a convent, and he and Paula became the heads of the two institutions. He continued the two great concerns he had undertaken at Rome. His lives of Malchus and Hilarion promoted the cause of asceticism, and the influence of the monastery was by no means confined to the works which emerged from Jerome's study, but there was active evangelization of the countryfolk around. Scholarship poured from him; the Vulgate and numerous Bible commentaries flowed from his pen. He kept his contacts with the world outside, corresponded regularly with his friends, and after an initial misunderstanding, formed a liaison with Augustine founded on a large and genuine mutual respect.

But, above all, these years were years of controversy. On the one hand lay his disputes over the Christian life, first with Jovinian, and then with Vigilantius. These stood aside from the extreme asceticism which Jerome maintained, and though they did not deny a place for such ascetic practices, pointed out the dangers involved in them, and more especially the danger of spiritual pride, and maintained that fasting and feasting, virginity and marriage might equally be undertaken to the glory of God. Jerome's replies are violent in the extreme. He speaks of Jovinian as "a dog returned to his own vomit" and his views as "the hissings of the old serpent," and writes of his death in these words : "This man, after being condemned by the authority of the church of Rome, in the middle of feasting on the flesh of pigs and pheasants, belched out (I will not say, gave up) his life." On the other hand was the great Origenist controversy with Rufinus. We do not need here to enter upon the complex chain of accusations and misunderstandings. Three points are important, however, in the understanding of Jerome's attitude to Pelagius. The first is that he had once been an immoderate admirer of Origen. He

[1] *Ep.*, 45, 3.

was concerned at the time with Origen's biblical scholarship rather than his theology. The result was that opponents of Origensim such as Aterbius began to accuse him of heresy, and in rebutting the accusations he turned against Origen with the same violence which he had once used in his defence, and threw himself headlong into the party of Epiphanius and Theophilus. We may suspect a certain uneasiness in the vehemence of his negations, as in Pelagius' attack upon the sin of pride. They both protest too much. The point is psychologically significant especially when we reflect that Jerome and Pelagius were at one in an earnest desire to foster the ascetic life. It should be remembered too that it was Jerome's own translation of Origen's περὶ ἀρχῶν that roused the fears of Orosius and his opposition to Origenism. Secondly, Rufinus, his principal opponent, had once been one of his closest friends and associates. With Augustine this might have meant gentleness and courtesy, with Jerome it led to bitterness and vituperation. Rufinus died in Sicily in 410, and Jerome wrote of his former friend : "The scorpion lies beneath the earth between Enceladus and Porphyrion; the many-headed hydra has at last ceased to hiss against me."[1] He continued to assail his memory long after his death,[2] and saw in Pelagius Rufinus incarnate.[3] Thirdly, the Origenist controversy had as one of its incidental results an alienation between Jerome and John, the bishop of Jerusalem. The latter, if not Origenist, was so near the position that Epiphanius advised Jerome to separate from him,[4] and forcibly ordained his brother Paulinian that the monks might not be without the ministrations of the Church.[5] At one time John denied the monks access to the holy places in Jerusalem, refused to baptize their converts, or bury their dead, used threats of excommunication against any who defended the validity of Paulinian's ordination, and even tried to obtain from the civil authorities Jerome's banishment.[6] This personal antagonism, and John's tendency to unorthodoxy, were to play some part in the next round of the Pelagian controversy.

---

[1] *Comm. in Ezech.*, Pref.   [2] *Ep.*, 125, 18; 133, 3.   [3] *Comm. in Jerem.*, Pref.
[4] Jer., *Contr. Ioan. Hieros.*   [5] *Ep.*, 51, 1.
[6] *Contr. Ioan. Hieros.*, 43, cf. *Ep.*, 82, 10.

JEROME AND PELAGIUS

Rufinus was dead, and the old lion was looking for some new adversary on whom to sharpen his claws when Pelagius came on the scene. After a long life of disputation controversy was his meat and drink; to abandon it would mean spiritual starvation. Jerome was a linguist of no mean ability, and a biblical scholar without peer, but he was not in the first place a theologian. If he held a chair to-day, it would be in Biblical Studies, not Systematic Theology. We have already seen how he was led by Origen's exegetical genius to a vehement advocacy without full realization of the intellectual position to which he was committing himself. For more than twenty years now he had been engaged in the refutation and opposition of the Origenists. Pelagius had been associated with Rufinus in Rome; it was but to be expected that Jerome would see in his teaching a further outbreak of the detestable heresy. There was a preliminary skirmish over Demetrias, to which we have already referred. Jerome warns her to be very careful of the company she keeps, and in particular to avoid abstract theological speculations of the school of Origen.[1] The words are those of a man who is not certain of what he believes, but knows what he ought to believe—the way of avoidance is safer than the way of refutation.

It may be that the way to the dispute was prepared by a still earlier clash. In the year 394 Jerome's writings against Jovinian reached Rome. Among those who criticized them was a young man, described as a monk, endowed with an eloquent tongue, at least in his own conceit, versed in the art of disputation, pleasantly corpulent and with the flanks of an athlete and having the entrée into the noble houses of Rome.[2] De Plinval identifies this monk with Pelagius.[3] Vallarsi does not accept the identification, and Haller suspends judgment. But it is at least plausible. The description of him battling "acuminato capite" is parallel with Jerome's description of Pelagius butting with his horns[4]; the passage in which he is said "canino dente rodere" reminds us that Jerome called Pelagius a great hound from the Alps[5]; the word "corpulentus"

---

[1] *Ep.*, 130.   [2] *Ep.*, 50.   [3] De Plinval, pp. 50 ff.
[4] *Ep.*, 50, 4; *Dial.*, i, 29.   [5] *Ep.*, 50, 1; *Comm. in Jerem.*, iii, 1.

is applied to both[1]; the comparison with a wrestler is used of Pelagius[2]; above all Augustine's words on the relations between Pelagius and Jerome, "De illo quidem sancto presbytero . . . non solet Pelagius iactitare, nisi quod ei tamquam aemulo inviderit" give every appearance of being taken from Jerome's account of this critic, "postquam Romam mea opuscula pervenerunt, quasi aemulum exhorruit."[3]   If this identification is right then Jerome saw in Pelagius a representative not of one, but of both the schools of thought he had spent the best part of his life in combatting.

It cannot be doubted that there is some confusion in Jerome's indictment of Pelagius.   The beginning of his commentary is obscure and disputed, but it looks very much as though he has mixed up the criticisms of Vigilantius, Rufinus and Pelagius; in any event, he does not spare the last and describes him as "snoring away and failing to understand the principles of commentary" and "sluggish, being weighed down with Irish porridge."   Confusion of the same kind is to be seen in the criticisms he now levelled at Pelagius.   He may have been misled by the Stoical trend visible alike in the thought of Rufinus and Pelagius; he may have overestimated the influence of the former upon the latter.   At any rate, he thought he could see in Pelagius' doctrine of sinlessness a resurgence of the doctrine of ἀπαθεία against which he had set himself in the writings of Evagrius Ponticus.   Evagrius asserted that the saint could raise himself to a position where he was insensible to temptation, where the πάθη of hope and fear, joy and sorrow, were annihilated in a kind of Nirvana, so that man became, in Jerome's words, "either a stone or a god," a view which as he rightly saw, derived from Stoicism.   Jerome's error in seeing in Evagrius a precursor of Pelagius is understandable but inexcusable.   This is nothing to do with Pelagius' assertion that at each moment when we sin it is through our own most grievous fault, and we could have acted otherwise.   Jerome has Origenism on the brain.

Pelagius, then, attempted the initiative in reconciliation, but only provoked Jerome into the offensive.   The latter wrote

---

[1] *Ep.*, 50, 4; *Comm. in Jerem.* iii, 1.   [2] *Ep.*, 50, 4; Oros., *Apol.*, 31.
[3] Aug., *Contr. Iul.*, ii, 36; Jer., *Ep.*, 50, 5.

immediately in reply to Ctesiphon a letter of some length in which he surveys broadly the theme of freewill and sinlessness with some detailed criticisms of Pelagius and Caelestius. With Jerome the attention turns from the question of infant baptism which has dominated the early stages of the controversy, but which in the Dialogue, for instance, is only briefly surveyed at the end, and without adding anything fresh to Augustine.[1] He now concentrates upon these broader issues, in which he detects sproutings from the seed of Origen, lumps together Pelagius with the Gnostics, Manicheans and Priscillian as well as with Origen and Jovinian, and describes his latest opponent as a rat, "quasi mus."[2] This was expanded into a treatise against the Pelagians, consisting of three books of dialogue between Critobulus, a Pelagian, and the more orthodox Atticus. His criticism of Pelagius is based upon the latter's volume of "Testimonia." Pelagius' position is presented fairly and accurately, but, as in the letter to Ctesiphon, Jerome misinterprets it, and is for ever chasing the spectre of ἀπάθεια, and the ghosts of Origen and Jovinian mock him from the pages of Pelagius. Jerome takes Pelagius' position to be a pretention to a wholly inhuman indifference to sin, and, though he allows Critobulus to explain the distinction between sanctification and deification,[3] he sarcastically represents the Pelagian as crying "I am without sin : I am stronger than the apostle Paul; I do that which I will. The kingdom of Heaven is prepared for me, or, rather, I have prepared it for myself by my own virtues."[4] The temper of the work is less bitter than many of his controversial writings. There is sarcasm indeed, but his chief weapon is the accumulation of biblical passages. In general, he takes the view that man, even if he can attain sinlessness for a short period, cannot sustain it; the diversity of gifts of the epistles implies an universal imperfection.[5] Unbroken sinlessness is reserved only for God.[6] An important passage, to which we shall recur, stresses the imperfections under which Christ laboured.[7] But Jerome does not hold the extreme predestinarian views of Augustine. He is rather a synergist, holding that God's grace and man's freewill come together in

---

[1] *Dial.*, iii, 17–8. [2] *Ep.*, 133. [3] *Dial*, i, 16. [4] *Ib.*, ii, 23–4.
[5] *Ib.*, i, passim. [6] *Ib.*, iii, 12. [7] *Ib.*, ii, 11, 14–7.

the work of salvation, and equating predestination with prescience, that is to say, interpreting the doctrine not in terms of an arbitrary fiat of the Almighty that A shall be saved and B damned, but to mean that God having in His Almighty perfection complete knowledge of past, present and future, foreknows that A will so live as to be saved, and B will so live as to be damned. But despite this comparative moderation, the ban he places upon the heresy is drastic and terrible; it is anathema alike in the Church and in the courts of Heaven.

This work was not completed in time for the dramatic events to which we shall in a moment turn, but the shadow of Jerome lay upon the assemblies. Orosius appealed to the authority of his condemnation of the doctrines, both in the letter to Ctesiphon, and in the work on which he was then engaged. John was no doubt governed in part by his antipathy to Jerome in his sympathy with Pelagius, and Jerome, who probably encouraged the appeal to Eulogius in the first place, calls the synod of Diospolis at which Pelagius was acquitted "miserable."[1] While Pelagius grew in the good esteem of many Christians in Jerusalem, Augustine tells us that the majority withstood him "in the cause of Christ's grace"[2]; again we may detect the authority and influence of Jerome in the background. A raid upon the monasteries at Bethlehem by a band of hooligans was put down to Pelagian resentment against his persistent hostility.[3] Buildings were burnt, and lives lost, and Jerome escaped only by taking refuge in a strongly built tower. It is unthinkable that Pelagius was concerned in the outrage. Not only was it wholly inconsistent with what we know of his character and temper, but if it could have been remotely laid at his door it would undoubtedly have formed a part of the indictment before Pope Innocent later. As it was Innocent wrote sternly from Rome to John, holding him accountable if there were further outbreaks of violence,[4] and to Jerome to assure him of protection in the future.[5]

Jerome's active part in the controversy was now over. A few letters refer to subsequent events in Palestine. Augustine had

---

[1] *Ep.*, 143. [2] Aug., *Ep.*, 176, 4.
[3] Id. *De Gest. Pel.*, xxxv, 66, cf. Jer., *Ep.*, 136, 137.
[4] Inn., *Ep.*, 32. [5] Jer., *Ep.*, 136.

written to him earlier about Pelagius, and warned him that his creationism might lead some to set him in the camp of Pelagius.[1] Now he wrote back to say that Christ has triumphed in Palestine without human aid, Pelagius has fled as Catiline fled from Rome, Lentulus-Ctesiphon is at Joppa, and though Nebuchadrezzar still rules in Jerusalem, the victory is won.[2] When the African bishops pressed hard upon Zosimus in the winter of 417-8, he wrote to Augustine words of admiring encouragement.[3] In the West Anianus, and in the East Theodore of Mopsuestia took the field against him,[4] but in 419 the old man's last illness came upon him, and he was precluded from replying.

Orosius

Paulus Orosius has been mentioned more than once already as one of Pelagius' most bitter opponents. He was a native of Tarragona[5] in Spain, and was born probably some time in the 380s. When the Alans and Vandals entered Spain in 409 he narrowly escaped falling a victim to their violence.[6] But even more dangerous in his estimation were the heresies of Priscillian and Origen, which began to make headway in Spain at about this time. Eutropius and Paul had already gone from Spain to Sicily and appealed to Augustine in their desire to refute Pelagian errors. Orosius, filled with a similar zeal, decided on his own initiative to follow their example, and in 415 made his way to Augustine in Africa. We obtain a vivid picture of him at this time from the pen of Augustine. He appears as a young man of religious bent, vigilant intellect, ready tongue, and burning zeal.[7] He is "sanctissimus et studiosissimus."[8] The description is as full of meaning in what it omits as in what it records. Orosius had faith and hope; he spoke with the eloquence of angels; he would gladly have given his body to be burnt and his goods to the poor; but we may doubt if he had much charity.

He came then to Augustine to consult him about the spread of Priscillianism and Origenism in Spain. Augustine was

---

[1] *Epp.*, 130; 131; 132.   [2] *Ep.*, 138.   [3] *Epp.*, 141–2.
[4] περὶ τοὺς λέγοντας, φύσει καὶ οὐ γνώμῃ πταίειν τοὺς ἀνθρώπους.
[5] Oros., *Hist.*, vii, 22.   [6] *Ib.*, iii, 20; v, 2; vii, 40.
[7] Aug., *Ep.*, 166, 2.   [8] *Ib.*, 169, 13.

impressed by the young man's ability and eagerness, gave him
a partial answer, referred him to his books against the Manicheans, and recommended him to visit Jerome in Palestine for
further consultation, at the same time using him as a bearer of
some letters to Jerome on the Pelagian controversy which had
already begun to engage his attention.[1]   It was not likely that
Augustine would fail to inform him of the contents of these
letters, or that he would not acquire some knowledge of the
dogmatic conflict which had been engaging the Church in
Africa.   In fact at the synod, and in his Apology, he shows wide
acquaintance with the part which Augustine was playing.
Orosius went to Palestine, arriving about midsummer, and
naturally made straight for Bethlehem, where he was warmly
received by Jerome as one whom Augustine had commended,[2]
and purposed to stay at the monastery and study under him for
some time.

THE SYNOD AT JERUSALEM

This was not to be.   On 28th July there was a diocesan
synod at Jerusalem, and Orosius was summoned to attend.   He
seems to have met Pelagius on his way to the synod, and had a
short talk with him.[3] Jerome was not present. He was ordained,
but preferred not to appear as a presbyter, and the sustained
tension between himself and the bishop readily explains his
absence.   It is clear that the activity of Pelagius in Jerusalem,
and the incipient conflict with Jerome had aroused speculation
and curiosity which the church could not ignore.   Orosius
was but recently arrived from Carthage where Caelestius and
Pelagius had first caught the public eye.   He was now asked
what he could tell the synod about them.   He recorded that
Caelestius had been condemned of heresy at Carthage, excommunicated and had shortly afterwards left Africa.   Augustine
had written a letter to Hilary in Sicily refuting Caelestius, (a
copy of which Orosius produced and read to the synod) and
was at that time engaged upon a treatise examining the whole
Pelagian position.   This is generally stated to have been
"De Natura et Gratia," which Orosius was able to quote at

---

[1] *Epp.*, 166; 167; see above.   [2] Jer., *Ep.*, 134; Aug., *Ep.*, 172.
[3] Oros., *Apol.*, 2.

length in writing his own defence later. But it was perhaps "De Perfectione Iustitiae Hominis" which followed up the situation in Sicily, and in which Orosius had a direct interest as it was occasioned by the appeal from his fellow-countrymen Eutropius and Paul.

The bishop thought it only fair to send for Pelagius in person and give him the opportunity of replying to the allegations against him. He entered the assembly moving slowly by reason of his weight, and was asked by the presbyters whether he really taught the doctrines against which Augustine had thrown his authority. He replied curtly "What is Augustine to me?" This profoundly shocked the majority of those present, for the reputation of Augustine as champion of orthodox and catholic Christianity against heresy and schism was now at its height. But the bishop was not disposed to allow an issue in his own diocese to be settled by appeal to the authority of a foreign bishop, however eminent, and making reply "I am Augustine here," invited Pelagius, layman as he was, to take his place in the synod.

He then called on Orosius to state his charges. Orosius declared that Pelagius had said to him personally "My teaching is that a man can, if he will, live without sin, and easily keep God's commandments." Pelagius acknowledged it. Orosius immediately denounced the doctrine on three counts : first that it was condemned by the council of Carthage : second, that it was opposed by the authority of Augustine; third, that Jerome himself in the letter to Ctesiphon and in the work on which he was at present engaged, equally set himself against it. We have to realize that the division between the churches of the East and those of the West was deeply rooted, and at this era we can already see the incipient conflict that was to sever them. Neither Carthage nor Augustine carried weight with John, and Jerome was his bitterest critic. The examples of Abraham, who was commanded "to walk before God and be perfect"[1] and of Zacharias and Elizabeth who "were both righteous before God, walking in all the commandments and ordinances of the law blameless"[2] were *prima facie* witnesses in Pelagius' favour. The bishop was not of a disposition to condemn him

[1] Gen. xvii. 1. [2] Luke i. 6.

G

out of hand and unheard on the authority of others, whereas Orosius and his associates Avitus and Posserius regarded the decision given at Carthage as final, and to pursue the matter was to them tantamount to acknowledging as still open a question which they believed to be closed. He therefore turned to Pelagius himself and asked him to explain more clearly what he meant by the possibility of sinlessness, urged by those in the synod who were murmuring against Pelagius as a heretic. Pelagius replied "I did not mean that human nature has a natural endowment of sinlessness; I meant that the person who is prepared to toil and strive to avoid sin and to walk in the commandments of God on behalf of his own salvation, is granted by God the possibility of so doing." There were at once further murmurings that this was inadequate; it gave no place to the grace of God. Pelagius answered in scriptural terms by quoting the words of Paul "I laboured more abundantly than they all, yet not I but the grace of God which was with me,"[1] and again "It is not of him that willeth nor of him that runneth but of God that showeth mercy,"[2] and again from the Psalm "Except the Lord build the house they labour in vain that build it."[3] The murmurs did not cease and Pelagius roundly anathematized anyone who should avow that apart from the help of God a man could advance in virtue.[4]

The tables were now turned. Pelagius' position seemed incontrovertibly Christian, and the bishop asked Orosius whether he denied the efficacy of Divine grace to free a man from sin. Orosius' answer could only be in the negative, and there was established a piquant situation in which the two antagonists had been brought to verbal agreement, without having come in any degree to a meeting of minds. Orosius saw that he would get no further under the presidency of John, and that John would not admit the authority of the churches of the West. The only possible court of appeal was to the bishop of Rome. The question had arisen in the West, it was affecting principally the Churches of the West, and might reasonably be referred to the chief bishop of Latin Christianity. This was agreed, and the synod dissolved.

[1] 1 Cor. xv. 10.   [2] Rom. ix. 16.   [3] Ps. cxxvii. 1.
[4] Aug. *De Gest. Pel.*, xxx, 54; xiv, 37.

The appeal to Rome was not however to come yet. Just under seven weeks later, on 12th September, Orosius presented himself at the Church of the Resurrection for the annual festival of the dedication, to assist the bishop at the altar. The latter, to his amazement, instantly denounced him for the blasphemy of maintaining that it was impossible to live without sin even by the help of God. Orosius flatly denied it, adducing the fact that in any case John did not understand Latin and could not understand what he said; he was not above accusing the bishop of seeking false witnesses in his despite. To clear himself he addressed an apologia to the priests of Jerusalem in which he combined an account of the recent proceedings with some arguments against Pelagianism, mainly taken from Augustine, and a virulent attack upon Pelagius himself. In this fresh conflict the appeal to Innocent's arbitration became impossible.

Two further points must be made about these events. One is that much of the business of the synod, and especially between John and Orosius, had to be carried on through an interpreter, and Orosius and his associates were ready to impugn the veracity of the interpreter in question. Whether they were justified in this we cannot tell, but it meant that the proceedings were bound to be unsatisfactory. Secondly we see the synod through the eyes of Orosius, for no minutes were taken,[1] and we have only slight indications of John's version in the pages of Augustine.[2] But Orosius was a fanatical partisan. He certainly misrepresents Pelagius as maintaining that he was himself without blemish or sin.[3] We have no real reason to doubt that the proceedings were fair. John was certainly hasty in his subsequent condemnation of Orosius, but he may, in his ignorance of Latin, have been misinformed. His conduct of the synod failed in fact to bring out the depth of divergence and gave a false and superficial impression of unity, but it was not biassed or unfair, as we can see equally from what happened at Diospolis.

THE SYNOD AT DIOSPOLIS

It is probable that Jerome was profoundly dissatisfied with the result of the synod, and took the opportunity of stirring up

---

[1] Aug., *De Gest. Pel.*, xvi, 39.   [2] *Ib.*, xxx, 54.   [3] Oros., *Apol.*, 16.

further opposition to Pelagius. Towards the end of the same year two deposed bishops from Gaul who had made their home in Palestine took up the cause. Heros, bishop of Arles, was a former disciple of St. Martin. He had been a bishop in Spain,[1] which thus provided a bond of sympathy between Orosius and himself. There he associated himself with the attempt of Constantine to usurp the imperial purple. He was forced by political circumstances to flee from Spain to Gaul, and was imposed upon the diocese of Arles by the would-be emperor in face of the opposition of both clergy and laity. Constantine was besieged in Arles, and during the siege Heros behaved with some gallantry.[2] But after Constantine's defeat and death he was driven out by the people and took refuge in the East. Heros appears as a man of some standing whose chief fault was to have chosen the losing side politically and remained loyal to it. Lazarus, bishop of Aix, is set in a more doubtful light. He too was an associate of Constantine, and was transferred by him from Veseo to Aix. There was suspicion that he was involved in the death of his predecessor; certainly his part in the condemnation of bishop Briccius of Tours on a false charge of adultery was unsavoury. While Briccius' appeal was still *sub judice*, he resigned and joined Heros in Palestine. There they appear as trouble-makers, and Zosimus dismisses them roundly as "turbines ecclesiae."[3] The way in which they brought accusations against Pelagius, and failed to appear to press them, suggests that they were not acting in their own behalf, but were the mouthpieces of Jerome and Orosius.[4] Heros, indeed, later was persuaded to drop his hostility to the Pelagians altogether.

These two studied carefully Pelagius' "Testimonia" and some of his letters, an anonymous work of Caelestius, and the records of events at Carthage and in Sicily. They drew up a formal indictment, and presented this "libellus" to Eulogius, metropolitan of Caesarea and thus the senior bishop in Palestine. He called a synod at Diospolis of the Palestinian bishops under his own presidency. John was, of course, present, and besides Ammonianus, Chromatius, Clematius, Eleutherius, Eutonius,

Fidus, Jovinus, Nymphidius, the two Porphyries, Zoboennus and Zomnus. The synod met towards the end of December. But the accusers did not appear: one was seriously ill, it was pleaded, and the other for some reason would not appear without him. Neither Orosius nor Jerome of course was present.

The "libellus" was translated into Greek, and presented to the court, and Pelagius was called to make his defence count by count. The first part of the accusation consisted of seven charges, each presented in the form of quotation from his writings, as follows:

1. That no man can be without sin except he have knowledge of the Law.[1]

2. That all men are governed by their own free will.[2]

3. That in the day of judgment there will be no mercy for sinners and wrongdoers, but they must be consumed in eternal fire.[3]

4. That evil does not even enter the thought.[4]

5. That the kingdom of Heaven is promised in the Old Testament as well.[5]

6. That man can if he will be without sin. (This was buttressed with three comparable quotations.)[6]

7. That the Church is here without blemish or wrinkle.[7]

The indictment shows no great acumen on the part of the prosecutors. It is dominated by obsession with past heresies, Origen and Donatus, and even as such is incompetently presented, for it was easy for Pelagius to turn with a "tu quoque" on the third count and say that anyone who denied it was an Origenist. Pelagius' defence on an unfavourable view might be charged with equivocation; on a kinder view he did his best to meet the position of the orthodox without surrendering that from which his whole thinking had started, his right to upbraid the moral laggard and urge him on to better things. The first statement he explained to mean that the Law assisted man to virtue, which, as Augustine points out, is

---

[1] *Ib.*, i, 2.   [2] *Ib.*, iii, 5.   [3] *Ib.*, iii, 9.   [4] *Ib.*, iv, 12.
[5] *Ib.*, v, 13.   [6] *Ib.*, vi, 16.   [7] *Ib.*, xii, 27.

not at all the same thing. For the second he argued that man
has free will. This was deemed orthodox. For the third he
maintained the irrevocable nature of the Final Judgment.
The fourth he denied stating : his position was that the Christian
must avoid evil thinking—again, as Augustine says, a very
different proposition. The sixth is the crux of the matter.
The three subsidiary quotations, taken from a letter to Juliana
of which he was generally believed to be the author, he dis-
owned. These seemed to attribute perfect virtue to their
recipient. When called upon to anathematize those who held
such views, he did so, while claiming that this was not a matter
of dogma, and they were fools not heretics. The central
proposition about the possibility of sinlessness he clung to, but
with two qualifications of the highest importance, the first that
sinlessness was only possible by a combination of personal effort
and the grace of God ("proprio labore et Dei gratia"), the
second that he had never said that you would find a perfectly
sinless man, but that such a phenomenon was not theoretically
impossible. The final count was easily disposed of : the baptismal laver cleansed perfectly, and it was God's wish that that
state of perfect cleansing should abide.

The second part of the indictment consisted of propositions
ascribed to Caelestius. These were varied. First there were
presented en bloc the propositions condemned at Carthage.[1]
Then followed the assertion that we do more than is enjoined
in the Law or the Gospel, which Pelagius referred to virginity,
pointed out that Paul did not claim Dominical authority for
this.[2] A series of contentions which Augustine describes as
"capitula capitalia" came next.[3] One maintained that the
grace and help of God were not given for individual actions, but
consisted of the general endowment of free will, the Law, and
teaching; one that the grace of God is bestowed according to
merit, a view which Augustine rightly regarded as negating the
true significance of grace; the third that if God's grace alone
enabled us to overcome sin, then He is responsible when we do
sin. These Pelagius anathematized, but in response to a
further quotation which suggested that all the graces and
virtues might be bestowed upon one individual, certainly

---

[1] *Ib.*, xi, 23.   [2] *Ib.*, xiii, 29.   [3] *Ib.*, xiv, 30.

seemed to make nonsense of his disavowal by arguing that the graces granted to Paul were a matter of desert.[1] A final group of passages maintained that to be a son of God was equivalent to being sinless; that forgetfulness and ignorance could not be accounted sin, belonging to the sphere of necessity not that of will; that free will meant the power to act or refrain from acting; that our victory comes from our wills; that if the soul cannot be free from sin then God cannot be free from sin either; and that pardon comes not from grace and mercy but from effort and merit which earn mercy.[2] In all this second section of the indictment Pelagius consistently adopts the same position. He is not responsible for the assertions ascribed to Caelestius, whether they were in fact the latter's or not, and he fully anathematizes those who hold them. Occasionally a modification of his former views comes in : he now distinguishes between a holy and just life and a life without sin in speaking of the patriarchs.[3] But as a whole it is hard to resist the conclusion that his strong desire to be accounted orthodox carried him further than it should have done in the direction of "accommodation" if he were to remain loyal to his real and strongly felt opinions.

Pelagius met the accusations to the satisfaction of the bishops, and was able in addition to produce letters from Augustine and other Church leaders written in terms of affection and friendship.[4] He uttered a general anathema upon all doctrines alien to that of the Church, and was acquitted of the charges laid against him, and declared to be within the communion of the Catholic Church.[5]

THE AFTERMATH

Augustine's immediate response was one of joy that the heresy had been abjured,[6] though there was a measure of uncertainty behind this pleasure. "Forsitan correctus est" he said.[7] Jerome considered the whole synod a wretched piece of botching. Pelagius on the other hand was naturally in a state of some elation. Augustine speaks of "epistola carnalis

---

[1] *Ib.*, xiv, 32.   [2] *Ib.*, xviii, 42.   [3] *Ib.*, xi, 26.   [4] *Ib.*, xxv–xxix, 50–53.
[5] *Ib.*, xx, 44.   [6] *De Pecc. Orig.*, xiv, 15.
[7] *Serm. Fr.*, i, 5, cf. *Ep.*, 177, 3.

ventositatis et elationis."[1] Pelagius had seen himself as a man with a spiritual mission, whose fulfilment presupposed the acceptance of certain ideas. At every point he found himself meeting with opposition, and, what was more, he could trace the links between the opposition in different parts of the world, the correspondence between Jerome and Augustine, the work of Orosius, linking Eutropius and Paul in Sicily, Augustine in Africa, Jerome and Heros in Palestine, the way in which Heros and Lazarus cited the Council of Carthage, and Orosius quoted from the writings of Augustine. There was a conspiracy against him. Now the decision of the synod had "broken up the whole band of conspirators." "Quae sententia contradictionis os confusione perfudit, et omnem in malum conspirantem societatem ab invicem separavit."[2] The words appear in a letter to a priest alleged to be by Pelagius. Augustine, into whose hands it came, already thinks that Pelagius is equivocating. Before the council he admitted to the statement that man can be without sin and keep God's commandments. Now he is inserting the word "easily" which conflicts on the face of it with the "laborare et agonizare" of his earlier statement. Pelagius would probably have denied the equivocation. He consistently maintained that the basic dogmatic issue was whether a man could live without sin. Qualifications of that— the means by which he could attain that, or the ease of the attainment—were secondary and subsidiary and obscured the real issue. To Augustine the workings of God's grace not the possibility of sinlessness, was what mattered. His interest was theological, Pelagius' anthropological. There is a sense in which these are the obverse and reverse of the same coin. But in much of the conflict each was looking at his own coinface and maintaining that he saw something different from the other. And it was precisely this refusal to see the other side of the picture which led each of them, Pelagius in occasional utterances, Augustine systematically, into an untenable position.

Pelagius was now writing again. First Charus, a fellow-townsman of Augustine, who was now a deacon in Palestine, brought him a document in which Pelagius gave his version of

[1] *De Gest. Pel.*, xxx, 55.
[2] *De Gest. Pel.*, xxx, 54.

the proceedings of the synod.[1] Augustine, during the proceedings at Rome, wrote to John for the official account of the meeting. He found some inconsistencies in the two accounts. For example, in the official record Pelagius said that the propositions condemned at Carthage were nothing to do with him, but for the satisfaction of the synod he anathematized them. In his own account the anathema is omitted. There is no need to see in this malicious perversion. Pelagius was probably writing from memory, and was not professing to give a verbatim report. There are discrepancies. If, as we can well imagine, Augustine has listed all he can find, they are surprisingly few, and certainly a deliberately false account would have produced more. However Augustine regarded the matter as serious enough to demand his intervention, and in the early part of 417 addressed to Aurelius, bishop of Carthage, a full and critical account of the proceedings, commonly called "De Gestis Pelagii" but more accurately "De Gestis Palaestinis."

Three facts emerge clearly from the proceedings at Diospolis. The first is Pelagius' genuine concern for orthodoxy. He does not regard himself as unorthodox. Nor does he suggest that his opponents are unorthodox. He regards the issue between them not as dogmatic, but as a legitimate difference of opinion on a matter concerning action in which there should be freedom of opinion. This is an important point which has rarely been understood. Augustine laid himself wide open to attacks upon his own orthodoxy. Julian, one of the ablest and most attractive of the Pelagians, saw this clearly, and took the offensive. This Pelagius never did. All he wanted was peace to propagate his concern for moral earnestness within the framework of the Church. But he could not instil that earnestness without providing an alternative to the predestinarian theories of Augustine. Secondly, as has often been said, the agreement reached at Diospolis was verbal only. It is too much to say that Pelagius obtained his acquittal by condemning Pelagianism. One would rather aver that the verbal agreement did not touch and even helped to obscure the underlying divergence. The difference between Pelagius and his critics

[1] *Ib.*, xxxii–xxxiii, 57–8.

remained. Pelagius was content that it should remain; the critics were not. Thirdly, it is true that the synod was hampered by having to use an interpreter,[1] though, in this case, there is no serious suggestion that the latter was unskilful or dishonest. It is true, too, that in these circumstances they were inclined, like the cricket umpire, to give the batsman the benefit of any doubt.[2] And it is true that the case for the prosecution was hampered by the absence of the prosecutors.[3] But it remains to be said, when all that is allowed for, that predestinarian theories had not made much headway in the East, that the bishops were not particularly concerned about a precise definition of the role of grace in the saving work of God, and that provided acknowledgment were made of the necessity both of grace and of free will, they were well content without further distinction or definition. The court was not biassed. Pelagius was acquitted, as Caelestius in different circumstances had been condemned, by a fair judgment of an impartial tribunal acting according to its own lights.

Principal Sources: See Chapter IV.

[1] *Ib.*, i, 2; xvi, 39.
[2] *Ib.*, iii, 8.
[3] *Ib.*, xvi, 39.

VII

THE JUDGMENT OF ROME

The Appeal from Africa

Orosius now left Palestine and returned to Africa, armed with two letters, one from Jerome,[1] and one from Heros and Lazarus. The first of these was written to Augustine; with it was another concerning the resurrection of the body, which for some reason he did not deliver until later[2]; he may also have had Jerome's book against Pelagius with him. The letter from Heros and Lazarus was delivered at a synod held at Carthage in June or July 416.[3] As a result of this letter and the testimony of Orosius the assembled bishops resolved to anathematize Pelagius, and Caelestius, who had at last obtained ordination at Ephesus, unless they in their turn anathematized the errors attributed to them. This judgment is of peculiar importance as the first official association of Pelagius and Caelestius in a joint condemnation. A letter was drawn up to Innocent, the bishop of Rome, asking him to add the anathema of the apostolic see in all its authority upon this blasphemous error which was spreading in all directions. They bluntly denounced Pelagius and Caelestius as authors of an abominable error, and argued that their exaltation of free will virtually did away with the need for grace and recourse to prayer, and that their attitude to infant baptism, by denying its necessity for salvation, was in effect condemning children to eternal death. The letter was signed by Aurelius, the bishop of Carthage, and sixty-seven other bishops.[4] The neighbouring churches of Numidia soon followed suit. They did not have the authority of the Carthaginian province, but with Alypius and Augustine in their number they carried a good deal of weight. They met at Milevum, with Silvanus Senex presiding over an assembly of fifty-eight bishops and drew up a document in similar terms, indeed in direct emulation of the church at

---

[1] Jer., *Ep.*, 134.   [2] Aug., *Ep.*, 180.

[3] Ince apud Smith's *Dict. of Chr. Biog.*, iii, 287, s.v. Pelagius, is wrong in saying "towards the close of A.D. 416."

[4] Aug., *Ep.*, 175.

Carthage, stressing what they saw as the two great dangers of the heresy, its derogation of prayer, and its denial of eternal life to infants.[1] This in its turn was forwarded to Innocent. In addition to these synodical letters, five of the most influential bishops, Aurelius, Augustine, Alypius, Evodius and Possidius wrote a personal letter to the Pope.[2] They did not seek in any way to diminish the authority of the Diospolis synod. But it was not just the personal faith of Pelagius which was at stake. It might be that he had in fact mended his ways, but the views attributed to him were still spreading. They pointed out the ambiguity of some of his language, and the difficulty of full understanding through the medium of an interpreter. He should ideally be summoned to Rome; in any case he should be made to give, not just a general profession of faith, but recantation of specific, individual and concrete dogmatic errors. They enclosed a copy of Pelagius' "De Natura" as exemplifying the views they wished condemned, marking particular passages which repelled them, and concluded that they felt confident that the authority of the bishop of Rome would weigh heavily with Pelagius, and that if he rejected the error of his ways his associates would no longer dare to speak against the grace of God and so disturb the simple, single-hearted faith of Christian people.

The whole operation is a model example of a pressure-group working upon authority. Meantime in Rome there was a measure of confusion. It was not to be expected that Pelagius' long residence in the capital would have left no impression, and the bishops writing to Innocent are concerned about the situation in Rome itself, for though there are those who cannot believe Pelagius to hold the views of which he is accused, there are others who accept these views for themselves.[3] One bishop from Africa, talking to a Pelagian in Rome, was horrified to hear him explain the prayer "Lead us not into temptation" as referring to physical, not to moral danger, "ne ruam de equo" or "ne latro me interficiat."[4] This Pelagius himself would hardly have said. Innocent himself apparently had

---

[1] *Ib.*, 176.   [2] *De Pecc. Orig.*, ix, 10; *Ep.*, 177.

[3] *Ep.*, 177, 2.   [4] *Serm. Fr.*, i, 1.

not come upon any Pelagians in Rome[1] : the Pelagians themselves claimed the adherence of the future Pope Sixtus III,
and other clergy.[2]   It is unlikely that Sixtus went all the way
with them, but, like John of Jerusalem, he showed his sym-
pathies.   Innocent did not act in haste.   He first called a local
synod to assist his deliberations, and finally replied in three
letters dated 27th January, 417.[3]   Each letter began with a
vigorous assertion of the primacy of the Roman see, and an
expression of satisfaction that the dispute has been referred to
him.   The letters contained two points of substance.   With
relation to the synod at Diospolis he had received a document
purporting to be the official record, but was uncertain of its
authenticity, and in the circumstance could neither approve
nor disapprove of the decisions there taken without further
evidence.   Augustine had some suspicion that the record was
being deliberately withheld, and wrote personally to John
requesting a copy[4] : the gentle courtesy of his language is in
marked contrast to Jerome's virulence.   With relation to the
"De Natura" Innocent found that it blasphemously denied the
necessity of real grace, and gave as his judgment that Pelagius,
Caelestius and their supporters ought to be excommunicated
until they should return to orthodoxy.   Forty-four days after
this solemn sentence he died.

PELAGIUS IN PALESTINE

Pelagius meanwhile decided that the strictures of Jerome
demanded a substantial answer.   This he presented in his
treatise on free-will.   The work itself, which ran to four books,
is unfortunately lost, except for a few fragments, but it is cited
and examined by Augustine in his works "De Gratia Christi"
and "De Peccato Originali" and we can obtain a fair estimate
of some of its contents, though we cannot now reconstruct its
ordered exposition.   This is a grievous loss, as it is clear from
what we possess that it contained the most systematic exposition
of his considered views.   Four points here deserve especial
mention.

[1] *Ep.*, 183, 2.   [2] *C. duas Ep. Pel.*, II, iii, 5; *Ep.*, 191; 194.
[3] *Epp.*, 181–3; cf. *C. duas Ep. Pel.*, II, v, 7; *De Pecc. Orig.*, ix, 10.
[4] *Ep.*, 179.

First he develops the view adumbrated earlier that we are born in a kind of morally neutral condition with the capacity for good and evil alike, but free from the actuality of either: all the good and evil by which we merit laud or censure is subsequent. In man at birth there is only what God has set there. "Omne bonum ac malum quo vel laudabiles vel vituperabiles sumus, non nobiscum oritur, sed agitur a nobis; capaces enim utriusque rei; non pleni nascimur, et, ut sine virtute, ita et sine vitio procreamur, atque ante actionem propriae voluntatis, id solum in homine est, quod Deus condidit."[1] Our moral self, in other words, is at birth a "tabula rasa," as some theories would have our minds to be. But whereas the mind is open from the moment of birth, and indeed, as we now understand, from the moment of conception, to all manner of impressions (the word, which has to-day lost its metaphorical sense, in fact continues the metaphor), no-one but we ourselves can write upon our souls, and we alone are responsible for what is found there written. This is a flat denial of original sin and an inherited taint, but Pelagius protested that it did not involve him in the admitted heresy of denying the efficacy and needfulness of infant baptism. This would be to refuse the children admission to the kingdom of heaven,[2] and share in the common redemption of mankind. This is to reiterate the old distinction between salvation and a higher sanctification, and is consistent with his characteristic assertion about infants who died unbaptized: "I know where they do not go; I do not know where they do go."

Secondly, he introduced a distinction of fundamental importance. Up till the present he had preferred to speak of God's help rather than God's grace, "Deo adiuvante" or "adiutorium" rather than "gratia." Now the force of Catholic orthodoxy had compelled him to subscribe to the tenet that God's grace was necessary to salvation, and he felt constrained to define more precisely what he meant by this acceptance. This alone should be enough to acquit him of the charge of double-dealing. He does not take refuge in ambiguity and equivocation, but chooses to come out into the open and define his terms, even though he knows that his position

---

[1] *De Pecc. Orig.*, xiii, 14.   [2] *Ib.*, xviii–xx, 20–2.

thus clarified is unlikely to be acceptable to Augustine and the bishops of the West. He distinguishes three elements in any course of action, "posse," "velle," and "esse"—the power, desire and realization. The power is in our nature, the desire in our will, the realization in the result. The first is bestowed by God; the other two come from our will and are our proper domain. For any right action man may rightly be praised, but God must be praised as well, for the power comes from him. That we are able to speak, think or act well, comes from God; that we do speak, think or act well comes from ourselves. If we attribute wrong action to ourselves we must also attribute right action to ourselves.[1] Nowhere is it more abundantly clear than in this passage that Pelagius is not interested in theory for its own sake, but in its moral implications. But all this is what the eighteenth century termed "natural religion." The God and Father of our Lord Jesus Christ goes further. He not merely gives us the power to act rightly. He helps those who are Christians by sustaining them in the action itself, by His teaching and revelation; by opening the eyes of our understanding, by showing to us the future for fear that we should be overwhelmed by present circumstances, by uncovering the wiles of Satan, by enlightening us through the gift of His heavenly grace in ways unspeakably various,[2] above all by the example of Christ.[3] It is this gift of illumination which is the proper object of prayer. This is Pelagius' answer to Augustine's castigation of his teaching as "a philosophy of this world."[4] It represents the furthest point to which he could possibly go in accommodation to the orthodox position.

Thirdly, he explained how he was able to pronounce the anathemas at Diospolis. He admitted, for instance, that Adam's sin did harm the whole human race, and not merely himself, but by example, not by physical transmission, and that children at birth were not in the same state as Adam before the Fall, because they, unlike him, were not yet endowed with the use of reason.[5] Augustine accuses him of making an ambiguous statement in public with deliberate intent to deceive, while he reveals his true meaning only to his disciples.

---

[1] *De Grat. Chr.*, iv, 5.   [2] *Ib.*, vii, 8.   [3] *Ib.*, xxxix, 43; xli, 45.
[4] *Ep.*, 186, 37.   [5] *De Pecc. Orig.*, xv, 16.

This is unfair, for Pelagius was here overtly publishing his full beliefs. His basic attitude remained consistent. Dogmatic orthodoxy required a general statement; its elaboration could rightly remain a subject of difference.

Fourthly he made an interesting examination of some passages in Paul. There were those who saw in Paul one who although a vessel of choice was driven to evil by necessity of the flesh. This was to open the door to Manicheism, and in denying the goodness of the creation to deny the goodness of the Creator. If we were driven by necessity to evil, then there was no justice in our punishment. This was not the lesson of the epistles. When Paul wrote "Those who do these things shall not inherit the kingdom of God," he implied that there were others who acted otherwise and did enter the kingdom. The conclusion of the epistles did not lie in moral defeatism; Paul himself was an example of one who because he had fought the good fight, merited the crown of justice.[1]

Pelagius had rarely been more certain of himself. He was acquitted by the bishops of Palestine. John alone might be suspected of favouring his view, but it would be hard to accuse the whole mass of the episcopal synod of corruption, incompetence or heresy. Further he was growing in the good graces of the people of Jerusalem.[2] He was able to expound his views publicly with confidence. Suddenly three events shook his security. The first was the raid on Jerome's monastery referred to earlier. There was no evidence where the responsibility lay. Jerome naturally attributed it to Pelagian hostility. He had no grounds for an official accusation: he did not hesitate unofficially to express his certainty.[3] Eustochium retained her influence with the Roman aristocracy; Jerome, whatever enmities he might arouse in the East, had been out of the West for thirty years, and was a figure revered from afar.[4] The incident caused a profound shock, and feeling turned more firmly against Pelagius. Secondly, the accusation of Innocent fell on him like a bolt out of a clear sky. Thirdly his protector

[1] Souter, *J. T. S.*, 1910, pp. 32–5; *P. B. A.*, ii, 437–9.

[2] Aug., *Ep.*, 176, 4.

[3] Jer., *Ep.*, 137, cf. 136; Aug., *De Gest. Pel.*, xxxv, 66.

[4] Oros., *Apol.*, 4.

and friend John was obviously nearing his end, and he could not foresee the consequences if that protection were withdrawn. He deemed it best to withdraw for a time, and Jerome exulted over his departure.[1]

He was not long gone; John died, and his successor Praylius proved equally sympathetic to Pelagius. Pelagius returned to Jerusalem, and set himself to write a letter in his own defence to Innocent.[2] In this apologia he protests his orthodoxy on all subjects from the unity of the Trinity to the resurrection of the Body. Augustine remarks sarcastically that these were not in question, but Pelagius was trying to keep a sense of proportion, and set his divergence from Augustine and Jerome in its perspective against the totality of the Christian faith. He directed Innocent to those works which alone he recognized as the true expression of his mind, notably a letter to bishop Constantius, his letter to Demetrias, and his recent composition on the freedom of the will. It was not to be expected that such an apologia would contain anything new. But he explained afresh the sense in which he spoke of freedom as freedom either to sin or to refrain from sinning, and protested that he recognized that the exercise of this freedom in right action depended upon the grace of God. Freedom belongs to all men; in Christians alone is it aided by grace. Turning to baptism he made an important admission in acknowledging one single baptism for children and adults, though he did not feel able to offer a more precisely defined view. He met the new accusations of Origenism by declaring that souls were the direct creation of God (this was incompatible with Origen's belief in pre-existence) and further met Jerome's criticisms in disavowing the position of Jovinian that man is incapable of sinning. This last destroyed the freedom of the will as effectively as those who said he was incapable of not sinning. He also had a sidelong thrust at Augustine and Jerome when he declared it to be blasphemy to assert that God commanded the impossible, or that His commandments might be fulfilled by the Church, but not by individuals, or to condemn marriage like the Manicheans, or remarriage like the Cataphrygians. He

[1] Jer., *Ep.*, 138.
[2] *Libellus fidei*; Aug., *De Grat. Chr.*, xxxi, 33, ff.

anathematized those who declared that Jesus limited his moral capacity by the incarnation. As we have remarked before, it is only rarely that points concerning the person of Jesus are introduced into the controversy, and they are at no time central. It may be that this failure stood in the way of the truth more than any other. Pelagius concluded with his central and definitive assertion : man has always the freedom to sin or not to sin, and always stands in need of the help of God.

It is most unlikely that this document could have induced Innocent to alter his decision, but his death and the succession of Zosimus opened a new series of events.

AUGUSTINE

Augustine meantime was not idle, and wrote a letter of some length and importance to Pelagius' friend Paulinus of Nola.[1] This was occasioned by the rumour that some people at Nola had declared "We will rather forsake and despise Pelagius for having given up his former views than give up those views ourselves." We do not know how Pelagius' views reached Campania. It may have been from the group of his adherents at Rome, or through his personal association with Paulinus, or by reason of some subsequent accidental contact. The situation was serious enough for Augustine to enter on a full examination of the controversy. He lays considerable stress upon the actual events, and tries to show by an account of the occurrences in Palestine that the decision of Diospolis was not definitive. But what is most important is the developed statement of Augustine's own theological position in criticism of Pelagius. He writes of predestination and of grace. Because of the sin of Adam the human race, who sin in Adam, (the old error about Romans v. 12) are under a just condemnation. Out of the mass of souls condemned God selects, arbitrarily and absolutely, a certain number for salvation. The infant who dies unbaptized is damned : it is a hard saying, but to say less is to denigrate the grace of God in mercy towards those whom He chooses to save. It follows that the first grace received by a soul is absolutely unmerited, though further grace may be merited by a soul which has already found justification through

[1] *Ep.*, 186.

faith. It is a grandiose scheme, dreadful and majestic, and we may well understand that by its side Augustine condemns Pelagianism as an essentially godless secular philosophy.

There is little doubt that he was the main force behind the appeal to Innocent, and it is at least probable that the letter from the five bishops was of his drafting. He had secured his verdict, or so he thought; but the heresy was not dead. On September 23rd, 417, he preached a sermon in which he reviewed the issues of the conflict up to the appeal to the apostolic see. The reply from Rome had been received, "Causa finita est." The debate was over. Would that one day the error might disappear! "Causa finita est". He little knew what lay over the page of time.

CAELESTIUS.

Since his departure from Carthage Caelestius had been in the background. Now he moved again to the front of the stage. How he had spent his time since 412 is uncertain. Augustine saw his hand behind the disturbances in Sicily, but there is no evidence of this. Certainly he spent some years in Ephesus, where he at last received the ordination he desired, and went from there to Constantinople. Here his persistence in propagating his ill-favoured view drew down upon him the opposition of the bishop, Atticus, and he was expelled from the city.[1] At the same time as the expulsion Atticus wrote letters about Caelestius to Asia, Carthage and Thessalonica, but not to Rome. Rome and Constantinople were not at this time in full communion with one another, because of a dispute, which does not here concern us, in which the name and person of Chrysostom were involved. The omission was to be significant later. Shortly after leaving Constantinople, Caelestius received the news of his condemnation by Innocent. Five years before he had thought of appealing from Carthage to Rome. Now the decision of Rome was given against him and he resolved to go forward in his own defence. He would go to Rome himself. But before his departure he found an opportunity to meet and turn from his hostility the worthier of his two Gallic traducers, Heros. This would probably, though not certainly, be in

[1] Merc., *Comm.*

Palestine.   If so he must have turned south after his expulsion,
no doubt relying on the judgment of Diospolis for his protection.
His encounter may have been accidental, but it is more likely
that Caelestius deliberately sought out Heros in the confidence
that personal contact brings conviction more readily than the
written word of one who is not personally known.[1]   If so it is
to be counted to his credit.   Lazarus is not mentioned : it may
have been he who fell seriously ill at the time of the synod :
apart from his condemnation by Zosimus he passes out of the
story.   The date of Caelestius' brief visit to Palestine is clear.
It must be set in the first half of 417 at the time when Palagius
had left the country for a short while.   If Pelagius were there
it is unlikely that they would have failed to meet, and unlikely
in the extreme that such a meeting of the heresiarchs would pass
unrecorded.   There is one last point of speculation.   We
cannot be certain whether Caelestius' resolve to go to Rome
followed immediately upon his condemnation, so that he
intended to appeal in person, as Pelagius had done in writing,
to the bishop who condemned him, or whether, as Mercator's
words suggest, it was the accession of Zosimus which led his
keen mind to see an opportunity for his rehabilitation, and sent
him off to Italy post-haste ("tota festinatione").   The former
view would redound more to his credit than the latter; it must
be frankly said that the balance of evidence is for the latter.

On arrival in Rome Caelestius drew up a document in his
own defence for submission to the Pope.   There is evidence in
this statement of close collaboration, no doubt by correspondence, between Caelestius and Pelagius, for the position it
takes up is very similar to that of the profession of faith which
Pelagius addressed to Innocent, and indeed to the whole of
Pelagius' revised credo.   Like Pelagius, he covered in minute
detail the whole field of Catholic dogma, protesting his orthodoxy on each several point.   He then passed to the articles
dealing with grace, and, again like Pelagius, sought to establish
the point that the differences between himself and Augustine
were not substantial differences of dogma, but subsidiary and

---

[1] This is not pure fancy, but deduced from the words of Zosimus' letter:
"Herotem vero, etiam satisfactione interposita, quod secus de ignoto et absente
sensisset, cum gratia recessisse."

incidental differences of interpretation in which scriptural truth and necessary faith were not involved. He returned to a point far more central to his thinking than that of Pelagius, namely infant baptism. He acknowledged that infants ought to be baptized, and baptized for the remission of sins, according to Church practice. But to attribute to human nature evil prior to any exercise of the will was to impugn the goodness of the Creation and hence, as we have seen suggested before, the goodness of the Creator. Sin came solely from man. It was not with him at birth, but was the result of his own free choice. Hence baptism for the remission of sins was justified not in terms of original sin, but on the grounds that from the very moment of birth the infant is capable of sinning. In this way he avoided the implication which might seem to attach to some of Pelagius' formulations, of establishing two different classes of baptism, one for remission of sins, and one for admission to the kingdom, and brought his theories more closely in line with the established practices of the Church, even if differences still remained. He maintained that on matters pertaining strictly to the fundamentals of Christian faith, he was in no sense a revolutionary, and submitted himself to the apostolic see for approbation or reprobation.

ZOSIMUS

Innocent died on 12th March, 417, and his successor Zosimus was raised to the pontificate on 18th March. He occupied the Holy See for less than two years, but they were twenty-one months of outstanding importance in the history of Pelagianism. Of his early life and background we know nothing. His name suggests that he came from the East, and we have already seen, from the synod at Diospolis, that the bishops of the East showed a sympathy towards the views of Pelagius, and a readiness to accept them and him within the fold of the Christian Church, that were wholly lacking in the West. Zosimus had before him, in addition to the appeal of Caelestius, the judgment of Diospolis, in which, as an Easterner, he would be more inclined to put confidence than in fifty Carthaginian synods; further, Caelestius was personally present. On the other side it is true that there was the judgment of Innocent, and it is surprising that Zosimus was so ready to put this aside. There was also the "libellus" which Paulinus has presented in accusing him at Carthage in 412. But the principal opponents of Pelagianism, Augustine, Jerome, Orosius, Heros and Lazarus, were all Westerners, and none of them in Rome, and the condemnation of Caelestius by Atticus of Constantinople, for reasons of high ecclesiastical politics, did not come into his hands. In addition Innocent's condemnation had been conditional on the heretics failing to return to orthodoxy, and it may be that at this point Zosimus felt justified in assenting to the re-opening of a case which Augustine considered already closed.

Zosimus called a synod in the Basilica of St. Clement. The documents were read to the assembly, and Caelestius, who presented his own defence, was carefully questioned. He added to his written apologia three points. First he declared himself willing to abjure and condemn all that the blessed Innocent had condemned in his rescript to the churches of Africa. On the other hand he spoke scornfully of the deposition of Paulinus and steadfastly refused to condemn the alleged heresies there contained. Finally he approached the Pope with mingled humility and confidence and expressed his readiness to submit himself wholly to the latter's judgment and correction. To err was but human, and he acknowledged the limits of his understanding. "Si forte ut hominibus, quispiam ignorantiae error obrepserit vestra sententia corrigatur." His presence before the tribunal betokened his sincerity, and Zosimus was impressed by his bearing. He found substance in Caelestius' contention that here were matters outside the central dogmas of the Faith, and regarded the whole dispute as a snare and delusion, more likely to shake the fabric of the Church than to build it up, arising on both sides from pressing too far a contagious curiosity and perverting their natural abilities of intellect and expression and their understanding of the Bible. He recognized that he had heard one side of the case only, and refrained from giving hasty judgment. But he roundly condemned, suspended and excommunicated Heros and Lazarus, regarding them as mere trouble-makers, who preferred charges against Pelagius and Caelestius, and then failed to appear in person to press them. Zosimus is often accused of injustice in undertaking this action upon the sole word of Caelestius.[1] This is most implausible. Not only is it improbable that the bishop of Rome would take such drastic action upon the unsupported word of a recently ordained presbyter, who was himself suspect, and whose case was still *sub judice*, but it appears that a major factor in their condemnation was their previous lives and characters, about which accurate information would be easily accessible in Rome, and the official records of the Diospolis synod, which reached Augustine some time before, were now available, and served as evidence of the part they had played and failed to play in these proceedings. At the same time his condemnation of them *in absentia* accords ill with his rebuke of the African bishops on precisely similar grounds. Pending further investigation he warned Caelestius and his associates to stand completely aside from these inessential and dangerous questions.

He delayed before communicating with the bishops in Africa. He was waiting for further evidence from Africa, perhaps also a defence of their action by Heros and Lazarus; his later words might suggest this. Doubtless in addition he was occupied with pressure of other business, as well he might be, and regarded the whole issue as comparatively insignificant. After two months he wrote to Aurelius and his fellow-bishops, recounted to them the action and decisions he had taken, and censured them for their haste and lack of charity in condemning Caelestius in a case in which neither defendant nor prosecutors were present. He made it clear that he had given no final pronouncement on the subject, but that he was personally satisfied with the faith of Caelestius, and gave them the opportunity to revise their judgment, an action of which they should never be ashamed if it were for the better.

In all this the name of Pelagius had not been mentioned. He however had drawn up for Innocent the "libellus fidei" analysed earlier, and despatched it with a covering letter, and a glowing testimony to his orthodoxy from Praylius, John's successor in the bishopric of Jerusalem. These naturally came now into Zosimus' hands. They were read in public assembly;

---

[1] De Plinval does not fall into this error, p. 316.

it was observed that Pelagius professed the need for God's
grace both prior to and throughout the course of action,
prevenient and co-operative in fact, though Augustine would
not have applied his terms to Pelagius' theology.   Zosimus
amid a scene of wild enthusiasm pronounced the creed of
Pelagius to be fully orthodox and catholic.   The Pelagians
were men of unblemished faith ("absolutae fidei").   As the
letters were read, and the references to God's grace unfolded
there were tears of joy in the eyes of those present.   The lost
sheep, they believed, was found; the prodigal returned.

Zosimus, this time with greater promptitude, wrote afresh to
the churches of Africa.   He criticizes them more outspokenly
for their hasty condemnation of virtuous Christians on the
grounds of idle gossip, and whisperings behind the back,
without any opportunity of self-defence.   He denounces Heros
and Lazarus more vehemently than before; their testimony
was worthless, and their moral character below contempt.
Pelagius on the contrary he asserted to be a layman who for
many years had been outstanding in good works and the service
of God; he was happy to declare that he was also theologically
sound and had never really been estranged from the Catholic
faith.

Zosimus is often blamed for his easy reversal of his predecessor's decision and his acquittal of Pelagius and Caelestius.
To speak thus is to fail in historical understanding.   In the first
place Caelestius had come before him in person; Pelagius had
submitted a statement.   None of their accusers, none of the
principal witnesses against them came forward.   "Ubi Heros?"
asked Zosimus, legitimately "Ubi Lazarus? erubescenda factis
et damnationibus nomina.   Ubi illi adulescentes, Timasius
et Iacobus, qui scripta quaedam, ut asserebatur, protulerunt?"
Even Orosius, who had once been ceaseless in the pursuit of
heresy, had turned to the writing of tendentious history and
the task of conveying the relics of St. Stephen to Spain.   We
shall pass presently to the refusal of Paulinus to come to Rome.
But, even allowing for the exigencies of autumn weather and
possible difficulties in navigation, it is hard to acquit the anti-
Pelagians at this stage, and the African churches in particular,
of a measure of coolness and indifference in following up the

charges they had made. Secondly, Pelagius was a Christian of blameless moral life and unimpeachable zeal for the cause of Christ. Caelestius was a controversialist, but we know nothing else against him. But two of their accusers were men of doubtful moral record at the least, and Zosimus was inclined to treat the whole accusation as either unscrupulous or frivolous. Thirdly, he was judging the Pelagians, and it is arguable that he was right to do so, on the basis of their most recent writings and statements, which were specifically designed to minimize the differences between themselves and the generally accepted faith of the Catholic Church. When Zosimus saw earlier documents in which the divergence was emphasized, he reversed the decision. Fourthly, of the most recent synodical decisions, the acquittal had been given by the bishops of the East, where Zosimus was more at home, and in the presence of Pelagius, the condemnation by the bishops of the West, and in the defendants' absence. Fifthly, on the theological issues involved, it should be observed that Augustine had moved or been driven into a position which went far beyond the letter of scripture, and might seem as inimical to the practice of Christian morality by its denigration of the human side in righteous action, as the views of Pelagius seemed to Augustine inimical to Christian faith by their denigration of the divine initiative. Zosimus felt that as long as grace and free will were both acknowledged the essential Faith was kept: the rest was unprofitable disputation.[1]

From Acquittal to Condemnation

The churches of Africa had appealed to Rome, and they had received the decision of Rome, but it was not to be expected that they would acquiesce without a murmur. They could not slight the authority of the Holy See, and Augustine generally passes over this action on the part of Zosimus without any mention. When he does speak of it, he treats it as an example of the virtue of leniency carried to excess, excuses Zosimus as having given his decision not in terms of their errors but of their expressed willingness to correct them if they were adjudged in the wrong, and implies that the Pope was imposed upon in

[1] This whole account is based principally upon Zosimus' two letters.

the simplicity of his goodness by the dishonesty and lack of scruple in the Pelagians.   This last was certainly unfair. Pelagius and Caelestius went as far as they could in the interests of preserving their orthodoxy.   But Caelestius, for example, blazoned forth his refusal to abjure the propositions condemned in 412.   There was no concealment or duplicity there.

The events which followed are a little confused, owing to an obscure passage in one of Augustine's letters,[1] and owing to the perverted ingenuity of some church historians,[2] who fashion Councils almost at will.   The main events are clear enough. Zosimus sent his second letter to Carthage by a subdeacon named Basilicus.   By the same hand he sent another letter to Paulinus, who, it will be remembered, had served as a deacon under Ambrose at Milan, and played a leading part in the original condemnation of Caelestius at Carthage in 412.   The "libellus" which he presented on that occasion had been among the evidence when Zosimus examined Caelestius.   Opportunity had been given for the accusers to appear in person at Rome, and they had not taken it.   Further, Caelestius had rejected any suggestion that this "libellus" involved him in unorthodoxy, and flung back the accusation of heresy upon his accuser.   Zosimus had half-decided that the accusations were malicious or frivolous.   He now summoned Paulinus to Rome to answer for his conduct.   The latter replied on 8th November, 417, in a letter which is extant, and daringly but respectfully refuses to go, regarding the case as settled.   He had charged Caelestius with certain heresies, for which he had been condemned.   The same charges were laid before him in Rome, and he still refused to abjure them.   There was no more to be said.

Meantime the bishops were stirred into action.   No individual might go to press their concern, but letters passed and repassed between Africa and Rome at alarming length and with alarming frequency.[3]   It may be that there was a semi-official synod hurriedly summoned in November; it may be that Aurelius, like Ambrose on another occasion, took it upon himself to act in the name of those who had subscribed to the

---

[1] *Ep.*, 215, 2.   [2] E.g. Garnier and Quesnel.

[3] Aug., *Contr. duas Ep. Pel.*, II, iii, 5.

decisions of the full synod in 416, perhaps confirming his actions by correspondence. It is clear that the Africans stood by their own verdict of that year confirmed by Innocent, and Augustine felt certain that if they were presented openly before him, Zosimus would condemn the same propositions which had offended Innocent.[1] After all they had been directly concerned in the business since it first attracted public attention; he had not. They had minutely and thoroughly sifted all the theological implications; in the pressure of official duties, this could hardly be expected of him, and so backwards and forwards the letters sped, and Jerome wrote from Bethlehem comparing Augustine with Lot preferring to leave the city of destruction, even if he lost all his companions, rather than stay with those who were doomed to the fire.[2]

In Rome also opposition to Caelestius remained. The "commilitones in Domino"[3] were Donatus, Mercator, Marcus, Januarius, Primus, Restitutus, Trajan; we hear too of Apronius[4] and Riparius.[5] Of these, Mercator, author of the "Commonitorium" was perhaps the leader.[6] These bandied texts, and fervently discussed the disputed scriptural passages. We hear too of Constantius who attacked Caelestius' views "sine scriptura," that is, presumably, on grounds of natural religion, (unless it means merely "vocally"): as some might think, meeting them upon their own field. On the other side was Caelestius. His case was not in fact decided, for Zosimus had left it to the African churches to change their verdict, and this they would not do. He was now supported by Julian of Eclanum, of whom much was to be heard in the future. The dispute grew fiery, and in a brawl extreme violence was laid on Constantius.[7]

Next, Zosimus addressed a further letter to the African churches. The letter was written on 21st March, 418, probably a day or two after a synod on the anniversary of his consecration. It falls very sharply into two parts. At the outset, he expresses his displeasure at their failure to accept his judgment, speaks in exalted words of the authority which the Roman See

[1] *Ib.* [2] Jer., *Epp.*, 141–2. [3] Jer., *Ep.*, 154, 3.
[4] *Id., Ep.*, 139. [5] *Id., Epp.*, 138, 152. [6] Aug., *Ep.*, 193.
[7] Prosp., *Chron.*, 418.

derived from St. Peter, and asserts his independence in un-
qualified terms. If he chooses to consult others, that is his
free decision : it does not arise because he either requires their
instruction as to future action or confirmation as to past action.
Such a beginning might be expected to prelude a fresh criticism
of their attitude to the Pelagians. It is in fact the grandilo-
quence which covers up a "climb-down." The substance of
the letter is that the case of Caelestius remained where it was :
he had neither approved him in all respects nor condemned
him : and he hints as to a possibility of reconsideration.

There follows the least savoury episode of the whole campaign. The arm of the State was called in to deal with the
heretics. It was a shadow of the measures John had once
threatened, but not effected, against Jerome; the pendulum
swung back, the punchball rebounded. The consequences of
Augustine's readiness to countenance coercion in the Donatist
dispute were now becoming evident. Action must have been
going forward before this last rescript of Zosimus arrived in
Africa. It is to be feared that it was taken in despair of
ecclesiastical authority; it is almost less charitable to suppose
that it was directed to pull a wavering Pope firmly off the
fence. Count Valerius was a personal friend of Augustine, who
speaks of the high services which he has rendered to the catholic
cause in a stand against professed Christians who were really
enemies of Christ, opposing their error while caring for their
salvation.[1] This is language peculiarly apposite to an opponent of the Pelagians. No doubt he took the initiative at the
instigation of Augustine. Certainly the African bishops were
closely involved, for in the following year Honorius writes to
Aurelius and says that his action was taken in deference to the
latter's judgment. Duchesne has reasonably suggested that the
attitude of Galla Placidia, sister to the emperor Honorius, may
have turned the scales.[2] The African party could point to the
attack upon Constantius, and disorder in the streets of Rome;
they could adduce parallel disturbances from Palestine and
elsewhere. These were the occasion of the emperor's intervention. On 30th April, 418, he issued a rescript from

[1] Aug., *De Nuptiis et Concup.*, i, 2.
[2] *Hist. de l'Eglise*, iii, p. 237, note 3.

Ravenna, addressed to the Praetorian Prefect Palladius, commanding the banishment of Pelagius (who was not in fact in Rome, but the sentence looked to the future as well), Caelestius and all their adherents. Honorius was not concerned with questions of high theology. He was concerned with civil order, and made this the ground of his judgment. But he was a weak emperor, unusually prone to favouritism, and no doubt willing to support his friends without examining too carefully the niceties of the case or the real justification of his action.

Events moved fast. Almost simultaneously with this rescript, in fact on the very next day (the coincidence is without significance) over 200 bishops met in council once again at Carthage. The number is variously given as 214, 226 and 203, but the first figure is generally accepted.[1] This Council first reconsidered the questions involved in the whole case of Caelestius and Pelagius, and in view of the fact that they had not given a categorical admission that we need the grace of God to empower us in each several action we undertake, but had confined themselves to generalities, felt obliged to reassert the adverse verdict of Innocent. After this they proceeded to the celebrated canons of Carthage, which were once attributed to the earlier assembly at Milevum (a compliment to the influence of Augustine). These nine canons defined clearly the orthodox position. Three dealt with original sin : the third, which did not allow the existence of Limbo, is sometimes missing, but Augustine's position is clear: "Non accipientes aeternam vitam utique consequenter alterna morte damnentur."[2] Three dealt with grace, and specifically anathematize the Pelagian view of grace; here again the hand of Augustine is apparent. Three dealt with the universality of sin and the true nature, meaning and purpose of prayer. By the time the three delegates from Rome, Faustinus, Philip and Asellus, appeared on the scene on May 24th the mind of the council was firm and determined.

Zosimus had been wavering, as his last letter showed. He

---

[1] Prosp., *Contr. Collat.*, 5; Photius, *Bibl.*, 53; Mansi, *Sacr. Conc.*, IV, 377. The full account of the synod is in the first of these.

[2] *Contr. duas Ep. Pel.*, II, iv, 7.

summoned Caelestius to appear before him.   We do not know
the date of this summons : Garnier conjectured April 15th, but
without real foundation.   It would be interesting to be sure of
its relation to the rescript of Honorius and the decision of
Carthage.   Julian is certain that the Roman clergy were
governed not by the rights of the case, but by the fear of
Honorius' edict, in their subsequent action—"iussionis terrore
perculsos."[1]   He is not an impartial witness, though it is
possible that the summons did in fact come between the edict
of banishment and Caelestius' compulsory departure : it is
perhaps more likely that it was a little before, at a time when it
was known that the emperor was likely to intervene.   Caelestius saw what was in the air, and not merely failed to appear,
but left the city itself.[2]   This may indeed be the clue to the
date.   For unless he feared the intervention of the civic
authorities, it is hard to see what he had to gain by leaving.   He
knew that if he disappeared, his excommunication was inevitable, knew it with the greater certainty because of the strictures
which Zosimus had spoken against Heros and Lazarus.   His
personality had impressed Zosimus.   The letter of March 21st
must have warned him that his theological position was pre-
carious.   His only chance was to face it out personally; he had
shown at Carthage that he did not lack the courage to do this.
But if he foresaw simultaneous action by Church and State,
then he might well fear and flee.   Consequently we shall do
best to date these occurrences to closely the same dates as the
other two.

Zosimus was now pushed off the fence.   Africa stood
solidly against Caelestius; the emperor had raised his hand
against him; he had failed in his own defence.   The pope's
hand was forced; the gale was too strong, and he must bow
before it.   In a *volteface* almost unprecedented in the history
of the papacy, he drew up an "epistola tractoria,"[3] issued it
perhaps in midsummer (it was September before Augustine
heard of it, and popes were not wont to draw up such documents in haste), and sent it out to Constantinople and throughout the civilised world.   The letter is lost; it is evident that it

---

[1] *Ib.*, II, ii, 3.   [2] *Ib.*, II, iii, 5.   Mercator, *Comm.*
[3] Mercator, *Comm.*, Aug., *De Pecc. Orig.*, xxii, 25; *Ep.*, 190, 22–3.

treated at length the whole question of sin and redemption and emphasised the hereditary consequences of the Fall: he does not seem to have treated the specific topics of sinlessness or of the damnation of infants. But he declared Pelagius and Caelestius to have transgressed the central tenets of the Christian doctrine of redemption, and thereby to be excommunicated. Since his earlier pronouncements, Pelagius' commentary upon the Epistles had come into his hands, and was especially censured. Like his predecessor, however, he opened the door for them to return in penitence if they recanted their previous errors. But in all the churches in his domain, subscription to the letter was compulsory.

The Results

The letter had a wide circulation and, as one would expect, was generally accepted. In Italy, the subscription was enforced under the authority of the prefect; in Africa, the measures were taken by Aurelius under the protection of the imperial edict. But eighteen[1] Italian bishops, led by Julian, bishop of Eclanum in Campania, found themselves unable to subscribe to it. Julian wrote twice to Zosimus in protest, and finally appealed to a general council, but was withstood through the offices principally of Augustine in the church and Valerius representing the secular power. The Protestants were deposed and banished. Some recanted; Julian remained firm and became the chief representative of the Pelagian position.[2]

Pelagius was deeply shaken by these events. He had been present at not one of the councils which had accused him, and that through no fault of his own. Indeed, Zosimus' condemnation of him in his absence after his earlier approval is strange in view of the pope's criticism of the Africans for similar action. Pelagius was passionately anxious to remain a loyal member of the Church. He wished to work for right living within the Church, not outside it. He had written strongly against heresy after heresy. Now he protested to two friends of

---

[1] Not nineteen as is sometimes stated.

[2] Mercator, *Comm.*, Aug., *Contra duas Ep. Pel.*, IV, xii, 34; *Contra Iul.*, i, 13; iii, 5.

Augustine that he did believe in the grace of God, active not merely hour by hour or minute by minute, but in our every action.[1] He longed for reconciliation with Augustine. It was useless. A synod was called under the chairmanship of Theodotus of Antioch, and he was pronounced excluded from the holy places of Jerusalem : his former friend Praylius weakly succumbed to the pressure and concurred in the judgment.[2] It is likely that he left Palestine for Egypt, partly because the bishop there had not pronounced against Pelagianism,[3] partly because he could count on some friends there, among the laity, if not among the monks. There in face of contumely he remained loyal to the truth he had seen.[4] One of the letters of Isidore of Pelusium looks as if it might be addressed to him.[5] It contains all the gibes of Orosius about gormandizing and fawning upon the rich. One would like to think, as de Plinval reasonably suggests,[6] that he ended his life in writing a commentary on Job and "De bono constantiae," in which he stands firmly against a Manichean condemnation of natural good, asserts the freedom of the will, and the power of a rightly ordered will to defy external circumstances—above all the commentary on the Song of Songs, in which he exalts, again in opposition to the Manicheans, true love, which is holy and noble.[7] He fades out of history with love on his lips, surrounded by abuse and contempt.

Caelestius makes two last startling reappearances. He always had more vigour, and more sense of the dramatic than his master, but less depth and less dignity. The first was in 423. Zosimus was long dead, as was his successor, Boniface, and Celestine was bishop in their stead. The civic authorities had temporal disturbances to engage their attention. In the midst of this, regardless of danger, Caelestius suddenly appeared in Rome, and demanded a fresh hearing. He was unsuccessful, and the sentence of banishment from the territory of Italy altogether pronounced upon him.[8] He appears again in Constantinople in 429. Atticus had pronounced vigorously

---

[1] Aug., *De Grat. Chr.*, ii, 2. [2] Mercator, *Comm.* [3] *Collect. Avellane*, 49.

[4] Aug., *Ep.*, 196, 7. [5] Isid. Pelus., *Ep.*, i, 314.

[6] De Plinval, p. 330. [7] Bede, *Comm. in Cant. Cant.*

[8] Prosp., *Contr. Collat.*, 21, 2.

against the Pelagians,[1] and at a synod held in Cilicia in the 420s, even Theodore of Mopsuestia subscribed to the general condemnation.[2] But Nestorius, the successor of Atticus, although he delivered some important and weighty homilies against those who denied the transmission of Adam's sin, was felt to be less intransigent. Julian, Florus, and some of the other deposed bishops made their way to that city as pilgrims in distress, and presented themselves to the bishop. Caelestius accompanied them, but remained in the background. Nestorius heard them sympathetically and patiently, and wrote to Rome for further information. His letter was ignored, and a second letter received a curt reply from Celestine saying that the heretics had been justly condemned, and he was not surprised that they had taken refuge with Nestorius.[3] All this became obscured in the controversy over Nestorius' own views which now came to a head. His sympathy with Caelestius was used against both of them. The dénouement came at Ephesus in 431. There at a great general council two hundred bishops, led by Cyril, pronounced condemnation on the views of Nestorius and Caelestius, without specifying them, and in the synodal letter of July 22nd wrote to Celestine to say that they fully approved all the pope had said with relation to the deposition (a strange word as applied to Pelagius, a layman, and even Caelestius) of Caelestius, Pelagius, Julian, Persidius, Florus, Marcellinus, Orontius, and those who held their ideas. Caelestius had fought his last battle of words and ideas, and lost it.

Principal sources—See Chapter IV.

[1] Mercator, *Comm.*

[2] Id., *Refut. Symbol. Theod.*

[3] Gore once wrote that "the Nestorian Christ is the natural Saviour of the Pelagian man."

VIII

THE THEOLOGY OF THE COMMENTARIES

It is time to turn from the broader theme of the history of Pelagianism to enquire more closely into the ideas which Pelagius taught and . propagated. To do this, it will be necessary, before selecting specific ideas for a more detailed examination, to study the commentaries on Paul's epistles, which by an irony of history, passed for centuries under the name of Jerome, but which are with very little doubt the work of Pelagius. The procedure has much to commend it. In the first place, the commentaries are the most substantial work which we have from Pelagius' pen. Secondly, in studying them, we are face to face with Pelagius himself, and not trying to look at him through the distorting mirror of an opponent of more or less scrupulosity. Thirdly, precisely because the commentaries are commentaries, they are tied to the letter of scripture, and are not liable to go off into flights of abstract speculation. But while there are these undoubted advantages, there is also need of a caveat. We have to remember that this work was written while Pelagius' mature thought was still forming. His thinking has not been refined in the fire of controversy, and cannot be taken as systematic. Further, there is no doubt that it has been pruned. The shears of Catholic editors have trimmed and shaped the luxuriance of free growth. Enough remains to show clearly the trend of the original thought: we cannot be sure that on point of detail we have Pelagius' full and precise expression.

ORTHODOXY

For one who reads with the subsequent history of Pelagius in mind, one of the most striking features of the whole book is its concern for orthodoxy. The author clearly regards himself as an exponent of the Catholic faith. Indeed faith to him means the Catholic or universal faith.[1] Heresy is to be shunned as contrary to religion; all converse with heretics is to be avoided; suspicion of heresy is perhaps the gravest of all

[1] 1 Tim. iv. 12. The scriptural references in this chapter refer to the appropriate passages in the commentaries.

suspicions.[1] He sees in the writings of Paul the main guard against those who stand to disturb the true faith and the peace of the Church, false apostles,[2] false prophets,[3] secular philosophers,[4] pagans,[5] or Jews.[6] He rebuts by name many of the heresies which had disrupted the Church. It is not surprising to find him speaking strongly against the Manicheans,[7] though it is important to observe that his later hostility to Manichean views was not merely a weapon of debate against Augustine, but a life-long personal conviction. We have seen some reason to suppose in Pelagius a degree of sympathy with Jovinian, and it may be that his interpretation of "modestum" as "qui omnia faciat cum mensura" points the same way.[8] But he anathematizes the Jovinianists as firmly as the Manicheans.[9] On Church discipline he stands with the orthodox against the Novatians.[10] On the dominant issue of controversy, the person and work of Christ, he renounces alike Arius,[11] Photinus,[12] and Apollinaris,[13] and shows their views to be contrary to the letter and spirit of what Paul writes. He did in fact write an early work upon the Trinity, of which some fragments remain. Marcion[14] and the Macedonians,[15] Callimachus and Parmenides[16] are all to be dismissed as heretics. He believes that Christ came to suffer for others,[17] to save sinners,[18] to redeem us from death,[19] and three times speaks against the irreligious views of those who try to deny the real

[1] Rom. xiii. 21; 1 Cor. xv. 4; Col. iv. 6; 1 Tim. vi. 4; 2 Tim. ii. 15; ii. 17; iii. 13; Tit. iii. 9.
[2] 1 Cor. arg; 2 Cor. ii. 17, v. 12, xi. 9; Gal. arg; Phil. arg; iii. 2; Col. ii. 11; 1 Tim. arg.
[3] Eph. i. 11; cf. De Div. xviii. 7.
[4] Col. ii. 8, ii. 23.
[5] Rom. xiii. 21; Col. iv. 6.
[6] Col. iv. 6.
[7] Rom. i. 2, vi. 19, vii. 7, viii. 7, ix. 5; 1 Cor. xi. 12, xv. 46; 2 Cor. iii. 7, xiii. 1; Gal. v. 21; Col. i. 16; 1 Tim. vi. 4, 16; cf. *Lib. fid.*, 10, 13; Aug., *De Perf. Iust.*, vi, 14; *De Cast.*, 16.
[8] 1 Tim. iii. 3.
[9] 1 Cor. iii. 8; 2 Cor. ix. 6; Phil. iii. 18; 1 Thess. ii. 3; cf. *Lib. fid.*, 13; *De Cast.*, 16.
[10] 1 Cor. iii. 17; 2 Cor. ii. 11, xii. 21; 2 Tim. ii. 26.
[11] Rom. i. 3, viii. 34, ix. 5; 1 Cor. i. 9, ii. 8, viii. 6, ix. 21, xii. 6, xv. 24, 28; 2 Cor. xii. 3, xiii. 13; Phil. ii. 5; 2 Thess. iii. 3.
[12] Rom. i. 3, viii. 3, ix. 5; 1 Cor. ix. 21; 2 Cor. viii. 10.
[13] 1 Cor. ii. 8, xv. 45.
[14] Rom. vii. 12; Eph. iii. 9; cf. Aug. *De Perf. Iust.*, vi, 14; Pel., *De Cast.*, xvi.
[14] 1 Cor. xii. 4–6.
[16] Tit. i. 12.
[17] Phil. ii. 5, ii. 21.
[18] 1 Tim. arg.
[19] Rom. iii. 24.

bodily resurrection of Jesus.[1]   All this is of a piece with what we read elsewhere.   To take but one example, in the book on the hardening of the heart of Pharaoh, he speaks in orthodox Trinitarian terms,[2] and though he is putting forward an interpretation on the basis of views which were subsequently regarded as heretical, he constantly appeals to the accepted orthodox and Catholic understanding.[3]

This is important.   We shall pass presently to unsystematized indications of what was later called Pelagianism.   For the moment we must note that when Pelagius put forward the views for which he was to become notorious he did so not to assail orthodoxy, but to defend it.   The book to which we have just referred is in its essence a defence of the words in Ezekiel "I do not wish the death of a sinner,"[4] and an attempt to harmonize Paul's words about Pharaoh with the totality of the Catholic faith.   Later still, as Bigg saw, when Jerome thought him allied to Origen, Pelagius saw himself as refuting the Alexandrian.[5]

The Quality of the Commentaries

For the most part the commentaries are a scholarly and accurate elaboration of Paul's own words.   They show wide and careful reading of the Bible, and are filled with illuminating allusions to parallel passages.   They are mercifully free from the higher and less profitable flights of allegory; the interpretation is generally at one with the spirit in which Paul was writing, and is rarely strained or forced.   Occasionally Pelagius is too subtle.   On Galatians ii. 19, "I through the law am dead to the law" he introduces an illegitimate distinction whereby he makes the first refer to the law of Christ, and the second to the law of the Letter.   Or again on Ephesians iv. 27, "Let not the sun go down upon your wrath" is given a spiritual meaning which strains the grammar, "Let not the light of true knowledge be lacking in your anger."   More reprehensibly, in the sixth chapter of the same letter he breaks off at the words "which is the first commandment," and interprets it to refer to the first commandment on the second

---

[1] Rom. i. 4; 1 Cor. xv. 4; 2 Tim. ii. 15.   [2] *De ind. cord. Phar.*, 2.
[3] *Ib.*, 9, 19, 24, 34.   [4] *Ib.*, 31.
[5] *Christian Platonists of Alexandria*, p. 323; cf. Aug., *De Gest. Pel.*, iii, 10.

tablet, in defiance of the unity of the whole phrase, of which he was well aware. But such passages are infrequent, and more often Pelagius is right at Paul's heart, as when "the children of light and the children of day" is seen to mean "the children of the knowledge of truth."[1]

The explanation of this is two-fold. On the one hand it is true that Pelagius was a careful and accurate commentator, anxious to uphold and preserve the word of God. But it is also true that he is less prone to fancifulness because the purpose of his writing is frankly moralizing; it is not historical, critical or metaphysical. For this reason it is of peculiar interest to compare his treatment of some passages in Romans with that of the famous hymn of love in the first letter to Corinth. The latter contains some of his most profound and exalted writing. Romans, on the other hand, though his most substantial commentary, and containing much moral insight, shows that he is not at home with Paul's cosmic speculations.

It should be said at once that he is aware of other problems. He notes a discrepancy over the manuscript reading,[2] or a linguistic question of the derivation of Maran-atha,[3] or a variation in Paul's language.[4] He twice notes an apparent contradiction between Epistles and Acts,[5] observes that it is uncertain whether in fact Paul visited Spain,[6] mentions that it is disputed whether the battle with beasts at Ephesus is literal or allegorical.[7] But he does not treat any of these questions critically, and when he does assert that the description of James as "the brother of the Lord" is not to be taken literally, it is purely on dogmatic grounds.[8]

There is a closely parallel passage in the treatise on riches where he records the opinion of some that the "camel" which could not pass through the needle's eye was not an animal, but a rope, only to dismiss it, largely on *a priori* grounds and without any real weighing of evidence.[9] The fact is that these questions neither concern nor interest him. Provided that the text is such as to form the basis for a moral exhortation or diatribe he is content.

[1] 1 Thess. v. 5.   [2] Col. iii. 15.   [3] 1 Cor. xvi. 22.
[4] 2 Thess. iii. 18.   [5] 1 Cor. xv. 32; 2 Cor. xi. 24.   [6] Rom. xv. 24.
[7] 1 Cor. xv. 32.   [8] Gal. i. 19.   [9] *De Div.*, xviii.·1.

USE OF SCRIPTURE

The principal academic virtue of the commentaries, then, is their use of scripture, and here Pelagius shows himself at his best. There are considerably over a thousand such cross-references, and any detailed analysis would take up a disproportionate amount of space; those who wish to pursue the matter further may find all the pointers in Professor Souter's monumental edition. But the most cursory of glances at Pelagius' use of these quotations gives a clear indication of the bent of his mind. Thus there are nearly three times as many citations of the New Testament as of the Old, and even when one allows for a large number of cross references within the body of the Epistles, the disproportion is striking. It shows that Pelagius is concerned with Christianity, the Christianity of Jesus and the Apostles, and the Old Testament takes second place to that, and is introduced only as illustrating and illuminating that. Whatever theoretical views Pelagius might hold about the plenary inspiration of holy scripture,[1] in practice he emphasized some parts of the Bible against others. Indeed in the treatise on riches he specifically says that we are to imitate Christ, not the patriarchs and prophets, and fulfil the ordinances of the New Testament, not the Old.[2] As so commonly with people of this trend of thought, within the Old Testament it is the devotional literature of the Psalms which makes the fullest appeal to him, and that, together with the creation story and type-legends of Genesis and the moralizing literature of Proverbs and Ecclesiasticus, constitutes his richest quarry. The historical books and the minor prophets hold few jewels for him. It is surprising that he does not find more in Hosea to meet his thought. The single oblique reference to the Song of Songs shows that he turned to this only late in life and makes the more impressive his final panegyric of love after a life which might so easily have turned to bitterness. Of the gospels he prefers Matthew. This again is not surprising. Mark attracts by its simple historicity, John by its metaphysical profundity, Luke by its anecdotal charm, Matthew by its moral fervour. Today we know Mark as primary among the Gospels alike in date and in historical reliability. Pelagius

[1] Cf. Rom. vii. 11–12.   [2] *De Div.* ix. 5.

refers to it no more than twenty times; to Matthew there are more than one hundred references. Among the epistles, as one would expect, Romans and First Corinthians predominate. A study of individual texts confirms the picture. The texts most beloved of Pelagius, and most frequently quoted, uphold a life of service and toil and humility and a readiness to accept suffering, inculcate the commandment of love, urge the danger of sin. There is almost prophetic insight in the repeated quotation about the apostles rejoicing because they were counted worthy to suffer in the name of the Lord.[1] The reader is reminded eight times of the humbleness of Jesus in taking the shape of a slave[2]; six times of the commandment to love our enemies,[3] and of the saying that perfect love casts out fear.[4] We are made in the image of God[5]; we shall live with Jesus[6]; when He appears we shall be like Him[7]; we are members of His body[8]; it is for sinners that the law was given[9]; through the law came knowledge of sin[10]; it is riches and wordly cares that stand between us and God.[11]   This confirms quite closely the picture given by de Plinval of Pelagius' use of texts throughout his extant writing.[12]   De Plinval divides those which appear most frequently under five headings—human freedom and responsibility,[13] the injunction to a life of love and virtue,[14] the need for works as well as faith,[15] the example of Christ and the precept of perfection,[16] and the difficulties and rewards of the Christian calling.[17]

An example or two, chosen almost at random, show the admirable use to which this knowledge of the Bible is put. Thus in commenting on Paul's warning to those who participate in the Eucharist in the wrong spirit, Pelagius refers to the

---

[1] Acts v. 41.

[2] Phil. ii. 7, cf. ii. 3 and ii. 8, which are also frequently repeated.

[3] Matt. v. 44.   [4] 1 John. iv. 18.   [5] Gen. i. 26.

[6] 2 Tim. ii. 11.   [7] 1 John iii. 2.   [8] Eph. v. 30.

[9] 1 Tim. i. 9.   [10] Rom. iii. 20.   [11] Matt. xiii. 22.

[12] Pp. 94–6.

[13] Deut. xxx. 15; Ecclus. xv. 14–7; Ezra xviii. 20, xxxiii. 12, 16.

[14] Matt. vii. 12, xix. 17; Luke xiv. 33; Jas. ii. 10; 1 John ii. 15.

[15] Matt. vii. 19–22; Rom. ii. 13; Tit. i. 16.

[16] Job xxvii. 6; Matt. v. 48; 1 Cor. xi. 1; Eph. v. 27; Phil. ii. 14–5; 1 Pet. ii. 21; 1 John i. 6.

[17] Matt. vii. 14, xiv. 43, xix. 28; Rom. viii. 18; Phil. iii. 13–4.

words of Jesus "If before the altar you remember that your
brother has anything against you, leave your gift before the
altar, go, first be reconciled with your brother."[1] Again not
only is the passage in Galatians treating of the Council at
Jerusalem rightly and accurately referred to the corresponding
account in Acts, but a valuable parallel is drawn between
Paul's words "that they might bring us into bondage," and
Peter's "Now therefore why do you tempt God, to put a yoke
on the disciples' necks."[2] A third illustration shows the meticulous detail of Pelagius' knowledge of the Old Testament.
He is dealing with Paul's command to slaves to serve their
masters loyally. He argues, if I understand him rightly,
that Christ did not come to alter the accidental status in which
men might happen to find themselves, but to straighten out
their essential nature where it was warped. Slavery does not
exist by nature (Pelagius' knowledge of Stoic thought comes
out here). Nor does it exist by God's fiat. For though the
curse of Ham might seem to suggest this, the careful reader will
find that the children of Ham became not slaves but kings, and
the curse was fulfilled in the defeat of the Canaanites at the
hands of the children of Israel.[3] One especially notable
passage is his comment on the verse "Does God take care for
oxen?" and his affirmative answer, linking Jesus' words about
the sparrows with God's care for the cattle at Nineveh.[4]

There is enough here to show that Pelagius' biblical knowledge, though subject to the bent of his own mind, was wide and
deep, and that his use of it shows a combination of careful
scholarship and devotional insight.

MORAL PURPOSE: (1) THE ROOT OF EVIL

We have already said that the central purpose of the commentaries is moral exhortation. The nature of this exhortation
requires further analysis. Like Calvin Coolidge's preacher,
Pelagius' theme is sin, and he is "agin it." Sin is the gate of
the devil, righteousness the gate of the spirit.[5] But in what
does this sin consist? Pelagius tackles the question more than

---

[1] 1 Cor. xi. 27; Matt. v. 23–4.   [2] Gal. ii. 4; Acts xv. 10.
[3] Eph. vi. 5; Gen. ix. 25, x. 10; Judg. i. 4.
[4] 1 Cor. ix. 9; Matt. x. 29; Jonah iv. 11.   [5] Eph. iv. 27.

once. We need not take his citation of a passage of Ecclesiasticus, suggesting that wine and women are the chief causes of apostasy, as representative of his best thought.[1] More significant are the four roots of false judgment—personal affection, personal dislike, fear and greed.[2] These are susceptible of a wider extension, and in one passage he suggests that the principal causes of wrongdoing are "iniquitas" and "malitia,"[3] in another "immunditia" and "avaritia."[4] We have not in English precisely equivalent terms to these. "Iniquitas" is probably to be taken here as a legal metaphor, and may be translated as "partiality," representing the personal affection and dislike of the other passage mentioned above.[5] "Malitia" stands for ill-will, spite, faults of temper and the like, and is fundamentally a failure in personal relationship, the absence of "caritas." "Immunditia" is impurity, and no doubt is conceived primarily in terms of sexual looseness. "Avaritia" refers to greed for gain, particularly riches and possessions, but also power of any kind.[6] With shrewd psychology Pelagius sees that this applies equally to security of possession, and desire to possess.[7] It is natural to expect that he will be constantly warning his readers of the danger of riches, and in fact he does.[8] In one passage of the treatise on riches indeed he follows Paul in making avarice the sole cause of all wrongdoing "fontem omnium malorum, radicem scelerum, culparum fomitem, delictorum materiam."[9] The warning against pride however is not so prominent here as elsewhere; in the "De Natura" he sums up the whole of sin under the single word "superbia," for all sin is rejection of God, and all rejection of God is pride.[10] He is not unaware of it in the commentaries and repeats the lesson of humility,[11] but he does not at this stage see it as the root cause of other sins.

MORAL PURPOSE : (2) THE POWER OF CONSCIENCE

Pelagius lays considerable stress upon the power of self-knowledge revealed in conscience. When we stand at the

---

[1] Rom. xiv. 21; Ecclus. xix. 2.   [2] Id., ii. 2.   [3] Id., i. 29.   [4] Eph. v. 2.
[5] Cf. Gaius, Inst., iv, 178.   [6] Cf. De Div., vi. 2.   [7] 1 Tim. vi. 9.
[8] Cf. Rom. v. 4, xv. 20; 1 Cor. xiii. 3; 2 Cor. iv. 2, xi. 12, 20; 1 Tim. vi. 9, ff.
[9] De Div., xvii, 2.   [10] Aug., De Nat. et Grat., xxix, 33.
[11] E.g. 1 Cor. iv. 6; 1 Tim. iii. 6, et passim.

Lord's Table, or ready to make our gift at the altar, we must examine our conscience to be sure that we are doing so worthily.[1] It is the testimony of his own conscience which approves a man, and a good conscience should exalt the spirit more than the flattering words of another.[2] Men know what may be known of God because it is revealed to their consciences[3]; it is our consciences which approve the saying that Christ Jesus came into the world to save sinners.[4] So too in a subtle and accurate interpretation of Paul's words "We write no other things to you than what you read and acknowledge" Pelagius makes a clear division, that what they read in his letter, they acknowledge in their conscience.[5] It will be already clear that Pelagius gives the word "conscientia" a wider connotation than our own "conscience." This is borne out when "in cordibus nostris" is accounted equivalent to "in conscientiis nostris"[6] and "legi mentis meae" is rendered "conscience" or "the divine law in the mind."[7] Indeed we do well to remember that the original meaning of "conscientia" is knowledge held in common with others. There is something here of the Quaker teaching of the Inner Light. It is objective and in that sense common to all, because it comes from God. But it is at the same time intensely personal, and represents the highest law whereby an individual can judge his acts from within himself.

This interest in conscience, self-knowledge, the speaking of God to our hearts, is common throughout Pelagius' writing.[8]

MORAL PURPOSE: (3) THE LAW OF LOVE

Of all the virtues the greatest is love.[9] Love is the law of Christ[10]; a prophet requires a combination of humility and love.[11] A Christian is compounded out of faith and love and peace, but faith without love is of little worth,[12] and indeed true faith works not through fear, but through love.[13] All justice consists in love of one's neighbour; injustice arises when

---

[1] 1 Cor. xi. 27. [2] Gal. vi. 4. [3] Rom. i. 19. [4] 1 Tim. i. 15.
[5] 2 Cor. i. 13. [6] 2 Cor. iii. 2. [7] Rom. vii. 23.
[8] Eg. De Div., x, 7; De poss. non pecc., ii, 1. [9] Gal. v. 22.
[10] Gal. vi. 2. [11] 1 Cor. xiv. 33. [12] Eph. vi. 23.
[13] Gal. v. 6.

we love ourselves above the rest of mankind.[1] Love makes perfect what is lacking in the law.[2]

Love starts from the love which God shows us. The great benefits He gives us arouse great love.[3] We know how He loves us because He treats us, rebel slaves as we are, as His sons.[4] Not only did He send His Son to death for our sins, but in addition gave to us His Holy Spirit, revealing to us the majesty of the things that are to come.[5] Our response is fourfold.[6] First we love God; we shall find indeed that the love of Christ, arising out of knowledge, surpasses all knowledge.[7] But the love of Christ is shown in fulfilling His commandments,[8] and the love of God in building up our brethren.[9] It is God who teaches us love towards one another.[10] His commandment was to love our neighbour as ourselves. It follows that the second and third parts of love are to love ourselves under God and in accordance with Him, and to love our neighbour. The fourth part too is specifically enjoined upon us, to love our enemies, and to pray for them not only with our lips, but in our hearts.[11] We are to love God more than ourselves, our neighbour as ourselves, our enemy as our neighbour.[12]

It is not surprising that some of Pelagius' finest exegetical writing is contained in the commentary on 1 Corinthians xiii. Paul points us to a more excellent way, the way of love, by which man reaches God. He directs us away from things which are outside our control to that which leads to true life and for which we shall be held responsible. Musical instruments require another to play on them, and bring pleasure only to the hearing. Love comes from within ourselves, and there is no good thing which it does not bring in its train. The capacity to foretell the future and to understand things hidden, and, greater than these, even the knowledge which is the knowledge of all things that have ever been or are to-day, are nothing without love; how much less that asceticism which prides itself on its self-sufficiency! What of faith? Jesus

---

[1] Rom. xiii. 9; 1 Thess. v. 8. [2] Rom. xiii. 10. [3] Rom. v. 5.
[4] Eph. ii. 4. [5] Rom. v. 5. [6] Gal. v. 14—a very important passage.
[7] Eph. iii. 19. [8] Rom. viii. 38. [9] 1 Cor. viii. 3. [10] 2 Tim. i. 3.
[11] Rom. x. 1; cf. *De poss. non pecc.*, i, 1. [12] Gal. v. 14.

says that as much faith as a grain of salt suffices to move
mountains; Paul speaks of "all faith." The faith of which
Jesus speaks is therefore perfect faith; the comparison with the
grain of salt refers not to the size but the quality of the latter
(an ingenious but unacceptable exegesis). Yet even this faith
is valueless without love. Love is the fulfilment of the law.
If I do not realize love in action I shall hear the words "I do
not know you, worker of iniquity." Martyrdom and contempt of worldly possessions are important, and it is to be
noted that the second is put on a level with the first, and is
one of the great and permanent responsibilities of the Christian
life. Yet neither this nor martyrdom is anything compared
with love. Indeed it is hard to see how anyone could undergo
martyrdom if he did not love God and were driven merely by
human ambition, or if he did not love his brother, thereby
disobeying the commandments of Christ, and dying with a lie
in his heart. Love is as long-suffering as a parent with his son,
always wishes well, sees the happiness of the loved one as his
own, keeps his due estate, does not swell out with pride nor
long to dominate his fellows, seeks not his own good but the
greatest good of the greatest number, is not roused to quarrell-
ing, so far from engaging in evil action does not even think evil,
is grieved in fellow-feeling at the sight of another's wrongful
actions, but rejoices at the sight of good actions or of faith in
the truth. Love suffers injury, trusts the man who seeks to
make good what he has done, hopes for his reformation, and
and waits patiently for him to make amends. Love alone is
unchanged in time to come, for there can be no end to true
love. Prophecy and knowledge are limited; they are stages
on the way to that perfection which is promised in the future
for God's saints. Just as we grow up physically, so we grow up
spiritually. Today there are faith, hope and love : in time to
come there will be left only love, love towards God, the angels,
and the company of heaven. So we are to pursue love with all
our energies, because it is within our power.

It would not be improper to call Pelagius the herald of
Love. This is the real centre of his message; in it he is very
close to the Mind of Christ; before it much of the controversy
that surrounds his name seems irrelevant. Before the battle

broke he was writing this magnificent panegyric. After the tumult and the shouting had died he turned again to the same theme, and in his commentary on the Song of Songs himself sang again the praises of Love.

MORAL PURPOSE: (4) FAITH AND WORKS

What has been said already is enough to show that Pelagius, like Jesus, could see no reality in an abstract faith which does not reveal itself in actual living. Jesus said time and time again that it was not the person who called on Him by name, but the person who lived in His way who inherited the kingdom of Heaven,[1] that the person who loved Him would keep His commandments,[2] that it is by our fruits that our true selves are revealed.[3] James declared that faith without works is dead,[4] and Luther dismissed his writing, as he would have dismissed Pelagius', as a "letter of straw."

It is true that Pelagius frequently repeats Paul's teaching that it is by faith alone that we are justified, not by the works of the Law.[5] But he makes clear that what he means is on the one hand that we are not to trust in good deeds which we do not possess,[6] and on the other hand that we are not to trust in the external ceremonies of the Law.[7] Real faith is not to be found except in the person whose life is just.[8] It is in our actions that we are to glorify God.[9] That faith is feigned which is expressed only through the mouth but denied in action[10]: that is to behave as the Gentiles behave.[11] If we do not realize our love in action we shall hear the words whereby Jesus disowns knowledge of us.[12] Our obedience to God must come from our whole selves. We must pray for our enemies not only with our lips but in our hearts[13]; we must love not only with our words but with our works and in truth.[14] Otherwise our lives will undo the good which our words may build up,[15]

---

[1] Matt. vii, 21–2.   [2] John xiv. 15.   [3] Matt. vii. 20.
[4] Jas. ii. 20.   Quoted by Pelagius: Rom. iii. 28.
[5] Rom. i. 17, etc.   Souter, p. 70, lists most of the passages, curiously including those in which the teaching is explained away—see under.
[6] Rom. iv. 5.   [7] Rom. iii. 28—an important passage.
[8] Gal. iii. 5.   [9] Phil. i. 11.   [10] 1 Tim. i. 6.
[11] Eph. iv. 17.   [12] 1 Cor. xiii. 2.   [13] Rom. x. 1.
[14] Rom. xii. 9.   [15] 1 Cor. viii. 11; Tit. i. 7.

whereas rightly to treat the words of truth is to confirm our words by our example.[1] To love Christ in fact is to keep His commandments[2]; to love God is to look after our fellows.[3]

MORAL PURPOSE : (5) THE FORCE OF EXAMPLE

When Souter edited the commentaries thirty years ago he wrote "No subject occurs with more persistence than the influence of example on conduct. The author is never weary of referring especially to the force of the Apostle's good example in the lives of his converts."[4] Certainly an independent investigation has amply confirmed this, and added very few to the long list of passages which Souter appends.[5] What is here needed is a brief analysis of the passages in question.

First, as Souter rightly says, Pelagius explains passage after passage in terms of the influence of Paul's example upon those to whom he is writing. His description of himself as a slave or servant at the beginning of Romans is an example of humility to them,[6] and he is continually setting them a similar example of humility.[7] Again Paul has suffered, and that suffering is turned to an example for them of the way in which to undergo suffering.[8] He gives to them an example of prayer,[9] an example of continence of every kind,[10] an example of a spirit whose only glory is God,[11] an example of a life in which preaching and practice are at one.[12] By his example he encourages the Philippians to strive for Christ even though it lead them to death.[13]

Secondly, Pelagius interprets Paul as directing his correspondents to the importance of their example on others, and leaves this as a message for his own readers. This comes out with particularly striking force at the beginning of the first letter to the Thessalonians. The brief summary which precedes this runs "Not only had the Thessalonians attained a personal perfection in all respects, but others had benefited

---

[1] 2 Tim. ii. 15.   [2] Rom. viii. 38.   [3] 1 Cor. viii. 3.   [4] Souter, p. 69.

[5] Col. ii. 15 is an important passage; so is Phil. ii. 9. He has missed one or two passages where the operative word is not "exemplum" or "forma" but the verb "sequor," e.g., Rom. v. 11 or "imitor", e.g. Col. iv. 13, 18.

[6] Rom. i. 1.   [7] E.g. 1 Cor. iv. 6; 2 Thess. iii. 11.

[8] E.g. 2 Cor. i. 6, 8; Col. iv. 18.   [9] 2 Tim. i. 4.   [10] Gal. iv. 16.

[11] 1 Cor. vii. 25.   [12] 1 Cor. iv. 17.   [13] Phil. arg. (not noted by Souter).

alike from their words and their example. Therefore the apostle by praising them challenges and urges them to things still greater." Paul himself says that they have become imitators of him and of the Lord, and thus examples to all that believe in Macedonia and Achaea. Pelagius picks this up with joy. Paul has commended his teaching by his own example of justice. Now their example ("exemplum") provides the pattern ("forma") for all believers, not only within their own province, so that when he begins to speak of their good example, his hearers say that they know well enough already.[1] So too in the second letter not only lesser lights, but Paul himself commends them for all to imitate, and calls on them further to give an example of how to wait for the righteous judgment of God.[2] In exactly the same way Timothy is warned of the danger of his bad example offending the conscience of weaker brethren,[3] and told rather that he is to be an example of love which will lead others on to better things.[4] It is in fact the power of a bad example which destroys Christians, of a good example which builds them up.[5]

Thirdly, Pelagius occasionally uses other illustrations of one person imitating another to develop his theme. Of these much the most important is the suggestion, typically Pelagian, to which we shall have to return, that it was by the example or pattern of his behaviour that Adam injured the whole human race.[6] In a similar vein, though without the profound theological implications, Pelagius, in commenting on Paul's view of marriage, suggests that it would not be desirable to imitate Adam who, so to speak, married his daughter.[7] So too on the other side we find the disciples of the apostles imitating their teachers and putting themselves out for others,[8] and Paul adduces the example of the prophets to support what he says to Timothy.[9] The last instance is typical: Paul's word is "testes"; Pelagius renders it "exemplis et testimoniis."

Lastly, but most important of all, there is the example of Christ. It is natural to expect that Pelagius will couple together the teaching and the example of Christ.[10] He sets us an example

[1] 1 Thess. i. 5–8.   [2] 2 Thess. i. 4–5.   [3] 1 Tim. iii. 3.   [4] 1 Tim. iv. 12, 15.
[5] Rom. x. 32; Tit. i. 7; 2 Tim. ii. 15.   [6] Rom. v. 11–12.
[7] 1 Cor. vii. 3.   [8] Col. iv. 13.   [9] 2 Tim. ii. 2.   [10] Rom. vi. 18.

of justice, humility, service and willingness to die.[1] Sanctification means living according to the pattern of Christ.[2] Christ's in-dwelling presence means our imitation of Him.[3] To follow God ought to follow naturally upon knowledge of Him.[4] Some of this is sufficiently startling. It is tempting to see the influence of Plato on Pelagius' teaching of the relationship between Christ and the believer. Just as Plato can speak indifferently of the particulars imitating the Forms or participating in the Forms, so Pelagius can speak indifferently of the believer imitating Christ and Christ living in the heart. Probably the resemblance is coincidental. But there is this essential difference. Plato was speaking of an abstract or inanimate relationship, and therefore, as Aristotle pointed out with some vigour, his language was poetry and idle metaphor. But Pelagius is speaking of personal relationship, and apart altogether from the question whether the relationship of the soul to God is real and present, language is important because it implies a difference of initiative, and Pelagius' language obscures the divine initiative. When we turn to the saving work of Christ we are faced with views more startling still. It is true that in one passage he seems to separate the work of salvation as something objectively accomplished by Christ from the progress to a higher glorification, won by our imitation of Him[5]: this is curiously parallel with the explanations of infant baptism later propounded. But this is not the fulness of his thought. Paul, he suggests, tells the Corinthians that Christ became poor for them, in order that by following His example they might be enriched with heavenly goods.[6] In the commentary on Ephesians he equates God's goodness to us in Christ with Christ's example to us.[7] In the second letter to Timothy he declares that light comes to men from the words and example of Christ. By His teaching and intercourse He destroyed the sins which were bringing death upon men and showed men how to seek true life without blemish.[8] It is in fact to the teaching not to the Cross that we are to look for our salvation. To follow his example is all that we need for life.[9]

[1] The quotations are all from Phil.—i. 11; ii. 5, 9, 21.
[2] 1 Thess. iv. 7.   [3] Rom. viii. 10.   [4] Eph. iv. 18.
[5] Rom. v. 10.   [6] 2 Cor. viii. 10.   [7] Eph. ii. 7.
[8] 2 Tim. i. 10.   [9] Col. ii. 6, cf. Aug., *De Nat. et Grat.*, xl, 47.

Even the preaching of the Cross brings the same message—that Jesus conquered on the Cross to give to us an example of how to conquer.[1] By His victory over death and sin He shows us the way to victory.[2] This is to say that Pelagius anticipated Abelard, and the "moral influence" theory, not systematically, because the nature of the Atonement was not yet a dominant issue of controversy, but in the clear implications of his unsystematized utterances.

This idea of the imitation of Christ, with or without its full theological implications, continues throughout his life. We are to follow Christ by being poor not rich, humble not exalted, by renouncing desire not clinging to it.[3] Perfect conformity with Him may be seen in the apostles: as He said to the paralytic "Rise and walk" so they said to the lame man "Rise and walk."[4] God's choice rests upon them who are formed in the mould of Christ.[5] Indeed the precise cause of Christ's suffering was to persuade us to follow His example so that we are ready to burn away our sin in the fire of suffering.[6] It is not surprising to find that one of Pelagius' favourite texts is "Be imitators of me, as I am of Christ."[7]

MORAL PURPOSE: (6) PROGRESS IN THE GOOD LIFE

Souter also draws attention to Pelagius' frequent use of the words "proficio" and "profectus" for progress in the moral life.[8] It is significant that both words are common in Rufinus' version of Origen's commentary on Romans,[9] and the verb is particularly frequently found in Ambrosiaster.[10] There is no need to labour the point. It embraces three basic ideas. One is the actual moral progress of the converts.[11] One is the challenge of the master to the disciples for their further progress, even when their faith seems already perfect[12]; the word used

---

[1] Col. ii. 15.   [2] 1 Cor. i. 18, ff., cf. Rom. v. 16, 19.

[3] *De Div.*, x, 1; cf. v, 2.   [4] *De Ind. Cord. Phar.*, 49.

[5] *De Ind. Cord. Phar.*, 14.   [6] *Ib.*, 20.

[7] 1 Cor. xi. 1; *De Ind. Cord. Phar.*, 54; *De Div.*, x, 7; *Ep. ad Caelant.*, 12. See de Plinval p. 95 where, however, the reference is wrongly given. Souter has not found any allusion to it in the commentaries. It is not directly quoted, but it seems to be in Pelagius' mind in several of the passages mentioned above.

[8] Souter, pp. 70, 108–9.   [9] Smith in *J.T.S.*, xx (1918–19), p. 148.

[10] Souter, *Study of Ambrosiaster*, pp. 129–132.   [11] E.g. 2 Thess. iii. 1.

[12] E.g., 1 Thess. arg. cf. Rom. i. 8; 1 Cor. i. 4; Phil. iv. 18; 1 Tim. iii. 2; 2 Tim. i. 16, etc.

here is generally "provoco." One is the joy which the response of the disciples to the challenge brings to the master.[1]

The Shadow of Pelagianism: (1) Grace and Merit

That the view subsequently known as Pelagianism was
formed out of the fire of controversy, and that it emerged
gradually as an implication of our moral responsibility can be
seen clearly at this stage. So far from there being anything
remotely resembling a systematic exposition of Pelagianism, it
is clear that there are two unreconciled strands in his thinking
which are mutually contradictory, one arising from his concern
for moral progress and moral righteousness, the other from his
correct understanding of the words of Paul.

On the one side he states emphatically that we are all alike
saved not by our own merits but by the free grace of God.[2]   So
too it is by the will of God, not by his own merit that Paul
is called to be an apostle.[3]   Those in Rome who are called to
be saints are so by God's calling of them, not by their own
deserts.[4]   A long list of passages demonstrates that we are
saved and justified "gratis," by the free gift of God.[5]   But
when we come to examine these passages more closely, it is
generally clear what Paul means, but it is by no means so clear
what Pelagius means. Romans iii. 21, is an illuminating
example. Justice comes to man by the free gift of God, not
because he pursues it. This might suggest that the virtues we
possess are implanted in us by God, and are in no sense our
responsibility. But Pelagius does not mean this: he means
that God gives us a pattern of justice which we are to follow.
The pattern is perfectly clearly revealed in Christ; the responsibility for emulation is ours. Several of the passages deal with
forgiveness of sins.[6]   Here again it should be remembered that
Pelagius never denied that having sinned we stood in full need
of free forgiveness, nor did he deny that we do sin; all he denied

---

[1] E.g., 2 Cor. vii. 13–4; Gal. iv. 21.

[2] Arg. omn. ep.; Rom. v. 1; Gal. i. 4.

[3] Eph. i. 1, iii. 7.   [4] Rom. i. 7.

[5] Rom. i. 7; iii. 21, 24; iv. 4, 5; viii. 29; xi. 6; 2 Cor. i. 12; Gal. v. 4; Eph. i. 9;
1 Tim. i. 2; 2 Tim. i. 9, etc.   Souter lists these passages, but seems insufficiently
aware of the limitations which circumscribe Pelagius' use of "gratis."

[6] E.g. Rom. i. 7.

was that such sin was inevitable. The relationship of grace, in the Pauline sense of the word, is not the only possible relationship between God and man.

And when we examine the connotation of the word "grace" as Pelagius used it, the same hesitation remains. Grace is indeed God's free gift in answer to sin; it is received in baptism[1]; and the enormity of the sin shows the generosity of the grace.[2] To trust in the Law is to denigrate grace.[3] Jesus alone is God's son by nature; we are His children by grace.[4] But though our redemption is free and not by merit,[5] there is left a measure of initiative with the sinner; it is the impious man *who turns*, who is justified by grace.[6] The Corinthians are not to receive the grace of God "in vain." The literal meaning of the phrase "in vacuum" is "into an empty space." Pelagius suggests that the person who is not making progress within the New Testament is so doing, and again implies a human initiative; there must be a prior virtue in the individual into which the grace of God can enter.[7] Further, Pelagius is ready here, as he was later, to use the word "grace" loosely to mean, in theological language, general rather than special grace. Thus it is by grace that Paul speaks, by grace that he is a minister of God.[8] And there is one significant passage in which God's grace is at least closely linked with, and might be understood to be mediated through, the force of teaching and example.[9]

On the other side there are one or two passages where the emphasis is overtly on human merit. Thus Paul is made to assert that he fought with wild beasts of Ephesus because of the reward he would obtain from God thereby.[10] But four passages set the whole question in a broader setting. In two Pelagius speaks uncompromisingly of deserving to receive or be guided by the Holy Spirit.[11] We shall have occasion in a later chapter to comment on Pelagius' understanding of the Holy Spirit. Here it will be enough to notice that although there are instances where Pelagius' theoretical belief in the Spirit is expressed in the most orthodox terms, as in his condemnation of the

---

[1] Rom. i. 5.   [2] Rom. v. 20.   [3] Gal. v. 4.
[4] Rom. i. 3, but cf. viii. 17.   [5] Rom. iii. 24.   [6] 2 Cor. iii. 6.
[7] 2 Cor. vi. 1.   [8] Rom. xii. 3; Eph. iii. 7.   [9] Rom. vi. 14.
[10] 1 Cor. xv. 32.   [11] Rom. viii. 14; 1 Cor. ii. 10.

Macedonians for denying the Spirit to be God,[1] and though there are passages in which theoretical belief is kindled into a lively faith, as when he asserts that our powers are weak unless helped by the illumination of the Holy Spirit,[2] in general his view seems to be that the Spirit comes—I almost said "automatically"—into the heart of the righteous, and even that to live righteously is identical with possessing the Spirit of God. Thus righteousness is called the gate of the Holy Spirit.[3] To call Jesus Lord in the Spirit means to confess Him alike in word and act.[4] The Spirit of Christ is the spirit of humility, patience and every virtue.[5] The language is at least ambiguous; it is consonant with the interpretation that the true presence of the Spirit is revealed by its fruits,[6] but it is hard not to feel that Pelagius is going beyond this. The tendency of his thought is in fact revealed by his preference for the adjective "spiritalis" "spiritual," to the genitive "spiritus," "of the spirit." Thus "caritas spiritus" becomes in his hands "spiritalis caritas"[7] and "gaudium in spiritu sancto" "spiritale gaudium."[8] This shows at least that his emphasis is on the fruits not on the giver, and probably that so far as effective living goes he makes no real distinction between the human spirit at its highest, and the Spirit of God entering his heart. This becomes even clearer when he renders "spiritu ambulate" by "spiritalibus actionibus ambulate."[9] The emphasis upon our Christian discipleship being worked out in life and action is good and healthy, but at this point there is an underlying theological weakness.

The other two passages to which we have referred are more striking still. Pelagius at the beginning of Romans has asserted categorically that Jesus alone is God's son by nature and all others become his children only by grace.[10] He does not contradict that. But it is clear that he regards grace as something that can be in some way merited, and speaks unequivocally of those who deserve to be sons of God, and because they deserve the sonship deserve also to be joint heirs with the true Son.[11] It is a simple comment of twelve words in the Latin,

[1] 1 Cor. xii. 4.   [2] Rom. viii. 26.   [3] Eph. iv. 27.   [4] 1 Cor. xii. 3.
[5] Rom. viii. 9.   [6] Cf. Gal. v. 25.   [7] Rom. xv. 30.   [8] Rom. xiv. 17.
[9] Gal. v. 16.   [10] Rom. i. 3.   [11] Rom. viii. 17.

but colossal in its assumption.   The second passage is of similar weight.   Pelagius sometimes readily accepts the validity and necessity of baptism.[1]   But in this passage he makes a radical and specific contrast of baptism with merit acquired through good works.[2]   Again the emphasis is not upon God's work but upon man's.

THE SHADOW OF PELAGIANISM : (2) BAPTISM

It is apposite at this point, in view of the later controversy in which Caelestius figures, to say something briefly about Pelagius' attitude to baptism.   In baptism, he says, the devil is drowned as Pharaoh and his host were drowned in the Red Sea.[3]   On the day of baptism we receive the seal, the hallmark, of the Holy Spirit.[4]   It is by baptism that we receive sanctification, and become God's saints, that is, those whom He sets apart.[5]   In baptism we receive remission of all our sins.[6]   It will be remembered that when their position was questioned the Pelagians made two distinct assertions about baptism— one that it was the mark of a higher sanctification, the other that sins were indeed remitted thereby, for from the moment of birth we had the power of sinning.   This is of a piece with the views here expressed.   And though the expressions above are compatible with what came to be accepted as orthodoxy, three passages show that Pelagius was inclined to diminish the weight attaching to baptism.   In one he contrasts the importance of preaching with that of baptism : the latter is relatively insignificant.[7]   In one, as we have seen, he contrasts the efficacy of baptism as a defence against sin with the strength acquired from meritorious action.[8]   In the third he suggests that baptism only washes the body, and it is from teaching that the soul finds its purification.[9]   If pressed, he would probably have rejected the full implications of this; for understanding of his bent of mind it is tremendously significant.

THE SHADOW OF PELAGIANISM : (3) THE LAW

One of the subsequent accusations against the Pelagians was that they regarded the Law as equally powerful to the Gospel in

[1] E.g. Gal. iii. 27.   [2] 1 Cor. x. 1.   [3] 1 Cor. x. 6.
[4] Eph. iv. 30.   [5] 1 Cor. i. 2; Eph. i. 1.   [6] Gal. iii. 27.
[7] Rom. i. 17.   [8] 1 Cor. x. 1.   [9] Eph. v. 26.

bringing men to salvation. I can find very little trace of this in the commentaries. On the contrary, Pelagius repeatedly states that to place hope of justification in the Law is to cast aspersions upon the grace of Christ and to say that his death was needless[1]; it is by the passion of Christ, not by the ceremonies of the Law, that our sins are done away.[2]

There are two major expositions of Pelagius' view of the Law at this time. One is in the second and third chapters of the letter to Galatians. There he says flatly that the works of the Law justify no man, though he covers some contingencies by adding the words "at present," implying that they might have done in the past, and that the Law had a certain validity until the coming of Christ; by the works of the Law he means (as Paul does not) circumcision, and sabbath-keeping and the like. He does not appreciate the way in which Paul is torn by the challenge of the Law to him and by his very obedience of it, and where Paul says that the Law pulls him in two directions, Pelagius sees a contrast between the Law of Christ and the literal Law. But when a man has been crucified with Christ, when Christ has died for him, when he has faith, when by the merit of that faith (an expression Paul could never have used)[3] he has received the Holy Spirit, then the Law has nothing more to give him. The Law was an interim measure to keep us from sin and to preserve us for the era of faith. There is much here that is fine, but it is alien to the thinking of Paul. The other important passage is naturally Romans vii. Here Pelagius sees that Paul is treating the Law as a problem, and seeking ways to encourage his readers to pass over from the fear which it inculcates to the free grace of God. He rightly interprets Paul's parallel of the wife who is freed from her husband's authority at his death, and illuminates it in his own way by speaking of the authority of Christ, who rose from the dead. He brings in now the lesson of asceticism : the Law, by promising the reward of worldly goods, fosters worldly ambition; in renouncing worldly things the disciples of Jesus became dead to

---

[1] Rom. vii. 25; Gal. ii. 21; v. 4.

[2] Phil. iii. 18.

[3] One good reason for denying the Pauline authorship of Hebrews. He nearly says it in Rom. iv, but grace comes into its own.

the world. The Law brought the knowledge and understanding of what sin is; it revealed sin and punished sin, and directed men to right action which is not separable from justice and justification. But it meant also that actions which before had sprung from ignorance now became culpable sins of deliberate commission. But within us is the Law of God. This is expounded in Stoic terms: it is to live in accordance with reason and not to be governed by animal passions in which reason has no place. It is the power of conscience which is the divine law in the mind. Grace frees the man whom the law could not free.

From this it may be said that, though Pelagius does not accord the Law the same position as he was later accused of doing, we can see the starting point from which such a development might grow. Thus in the Galatians passage he seems to leave it open to himself to assert that before the coming of Christ the Law might have brought justification,[1] and by limiting the works of the Law to the external observances, or at least exemplifying them thereby, he allows himself the freedom to accept Paul's language without losing the idea of merited salvation.[2] In the Romans passage there is still higher praise for the moral ordinances of the Law; it is good and holy and Pelagius has no truck with Marcion or others who attack the Old Testament. There is to be no contrast between goodness and justice.[3] It may be that in this spirit we should interpret an obscure comment in Galatians. Paul's words are "Lex autem non est ex fide." Pelagius' comment is "Non iustificat solam fidem."[4] The reading is not absolutely certain, but if it is right the words should mean "It is only faith which the Law does not justify." That is to say that Pelagius makes the Law take second place to faith, but to nothing else.

THE SHADOW OF PELAGIANISM: (4) PREDESTINATION AND FREE WILL

It is impossible to burk the fact that Paul speaks explicitly of predestination, but Pelagius found it equally impossible to

---

[1] Gal. iii. 19. [2] Gal. ii. 16; Phil. iii. 18.
[3] Rom. vii. 11–12. [4] Gal. iii. 12.

brook the idea. So though he can speak of Paul going up to Jerusalem not of his own free will but by the imperious necessity laid upon him by God,[1] and see the hand of God alone in Paul's conversion,[2] he has to find some way round the more distasteful theological implications of the theory. This he seeks in an identification no doubt suggested to him by Ambrosiaster, whereby he equates pre-destination with prescience. "Praedestinare est idem quod praescire."[3] God separated Paul from his mother's womb, because he foreknew Paul's life that was to be.[4] This prevents God from appearing an arbitrary tyrant (a problem with which Pelagius wrestles again in writing on the hardening of Pharaoh's heart) and enables Pelagius to reconcile the scriptural words of predestination with freedom of action and a merited salvation. Indeed he is so anxious to stress this that he points it in words which are very nearly contradictory: "The foreknowledge of God does not pass sentence beforehand on the sinner if he shall have shown readiness to be converted"[5]—the use of the future perfect is full of meaning. What he means, of course, is that the foreknowledge of God includes the whole of a man's life, and does not prejudge a part of it in isolation.

On the other side Pelagius maintains without qualification the freedom of the will. The Corinthians have perfect freedom to choose life or death, as they will.[6] Paul uses his freedom for the sake of others.[7] An important passage in Romans emphasized this. "God called those who he foreknew would believe. But his calling of them brought them together of their own free will, not against it."[8] This demonstrates with pellucidity the relationship between predestination viewed as foreknowledge, and man's free choice. Man's choice is logically prior and one might almost say casually prior; the act of predestination is prior only by chronological accident, and if Pelagius were aware of Origen's argument that God is outside and beyond space and time[9] (he is hardly as Origenistic at this point as Jerome makes out), he would surely have used it to make his point still firmer. He still has, however, to explain the

---

[1] Gal. ii. 2.   [2] Gal. i. 23.   [3] Rom. viii. 29.   [4] Gal. i. 15.
[5] Rom. ix. 12.   [6] 1 Cor. iii. 23.   [7] 1 Cor. ix. 19.   [8] Rom. viii. 30.
[9] *De Princ.,* iv. 28.

words "It is not of him who wills or him who runs, but of God who shows mercy," and "He has mercy on whom He will, and hardens whom He will."[1] He disposes of these, as in the "De Induratione"[2] by the ingenious but illegitimate process of assigning them to an interlocutor; he does this not arbitrarily but by an attempt to demonstrate that these words are not to be reconciled with what Paul writes elsewhere.

It is convenient at this point, for purposes of comparison, to give a brief account of the treatise just mentioned, as it treats these last two points with some fulness. Pelagius sets out his scheme of working at the beginning. He sets himself five interrelated critical problems, the Decalogue text "I shall visit the sins of the fathers upon the children,"[3] Paul's account of Pharaoh, the story of Esau and Jacob, the vases of honour and dishonour, and predestination and prescience. The treatment is thorough, though not completely systematic; his purpose is not academic but avowedly moralistic. He begins with a discussion of the Law. The law of human nature was shattered by the devil's influence, and God gave the Mosaic Law as a guide to life; it was out of this old covenant that the new covenant in Christ sprang. The Law of the two covenants did not succeed in converting all human nature, because free will is the furnace in which human nature is tested. But through the Law man was able to begin again; the Law was our schoolmaster.[4] Some of the commandments are clear; the one referred to above is more difficult. It must be read in the light of other words, "The son shall not bear the iniquity of the father"[5] and that there is no contradiction we may be sure from the character of God who is true and good and prescient. The words are to be taken as a salutary reminder of the force of a bad example, and a consequent deterrent.

He passes to a short consideration of the story of Jacob and Esau, in which God's choice is vindicated by His prescience, and a fuller account of Pharaoh. The accepted theory of predestination is insupportable. It makes nonsense both of God's desire that all men will be saved, and of His moral commands, if these cannot be fulfilled. Pelagius in his

---

[1] Rom. ix. 16, 18.   [2] *De Ind. Cord. Phar.*, 18 ff, 39.
[3] Exod. xx. 5.   [4] Gal. iii. 24.   [5] Ezra xviii. 20.

explanation makes four points. First in the Pauline passage, as above, the words are not Paul's but pertain to an imaginary antagonist. Second, in the corresponding passage of Exodus God says that He will harden Pharaoh's heart, not that He has already hardened it : this shows Him to refer to prescience not to arbitrary predestination. Third, Pharaoh's antecedents and character show the justification for his fate. Fourth, if an external agent for the hardening must be sought, it is the devil, not God.

The remainder of the book, just under half, comprises a general discussion of the issues involved, based on the text about the vessels of honour and dishonour.[1] Here Pelagius is at pains to point out that earthly status is no indication of status in the eyes of God : there is a strangely modern ring about his comparison of the aristocrat and the sewage-worker. As to man's eternal destiny he starts from two great principles, the inexhaustible goodwill of God and the freewill of man. When a man acts contrary to God's will, the Holy Spirit leaves his heart, and he is no longer sanctified. In this sense God may be said to make him a vessel of dishonour : he becomes a vessel of dishonour because through his own fault God leaves him. This interpretation accords precisely with that in the commentaries where the condemned become vessels of wrath rightly because they pursue their sins to the end, and with their own hands prepare their own destruction.[2] Men are called to obey God of their own free will in whatever earthly position they find themselves : in that resides true freedom. They are called to the imitation of Christ, to form themselves after this pattern, and they will become one with Him. "Hi sunt igitur ad supra dictam conformationem Christi praesciti, praedestinati, vocati, iustificati, ut conformes fierent per omnia Christo, ad commoriendum et ad convivendum ei, qui eos praescivit robusta mente omnia, quae pro eius nomine passi sunt, immobiles perdurare."[3]

It is obvious that this book is closely associated with the commentaries, especially that on Romans. It was certainly written at Rome. Internal evidence suggests that it was after the commentaries, or at least after Romans. The handling of

---

[1] Rom. ix. 21.　　[2] Rom. ix. 22.　　[3] *De Ind. Cord. Phar.*, 51.

the texts is surer, the theological position more definite. But the idèas are common to both. To repeat the essential points, Pelagius treats as absolute dogmas the propositions that man enjoys freewill and that God does not will the damnation of any man. Two propositions follow as inevitable conclusions, that men damn themselves by severing themselves from the love of God, and that the only sense in which God can be said to predestinate men is by his foreknowledge of the lives they will in fact lead.

THE SHADOW OF PELAGIANISM : (5) THE SIN OF ADAM

We pass now to consider the chapter upon which much subsequent disputation was to turn, Romans v. In the latter part of that chapter Paul argues that through Adam sin entered the world, and through sin death, and from that time sin and death passed on to all mankind. In Jesus Christ these consequences are annulled. One act of sin exposed the whole of the human race to condemnation; one act of righteousness presents all men freely acquitted in God's sight. What one man's disobedience had destroyed, one man's obedience rebuilt.

The important points in Pelagius' interpretation are as follows : First, he accepts that death entered the world through Adam, because he was the first to die,[1] and indeed through his sin.[2] There was later some inclination to deny this, but here the direct statement must be Pelagius' own; there is no possibility of it being later interpolation, as in both passages it is inextricably embedded in unquestionably Pelagian material. But death did not in fact pass to all men, for Jesus said of Abraham and Isaac and Jacob that they are still alive.[3] The word "all" he suggests is loosely used meaning "the vast majority"[4]; there is the implication that if death is the punishment for sin, the rare examples of freedom from death are also examples of freedom from sin. Secondly, although Pelagius has the reading "in quo" at v. 12, which the Pelagians subsequently and more accurately rendered "quia" or "propter quod" (the Greek being ἐφ' ᾧ), he states simply and without question that it was by his example that Adam passed

---

[1] 1 Cor. xv. 22.
[2] Rom. v. 12; 2 Tim. i. 10.
[3] Rom. v. 12; Luke xx. 38.
[4] Rom. v. 12, cf. iii. 4.

on the legacy of sin to all mankind.[1] He implies that the saving work of Christ consists in giving an example of absolute and perfect obedience and justice which those who follow work out their own salvation,[2] though this is not integrated with the exaltation of the power of Christ as greater than that of Adam, because His influence lay not only upon posterity but also upon His predecessors. Thirdly, we are presented on v. 15 with some of the characteristic Pelagian dilemmas, the question, for instance, how, if baptism washes away original sin, the children of baptized parents can be born in original sin, and whether if the sin of Adam harmed those who did not themselves sin, the justifying work of Christ should not be held to benefit even those who did not believe. These are presented as the views, not of the author, but of those who oppose belief in inherited sin. It is not absolutely impossible that Pelagius is either putting the views of others on which he has not yet finally made up his own mind, or that he is not yet prepared to challenge orthodoxy by a dogmatic expression of them. But it is far more likely that here we have something that is either a modification of the original comment or substituted for it. We can at least be fairly certain that these dilemmas are in the spirit of the view of the passage Pelagius wished to propound.

THE SHADOW OF PELAGIANISM: (6) THE POSSIBILITY OF PERFECTION

We have seen in this last passage a possible implication that Abraham, Isaac and Jacob lived sinless lives. Pelagius with his concern for morality directs his readers to seek a similar perfection by their native efforts. We are to strive by our actions at this present time to achieve that state of perfect sinlessness we shall enjoy in the kingdom of God,[3] just as Paul directs the Philippians to be pure from all corruption and rich in the fruits of justice after the pattern of Christ,[4] and just as the Thessalonians actually achieved perfection.[5] In fact it is to sinlessness that we are called. Man was made in the image of God so that he might be just and holy and true no less than God.[6] We are to come to the knowledge of the Son of God,

---

[1] Rom. v. 12, 16, 19.   [2] Rom. v. 16, 19.   [3] 2 Cor. v. 9.
[4] Phil. i. 11.   [5] 1 Thess. arg.   [6] Eph. iv. 24.

and that knowledge consists in living without sin because everyone who sins does not know him.[1] If we have love and a pure heart we shall not find it easy to sin.[2] Pelagius would not at this stage state categorically the perfectibility of human nature, but it is implicit in much of his moral exhortation.

CONCLUSION

We have then here a shrewd, scholarly and scriptural commentary upon the epistles. Its purpose is to enable its readers to live better lives. Its emphasis is therefore exhortatory rather than didactic or dogmatic, and doctrinal implications subserve moral encouragement. We can see, if we will look, the embryonic propositions which were later condemned, and in Romans, Pelagius is inevitably involved in some attempt to explain Paul's metaphysics in a way congenial to his purposes, but they remain subsidiary. The most exalted passages are those which deal with the Christian life as a life of love[3]; there is yet deeper understanding when he writes "Perfecta fides est non solum Christum sed et Christo credere."[4] Intellectual assent is not enough; there must be a turning of the whole personality towards God. The full Christian is compounded of faith and peace and love; love is incomplete without faith, faith without love.[5] Here is the apogee of Pelagius' outlook, and it is lofty and inspiring.

Principal Source: A. Souter, *Texts and Studies* IX.

[1] Eph. iv. 13; 1 John iii. 6.   [2] 1 Tim. i. 5.

[3] E.g. 1 Cor. xiii. 3; Eph. vi. 23.

[4] Gal. iii. 11, cf. *Ep. Humanae*, 3, and *De poss. non pecc.*, v, 1, where he makes the same point.

[5] Eph. vi. 23.

IX

PELAGIUS' CONTRIBUTION TO CHRISTIAN THOUGHT

We may now pass from the detailed consideration of a single work to a broader attempt to draw out the issues which Pelagius brought to the fore. In so doing we shall endeavour to rescue from oblivion some points which have been swamped in the turbid waters of controversy.

THE VOCATION OF A LAYMAN

It will be remembered that at the very outset of his adult life there is some evidence of a conflict between Pelagius and his father, apparently because he was set upon a religious calling and his father directed him towards a secular career. The way in which he established a reconciliation between the two callings is of high importance. His wide knowledge of medicine suggests that his father wished him to follow that career.[1] His presence in Rome, and some references in his writing suggests that they compromised by directing him to a course of rhetorical and legal training.[2] But he went further and sought to combine a religious profession with a lay status. We have noted that Pelagius insisted on being called a layman. Jerome and Caelestius might take priestly orders, and we have seen, for example, in Orosius' shocked surprise that John should admit a layman to the synod at Jerusalem, some indication of the disadvantages that might attach to the laity; but Pelagius stood upon his principles. He abjured even the title of monk (though he was given it from time to time[3]) and Zosimus describes him as "laicum virum ad bonam frugem longa erga Deum servitute nitentem." The calling of a monk was a specialized calling, and the title should not be loosely extended. Pelagius writes in one of his treatises "Ego te christianum volo esse, non monachum dici, et virtutem propriae laudis possidere magis quam nomen alienum, quod

---

[1] For references in the commentaries see Souter, pp. 73–4 and cf. *De Div.* iv, 1, vii, 1; *Ep. De Mal. Doct.*, ii, 1. xvi, 6, xvii, 1; *De Cast.*, iv, 7, ix, 2, x, 3 and elsewhere.

[2] E.g. *Comm.* in Rom. ii. 2; *De Div.*, xiii, 5, etc.

[3] Cf. Jer., *Ep.*, 50, 2; Aug. *De Gest. Pel.*, xix, 43, etc.

propriae laudis turba commorantibus imponitur, cum a Graecis solitarie viventibus legitime deputetur."[1] Similarly the priesthood was a special vocation, the pastoral vocation; but the office of teacher was open to all who were capable of fulfilling it.[2] So, though a layman, he takes upon himself responsibility for instruction in the Christian life,[3] and quotes in his defence the admonition to mutual edification and encouragement in 1 Thessalonians v. 11, on which his comment is to observe that it is an injunction for laymen, the corresponding exhortation in Colossians iii. 16, upon which his comment is similar, and Romans xv. 14, where he points the relevance to all Christians. In exactly the same way his comment upon Ephesians iv. 29 shows that the whole Church has the responsibility for edification, and at 2 Corinthians xiii. 11 and 1 Thessalonians iv. 18, he calls on the laymen to encourage and instruct one another in the faith.

In other words Pelagius sees a difference between the clergy and the laity,[4] and would not deny that the clerical was the higher calling.[5] But it is fundamentally a difference of vocation. There is no moral difference[6]; the position of teacher was not one to which the pastoral and sacerdotal vocation was necessarily relevant; and above all it was essential to retain the unity of the whole church, and not to imagine that the profession of Christianity must lead the believer to special ordination. There were lay "saints" and clerical "saints,"[7] different limbs of the one body, and Pelagius was principally concerned with working out the challenge of Christian living to the former. To see the importance of this we have to understand the trend of contemporary history within the Church. Ever since Constantine had exempted the clergy from certain legal disabilities, they had been growing in power, and were tending to become an exclusive and superior set. At Rome especially the hierarchy was in the ascendant, and Innocent missed no opportunity of asserting the primacy of the

---

[1] *De Div. Leg.*, 9.   [2] *Comm. in Eph.* iv. 11.

[3] *De Mal. Doct.*, i. 4.

[4] Cf. *Comm. in 1 Tim.* iii. 1; v. 19; *De Div.*, xv. 3; *De Cast.* iii. 3.

[5] Cf. *Comm. in 1 Tim.* iii. 1.   [6] Cf. *Comm. in 1 Tim.* iii. 2.

[7] Cf. *Comm. in 2 Cor.* ix. 2.

Roman see. Ambrose, in his speech against Auxentius, speaks of the "soldiers of Christ" and the "servants of God," and says that the only weapons they may use in their defence are tears and prayers. But the soldiers of Christ and servants of God are the clergy. The laity are the soldiers of this world, and servants of who knows whom?—and their moral vocation is different. It is this sort of view against which Pelagius is protesting, not merely in his stand against coercion,[1] but in his insistence upon the moral responsibility of all Christians. It is interesting to note that Timasius and James seem to have remained laymen.

Our own century has seen something of a rebirth of concern over the Christian vocation of a layman. In France the Catholic Jocists and the Protestant *Christianisme Social* have directed attention in that direction. In Greece the Christian Union of Professional Men with their widely-circulated journal *Aktines* have reasserted the influence of the laity within the Orthodox Church. In our own country the Christian Frontier Council, with its Fabian tactics, despite its predominantly middle-class composition, is steadily permeating our national life. Pelagius had not reached the point where he could ask what was the peculiar service which the individual could give to Christ within his profession. But he was certain, as the Independents of the sixteenth and seventeenth centuries were certain, that the vitality and health of the Church was to be seen in the vitality and health of the ordinary members. He was certain that the laity had a responsibility in the Church which was being neglected. And he was certain that the higher flights of academic scholarship and abstract theology must give place to the work of edifying the layman and challenging him to the full service of Christ in the Church and in the World. It is a major disaster that the disruption caused by his teaching of moral perfectibility turned even his own attention away from this message, and buried it in the ashes of obloquy which were heaped upon him, for in this he might have made a great contribution to redirecting the life of the Church along healthier channels.

---

[1] *Ep. ad Dem.*, 2.

THE RENUNCIATION OF RICHES

We have seen already that Pelagius probably was the young Christian who attacked Jerome for his criticisms of Jovinian. He could not go all the way with Jovinian, but it cannot be doubted that he found much in his views to commend itself, and it may well be that the moderate asceticism which he preached owed something to the other's teaching that to take food thankfully is good in the eyes of God equally with abstinence.

Pelagius was emphatic in preaching the renunciation of riches. The service of wealth and the service of God, the service of Mammon and the service of Christ, are incompatible.[1] In the commentaries wealth is repeatedly attacked.[2] An important passage in 1 Corinthians xiii. argues that Paul's linking together martyrdom and the renunciation of riches shows that the latter is to be taken seriously as an essential part of the Gospel; a subtle analysis at 1 Timothy vi. shows that avarice may be displayed not merely in the desire for more, but in the desire for continued possession. Gold may degrade a man to the level of the brute beast.[3] He holds in the commentaries that the truly Christian attitude towards material possessions is that they should be held in common.[4]

This demand for the renunciation of riches remained one of the essential points of Pelagius' message. It appears as one of the five ideas whose circulation in Sicily troubled Hilary: "The rich man who remains in possession of his riches cannot enter the kingdom of God, unless he sells all that he has, and it can do him no good if by any chance he actually uses the riches to fulfil the commandments of God."[5] Similarly we know that Timasius and James were induced by Pelagius' teaching and example to give up prospects of secular advancement for an ascetic life.

But Pelagius' views upon the renunciation of the world are seen most clearly in two places. One is in the several letters and treatises which he wrote commending virginity and the

[1] *Comm.* in 1 Tim. vi. 11.
[2] Rom. v. 4, xv. 20; 1 Cor. xiii. 3; 2 Cor. iv. 2, xi. 12, 20; 1 Tim. vi. 9, 11, etc.
[3] Rom. v. 4.   [4] 1 Cor. xii. 13, cf. xi. 21 and *De Virg.*, 13.
[5] Aug., *Ep.*, 156, cf. *De Gest. Pel.*, xi, 23, xxxiii, 57; *De Pecc. Orig.*, xi, 12.

L

renunciation of worldly pleasure. Much of these consists, as one would expect, of moral exhortation and of detailed moral instruction, but there are passages which throw light on his wider views. Thus in the letter to Demetrias[1] he contrasts the life she is leaving in which she would have ensured that no one surpassed her in wealth, ornament or splendour with her new life, where she must endeavour to surpass all in moral character, virtue and right living, and says that the bride of Christ must not be less particular of her perfection than the brides who go to enormous pains in make-up and expensive accoutrements. In the same letter, in the letter to Caelantia, and in the treatise on virginity he gives warning that the Christian should show no pride in noble birth, since the baptismal laver brings all into a state of equality.[2] In the treatise on chastity he speaks scornfully of Christians who are "voluptuosi et luxuriam potius quam Christum amantes."[3] The truly Christian way is to renounce the power and pleasures of the world. It is naturally in the treatise on riches that Pelagius' outlook appears in its fulness. In this treatise he starts from his usual clear grasp of the centralities of scripture, and there is no difficulty in providing a large and weighty body of evidence, relating especially to the New Testament, which condemns riches and the possession of riches in no uncertain terms. The love of money is the root of all evil.[4] We cannot be disciples of Jesus unless we renounce all that we have; He became poor, although He was rich, and if we claim to abide in Him, we must tread in his footsteps.[5] Therefore, if riches increase, we are not to set our heart upon them[6]; if we love the world, the love of God is not in us[7]; riches are a grave occasion of stumbling.[8] Hence it was that Jesus encouraged the wealthy to give up their riches[9]; hence that He cried "Woe!" to them that were rich[10]; hence that it is easier for a camel to pass through a needle's eye than for a rich man to

---

[1] *Ep. ad Dem.*, 10, 24.   [2] *Ib.*, 22, *Ep. ad Cael.*, 21. *De Virg.*, 13.
[3] *De Cast.*, xi, 1.   [4] *De Div.*, iv, 1; 1 Tim. vi. 9–10.
[5] *De Div.*, v, 3; Luke xiv. 26; 2 Cor. viii. 9; 1 John ii. 6.
[6] *De Div.*, vii, 2; Ps. lxii. 11.   [7] *De Div.*, x, 8; 1 John ii. 15-7.
[8] *De Div.*, xix, 3; Ecclus. xi. 10.
[9] *De Div.*, x, 1; xi, 6; Matt. xix. 21; Luke xix. 6.
[10] *De Div.*, xvi, 1; Luke vi. 24.

enter the kingdom of God.[1] With God all things are possible, but it cannot be doubted that a humble and dedicated poverty is more pleasing to Him than the inequitable and haughty arrogance which so often goes with wealth.[2]

In this way Pelagius establishes his general thesis in terms of a fair and accurate presentation of the central tradition of the New Testament. In so doing he sets first things first. He is aware of difficulties, some of which are scriptural, some difficulties of application. But he is also aware, and assuredly with justice, of the necessity of accepting a central truth and seeing the difficulties in the light of that. In so doing he is establishing an obvious principle, but one which is too rarely followed. The Christian's certainty of God and understanding of His ways and His calling to us depends upon Jesus. Different sections of the Church have sought absolute authority in the Bible, in the historical and organized Church, or in the Inner Light which shines within each of our hearts. But the Christian owns one authority only which is absolute, that of Jesus; these others have their validity only in so far as they accurately mediate His will to us, and it is precisely the infallibility of this mediation which is in question. None the less we may fairly, with Bishop Butler, work on probabilities, and if we have decided with a high degree of probability the words and way of Jesus, that has a compulsive power upon us. It is from there that we must start, and subsidiary considerations must be aligned with this. Those who start from the difficulties and problems, real as these are, will not arrive at the truth. They are like the Englishman, lost in Ireland, who asked a peasant the way to Ballyhoolin, and received the reply "If I wanted to go to Ballyhoolin, I shouldn't start from here." The difficulties may be real, but human beings find it frighteningly easy to rationalize in their own favour, and Pelagius sees through such rationalizations. "Sic tractant, sic argumentantur, sic disputant, qui incubare divitiis malunt, quam Christi mandata servare, et qui pecunias magis quam regni gloriam diligunt."[3]

In just this way Pelagius starts from the right place, and meets his critics with firm ground under his feet. He sees for example

---

[1] *De Div.*, xviii, 1, 9; Matt. xix. 24.   [2] *De Div.*, xviii, 4.   [3] *Ib.*, x, 2.

that Joseph of Arimathea is called a rich man; how is this compatible with his following of Christ? He solves the problem with ingenuity, perhaps with too great ingenuity. Matthew is called "the tax-gatherer" after he has renounced the profession. Abigail is described as Nabal's wife after her husband is dead. They are described not in terms of what they are now but of what they have been in the past. In exactly the same way, Pelagius suggests, Joseph is called rich, not in virtue of what he now is, but in virtue of what he had once been.[1] The explanation is a little implausible, though not impossible, and it might have been better, as he does elsewhere, to leave an unreconciled contradiction, merely asserting that the majority of the evidence points in one direction, though an occasional passage seems to contravene this. But it is an interesting example of Pelagius' method in two ways. First, it shows his establishment of his central certainty, and his subsequent attempt to establish concord with recalcitrant passages. Secondly this attempt is carried out by reference to scripture and scriptural analogy. Both are sound principles of criticism.

Pelagius does not shirk the difficulties. He puts the case of the objector strongly and cogently. To those who say that the possession of riches is not in itself greed for gain he replies with a flat denial that the two can be separated.[2] To those who ask whether riches come from God or not he makes answer, perhaps less happily, that this depends upon how they are obtained, and goes on immediately to suggest, in a passage of fine insight, that if they are obtained at the expense of others who remain poor then their acquisition cannot be just and they do not come from God.[3] The subtlest objection with which he has to contend is one still common to-day, that to remove riches is to remove works of mercy and ability to help the poor. Pelagius has one of his infrequent lapses from the thorough understanding of Jesus when he speaks with half a sneer of those who put the poor before God. Jesus knew that those who cared for the needy, whatever their religious professions, were not far from the kingdom of God. He is on surer ground when he points out that the inequitable division of

[1] *Ib.*, xi, 5. [2] *Ib.*, ii–iii. [3] *Ib.*, viii, 2–3.

wealth itself causes poverty. Twentieth century economists doubt whether the redistribution of existing wealth would have very much effect, though they forget that a comparatively small rise of standard may be substantial at the lowest level. But in Rome the property qualification for the senatorial order was 1,000,000 sesterces, and for the *equites* 400,000, and where so many of the poor received their livelihood in the form of doles from the rich it seemed obvious that a redistribution would lead to an adequate standard of living by right. The argument indeed shows a sense of the social and political implications of the Gospel not commonly found among ancient writers. Pelagius proceeds to face such objections as the inability to give alms, which he counters with Jesus' words "Blessed are the poor," and the source of future sustenance, which he meets with "Take no thought for the morrow." He does not see anything necessarily wrong or illogical in living on the gifts of others, and cites the examples of Paul and the apostles.[1]

Constructively he makes three points of considerable importance. The first is in his understanding of what is meant by riches. There are, he says, three states of man—wealth, poverty, and sufficiency. Wealth consists in possessing more than necessity demands, poverty in less. Sufficiency holds the Aristotelian mean, and indeed Pelagius describes it in terms of the peculiarly Greek virtue of *temperantia*, that is σωψροσύνη. He seems aware that here is something fresh and original in Christian thinking, as he immediately seeks scriptural justification for it, which he finds in the book of Proverbs, coming a little strangely from the lips of its supposed author Solomon.[2] He drives the point home in a brilliant and memorable epigram "Tolle divitem et pauperem non invenies," to which he adds "Nemo plus quam necessarium est, possideat, et quantum necessarium est, omnes habebunt."[3] It is superfluous possessions which are forbidden.[4] This no doubt comes to him partly from his own rooted common sense, partly, as I have suggested, from his knowledge of Greek philosophy, partly from the early influence of Jovinian's rejection of the extremer

---

[1] *Ib.*, xii–xv.
[2] *Ib.*, v, 1–2, cf. Prov. xxx. 7.
[3] *Ib.*, xii. 2.
[4] *Ep. Humanae*, 5.

sorts of asceticism. The danger, of course, lies in defining the necessary standard of living. The luxuries of one age so quickly become the necessities of the next. At the same time the precept has an essential soundness and fidelity to the New Testament which much of the extreme asceticism lacked. For Jesus does not condemn possessions out of hand. He condemns domination by possessions; He condemns great possessions as almost inevitably corrupting; and He condemns a selfish attitude to possessions. Pelagius attempts to reflect his Master fairly.

Secondly Pelagius stands for what is to-day described as "levelling-up." He sees clearly what the late Dr. Alex Wood once called "the divisive effect of different standards of living." He argues, in one of the ablest passages of the treatise, that God made men equal in the great things and could not wish for inequality in other regards. He points to the air, the heat of the sun, the drops of rain, the shimmering light of moon and stars, and beyond them, with more profundity, to the mystery of the sacraments : in none of these is there one law for the rich and another for the poor.[1] (One asks, in passing, if this is the first appearance of this particular phrase.) Hence his ideal of society is that mentioned above—"Let no-one possess more than is necessary, and all will enjoy the necessities of life."[2] In some ways one wishes Pelagius had been born into an age when the commandments of the Gospel were being worked out in terms of the economic ordering of society : one feels he would have been a strong ally for Kingsley, Maurice and the Christian Socialists of a later generation. For him the challenge was personal, and indeed, whatever the political implications, the personal challenge must remain. But it is a pity that he was not more concerned at least with the possibilities of response by groups or fellowships. He nowhere in this treatise refers either to the disciples sharing a common purse with their master, or to the Early Church holding all things in common. But he does state clearly the principle of the Christian fight for social justice, and the foundation on which groups, in these days of sophisticated economics, have built in seeking to share incomes, or to maintain their standard of living at the national average.

[1] *De Div.*, viii, 3.   [2] *Ib.*, xii, 2.

Thirdly, though the reference to it is incidental, Pelagius sees that what is true of riches is true of power in a wider sphere.[1] It is a major defect in Plato's "Republic" that he seems to have lost the vivid awareness he possessed of this truth when he wrote the "Gorgias." The "Gorgias" is a scathing indictment of the corrupting effects of power and ambition. In the "Republic" he takes immense precautions to see that the ruling-class is secure from the temptations of wealth, but does not allude to the equal or more insidious temptations of power. To-day we know that many of the most dangerous dictators, including Hitler himself, have lived lives of considerable self-abnegation, and have been driven either by false ideals or by glory in power, and very often by both. It shows shrewd insight therefore on the part of Pelagius to realize the temptation of "potestates ambire terrenas,"[2] as well as of seeking gold itself, even though he presents the former as part of the latter.

In all this again there is much that speaks to our present need. In England to-day the grosser extremes of wealth and poverty are no more. But this is not true in other parts of the world, and there are countries in which the Christian teaching on the subject of riches seems confined to the parable of the talents. Even in England, where the social challenge of Jesus has been generally faced, we are not so happy about its personal implications. The pacifist minority who challenge the Church to take literally the way of Jesus over war rarely present such a forthright challenge over riches. Too many of our churches are predominantly middle-class in composition, and too often there is no real fellowship between these and the industrial worker. We do well to remember that it was to the poor, the down-trodden, the oppressed, the bruised, the prisoners, the slaves, the peasants and labourers that Christianity first came as a message of hope, and in the Early Church there were not many wealthy or noble. The insistent words of Pelagius, with their loyalty to the New Testament, their sturdy commonsense. and their demand of a full commitment are still relevant to-day.

---

[1] *Ib.*, vi, 2, cf. *Ep. Humanae*, 5 "non in terrenis honoribus aut facultatibus gloriari".

[2] *Ib.*

QUALITY OF LIFE

Pelagius enumerates three things which ought to be found in every Christian—knowledge, faith and obedience.[1] By knowledge we recognize God, by faith we believe in Him, by obedience we serve Him. Each of these may again be subdivided into two. We may know that God exists; we must also know His will; we may believe that God exists, but we have also to trust Him; we may refrain from evil, but we must also do good. This second distinction, which is repeated elsewhere,[2] is one of real insight; upon it depends the reconciliation of Paul's justification by faith alone with James' "Faith without works is dead"; they mean different things by "faith."

Pelagius then asserted that the Christian must turn to God with his whole self. Knowledge represents the movement of the intellect, faith the movement of the spirit, obedience in one sense the movement of the will, in another that of the whole physical being animated by the will. A substantial section of the letter on evil teachers is devoted to the proposition that true faith must find its fruits in action.[3] It is easier to aver faith in tenuous words than to demonstrate righteousness in action; but the visible testimony of deeds is needed to display the invisible motives of the heart. He makes some play with the text "My just man lives by faith"—that is not everyone, but those who combine their faith with righteousness of living.

It is of importance to realize that Pelagius begins his thinking not from abstract considerations about the freedom of the will, but from the fact of the sinfulness of man. "We claim to abstain from things permitted, and perform things which are not; we condemn what is not forbidden and commit acts which are. We attack marriage, and hate our brothers. We abstain from meats, but not from ill-will, refrain from drinking wine and become intoxicated with anger, find it easier to refuse to eat without reason than to refuse to hate. We put on the trappings of humility and wear pride within. Nowhere is there true humility, innocence, piety, pure and unadulterated singleness of heart. On all sides are wars, battles, discord, litigiousness, hatred, bickering, hostility, dissension. Nowhere

[1] *De poss. non. pecc.*, v, 1.   [2] *Ep. Humanae*, 3; *Comm. in Gal.* iii. 11.
[3] Explicitly *De mal. doct.*, v–vii; implicitly throughout.

is the bond of true peace, the unshakable foundation of the covenant of love. Everyone seeks glory for himself, and pursues position at his neighbour's expense. Everyone imagines that praise of another detracts from himself. In us is fulfilled the words of scripture, all seek their own, not the things that are Jesus Christ's."[1] It is from this point that he begins the moral exhortation with which this particular letter, like most of his works, is filled. I suspect that many who dismiss Pelagius for the alleged shallow optimism of his view of human nature would be surprised to read that passage. The truth is —a point to which we shall recur—that Pelagius takes a more serious view of sin than his opponents, because he both takes a gloomier picture of the general standard of contemporary morality and attributes it to a failure on the part of each individual. And he looks into his own heart, as he looks into the hearts of others, and with humility sees the same failure there.[2]

His positive teaching remained constant throughout his life. We have already analysed it thoroughly as it appears in the commentaries, and it is not varied over the range of his miscellaneous and general writings. Here is the same emphasis upon conscience and its power,[3] the same concern for moral progress.[4] Love is the centre of all moral life : the letter on the possibility of sinlessness starts from love.[5] Above all, Pelagius reiterates in letter after letter, and passage after passage his teaching about the power of example and the need to take Christ as our pattern.[6] Two of the more important passages may be taken to illustrate this. One is from the letter on chastity.[7] He has been adducing illustrations of his theme from the Old Testament, and passes now to the New. There he finds the supreme

---

[1] *De Mal. Doct.*, xi, 1—summarized and paraphrased.

[2] *De poss. non. pecc.*, ii, 1.

[3] *De Div.*, x, 7; *De Mal. Doct.*, i, 3, v, 3, x, 3, xviii, 1–2; xxiv, 3; *De poss. non pecc.*, ii, 1, iv, 2; *De cast.*, x, 3, 8, etc.

[4] *De Mal. Doct.*, xi, 1, xviii, 3; *De Cast.*, iii, 5, etc.

[5] *De poss. non. pecc.*, i, 1.

[6] On the example of Christ : *Humanae*, 5; *De Div.*, v, 3, vi, 1, x, 1; *De Mal. Doct.*, xviii, 3; *De poss. non pecc.*, vi, 3; *De Cast.*, vi–vii, ix, 1, xvii; Aug., *De Grat Chr.*, xxxv, 38, etc.
On the force of example in general : *De Div.*, xviii, 6; *De Mal. Doct.*, xii, 1; *De Cast.*, ii, 1, iii, 3, 5, x, 4, 15 etc.

[7] *De Cast.*, vi–vii.

example of chastity in Our Lord Himself, who sanctified chastity alike in woman and man, "qui tam permanere virgo voluit, quam de virgine procreari." Surely when chastity is commended by examples such as these it should begin to be more attractive. Moses gave the Jews their laws, Christ the Christians. Surely then Christians should not be less willing to imitate Christ than Jews to imitate Moses. And if an objector protests that this is example, not precept, Pelagius replies that the example of Christ is no less to be followed than his precepts, and cites the words of John: "He that says he abides in Him, ought himself also so to walk as He walked."[1] The other passage is from the treatise on riches. Here again he is passing from the Old Testament to the New, and links closely the example and the precepts there given. The eloquent cadences and neat chiasmus merit quotation of the Latin. "In quo ergo Christus nobis imitandus est? In paupertate, nisi fallor, non in divitiis, in humilitate, non in gloria saeculi, non concupiscendo, sed contempnendo. Et quae novi testamenti praecepta observanda sunt? In primis illa, quibus per divitiarum contemptum peccatorum aufertur occasio." The disciple must be like his Master: if the Master is homeless, so will His followers be, if the Master is poor, His followers will be poor also.[2] The example of Christ is the norm of our living.[3]

The contents of the moral life are briefly summarized in the letter on the possibility of sinlessness.[4] Pelagius starts from the two texts "Whatever you do not wish to be done to you do not do to another,"[5] and "Whatever you wish men to do to you, do you also likewise to them."[6] We want respect, freedom from injury, mercy; we should therefore show them to others. We seek to avoid hatred for ourselves; we must love our enemies We may not lie or slander, swear, meet evil with evil, flatter, make distinction of persons, or hate our enemies. We may not be avaricious, or seek wealth or worldly power. Christ is our example of poverty, humility, and chastity. This short analysis shows clearly that Pelagius is not an abstract moralist, but bases his teaching closely upon the words of scripture.

Perhaps the most powerful piece of moral exhortation which

---

[1] 1 John ii. 6.   [2] *De Div.*, x, 1.   [3] *Humanae*, 5; *De poss. non pecc.*, vi, 3.
[4] *De poss. non pecc.*, vi.   [5] Tob. iv. 16.   [6] Matt. vii. 12; Luke vi. 31.

he ever produced was the conclusion to the letter on evil teachers.[1] There are not many passages of comparable power in the whole library of Christian literature. It is a depiction of the Last Judgment. Mankind stands before the tribunal of the Son of God. Pretence is stripped away. Words are now of no avail; the inner knowledge of the truth prevails. Jesus speaks. "I created you after My own image, that you should follow Me in all things and mould your characters after the pattern of God. I gave you reason and intelligence to know and pursue the good, and to understand and shun evil. Then I gave you laws spoken and written, that visible and tangible evidence might be added to the testimony of your inner conscience. I sent prophets to recall you to those standards which law and conscience alike attested. I Myself came down to earth, took the shape of man, and suffered all manner of ignominy to give you examples of single-mindedness, guiltlessness, devotion to God, and gentleness, and to demonstrate in practice the fulness of My precepts. Yet you have disregarded My commandments, slighted My sufferings, and turned instead to a life of vice, sin, self-regard and lovelessness." Then in turn Peter, Paul, John and James rise and tell in the language of the epistles how they had called men away from sin and towards God. The deliberate hammer-blows of sentence after sentence beginning "ego" formidably mark the counts in the indictment. What answer dare we make? If we reply "We acknowledge our guilt and are without excuse, but we plead to be justified by our faith, because we have called on the name of Jesus and in that name cast out devils," we shall hear the words "Not everyone that says to Me 'Lord! Lord!' will enter into the Kingdom of Heaven, but he who has performed the will of My Father who is in Heaven shall enter into the Kingdom of Heaven. Depart from Me, you who work iniquity." Then there will indeed be weeping and wailing and gnashing of teeth, of which Pelagius speaks at some length, but without any overtones of emotionalism, and with none of that fierce sadistic delight which mars some parallel passages in Tertullian. Rather there is a deep sense of self-identification with those who have excluded themselves from Heaven; it is "nobis

[1] *De Mal. Doct.*, xviii–xxv. What follows is much condensed.

peccatoribus" of whom he writes.[1]   But this is not his last word.   "Let us then, my dear friends," he says, "ponder these things day and night.   It is a great thing to be a son of God; the joys of heaven are infinitely greater than those of earth; to possess eternal life in all its richness and all its fulness is to shine with the splendour of the sun[2]; to reign with God is a prospect brighter and more glorious than anything else; the grandeur of that future is ineffable and unbounded.   The condition of enjoying it is to live justly.   Let us be drawn either by the desire for such rewards, or at least by the fear of the alternative and the shame of hearing our secret sins brought to the light in the presence of God and the Powers of Heaven, patriarchs, prophets, martyrs and all those others He has set apart.   Let us then run while we may, and strive with all the powers at our command to overcome our habits of sin and dip ourselves deep in activities of holiness and righteousness, that we may not undergo the sufferings of the damned, but may enjoy the blessed state together with the righteous."

It is a powerful plea, and no passage expresses better the moral fervour of Pelagius.

The Possibility of Sinlessness

We have now examined three of the points upon which Pelagius laid much stress, and which have become obscured because of the controversy which surrounds his name.   It remains to look more closely at the theological issues of the actual controversy.   This will require a chapter to itself.

Principal Source : Pelagius.

[1] *De Mal. Doct.*, xxiii, 2.
[2] Cf. Matt. xiii. 42.

X

THE ISSUES OF PELAGIANISM

The last chapter has been an attempt to show that Pelagius made a contribution to Christian thinking wider and more constructive than is commonly supposed. He was not first and foremost a controversialist, but a reformer, and his concern lay not primarily with abstract problems of theology, but with Christian living. Thinking about the latter involved him in formulating an ethical philosophy. But though his contributions in this field were substantial, and though in his conception of the responsibilities of the lay Christian he was breaking fresh ground and feeling his way along original paths of thought, it remains true that his most important as well as his most influential contribution rested in his denial of original sin, and his assertion of individual responsibility and the possibility of sinlessness. We have already examined in some detail the progress of the controversy to which this gave birth. It remains to look more closely at some of the theological issues involved.

SIN

It will be remembered that the dispute between Pelagius and Augustine began effectively when Pelagius turned violently aside from Augustine's prayer "Da quod iubes et iube quod vis,"[1] as destructive of all moral effort. To Pelagius the vast majority of professing Christians were taking one of two views. Some argued the inevitability of sin, some that only the grace of God could overcome it. Either led to moral sloth. The former tended to an acquiescence in low standards and evil living on the grounds that they could not in any case be avoided: the latter meant a complete dependence on God which sapped the moral fibre of the individual human, an attitude of "leave it all to God without my stir." The low moral standards we have seen prevailing alike among clergy and laity led Pelagius to reassert individual responsibility for sin. It was from this point that the controversy began.

[1] Aug., *Conf.*, x, 29.

The first question then at issue was the nature of sin. Pelagius asserted that sin was not a "substance" which could be handed on and itself act upon human nature, but a quality to be discerned in individual actions.[1] He asked whether sin could be defined in terms which made it an inextricable portion of human nature and therefore inevitable,[2] or whether on the other hand sin did not always imply a degree of moral responsibility and of blameworthiness. In our own time F. R. Tennant has claimed that the only satisfactory definition of sin is "moral imperfection for which an agent is, in God's sight, accountable." As Pelagius remarks with some wit, there are enough things for which we are morally accountable, without blaming us for things for which we are not.[3] This point is lucidly made more than once in the dilemmas which Eutropius and Paul found disturbing the serenity and faith of the Church in Sicily, and was not adequately answered by Augustine. The first of these dilemmas, for example, runs as follows. "Above all, if anyone maintains the inevitable sinfulness of man, we must ask him what is a specific sin, something which can be avoided or something which cannot. If the latter, it is not sin; if the former, man can live without sin, seeing that it can be avoided. For certainly neither reason or justice could ever allow that which can by no means be avoided, to be called sin." Augustine's answer is that sin can be avoided if the taint in our nature is first removed by God's grace through our Lord Jesus Christ.[4] But this answer, while it points the way to regeneration for the individual sinner, does not meet the real difficulty. For, firstly, it means that in our temporal existence before the coming of Christ it was absolutely inevitable that life should be riddled with sin—there was no other possibility. Secondly, to Augustine the mediation of God's grace lay through the sacrament of baptism *ex opere operato*. This meant that in Augustine's thinking the individual, resolved on baptism, was still unable to live righteously until the sacrament had been performed. Thirdly, as Pelagius so often remarked, a man before and after baptism is confronted with precisely

---

[1] Aug., *De Nat. et Grat.*, xix, 21.
[2] Pel., *De poss. non pecc.*, iv, 1.
[3] *Ib.*, ii, 1.   [4] Aug., *De Perf. Iust.*, ii, 1.

the same alternative courses of action. If then, there is the possibility of sinless action after baptism there is that same possibility before baptism, even if we do not in fact take it. Where Pelagius' analysis is inadequate is in his failure to distinguish between the nature of an action, and the moral quality of the motive from which it springs. He was reacting against those who claimed to have faith, and were therefore indifferent to the actions which should have sprung from that faith had it been genuine. He saw the importance of Jesus' words "By their fruits you shall know them." The Christian should be distinguished from the pagan or from the indifferentist by the quality of his living. "Non eloquimur magna sed vivimus."[1] "See how these Christians love one another." The actions of a Christian should make him marked off. It is interesting to notice that Clement of Alexandria, who did not believe in any inherited depravity of human nature, maintained that evil was not a Power but an act. It was not the Platonic lie in the soul, nor the Pauline law of sin. Vice consists in acting the lie, and we need not act it unless we so choose. And in this they were laying down a vital truth. One of the more distressing features of that school of contemporary Christian thinking which urges the necessity that the Christian shall compromise his absolute standards in order to live effectively in the world is that it blurs and blots out this distinction. They are far more thoroughgoing than Augustine. Augustine argued that sinfulness is inevitable outside the Church; they argue that sinfulness is inevitable within it. Against this the ethical zeal of a new Pelagius is needed. But there is another truth, namely that the moral content of an act is not always fully discernible in the act itself. Two men make a stand as conscientious objectors, one because he is a coward, one because he feels his absolute loyalty to Christ demands it. Two men join the army, one because he is drifting with the mass and afraid of public opinion if he does not, the other because he feels his duty as a citizen calls him to make that sort of stand against tyranny and aggression. The actions may be identical, but the motives from which they spring are very different. It is thus reasonable to say that right *action* is possible at all

---

[1] Minucius, *Octavius*, 38, 6.

times, but freedom from sin depends on something happening within the personality.

It is possible indeed to go further, and to say that the right action is there to be done, but something within us stops us from doing it, and unless we have a motive power from God, we are helpless. This is the teaching of the tenth article of the Church of England : "The condition of man after the fall of Adam is such that he cannot turn and prepare himself, by his natural strength and good works, to faith and calling upon God : Wherefore we have no power to do good works, pleasant and acceptable to God, without the grace of God by Christ preventing us, that we may have a good will, and working with us, when we have that good will."

In other words, the dispute turns upon the definition of the word "sin." If sin is defined in terms of guilt, then Pelagius has the argument all the way, because guilt implies moral choice wrongly made, and that implies the possibility of a right choice. If sin is defined as a barrier between man and God, then it is perfectly possible to say, provided that it is said with responsible awareness of the seriousness of the statement, that there are such barriers for whose existence we are not guilty, and our task is to overcome them, or so to submit ourselves to God that they are overcome (already we are back on problems of initiative). Such a barrier might be called "original sin." But if this be argued, it would be far less confusing to alter the nomenclature so that it is clear that this is nothing to do with sin in the accepted sense of the term. This Augustine would not do, and his weakness at this point was in seeking to lay moral responsibility on each individual for something for which, in his own terms, there could be no such moral guilt. The grandeur of the conception of the solidarity of mankind by which he seeks to work this out should not conceal its basic illogicality.

ORIGINAL SIN

The indictment brought against Caelestius at Carthage contained the count "That the sin of Adam injured himself only and not the human race." Later the Pelagians were prepared to admit in concordance with the language of scripture that Adam's sin did injure his descendants, but by imitation, not organically. In this they were following the Alexandrians, who maintained that Adam was the type but not the source of sin.[1] They also accepted that infants now born are not in the same state as Adam before the fall, but again only meant that Adam, being adult, was endowed with reason. Augustine, on the contrary, misled, it will be recalled, by the Latin version of Romans v. 14, maintained that the whole world was condemned in Adam. "Quia vero per liberum arbitrium Deum deseruit, iustum iudicium Dei expertus est, ut cum tota sua stirpe, quae in illo adhuc posita tota cum illo peccaverat, damnaretur."[2] The father had eaten a sour apple, and for all time the children's teeth were set on edge. This was more than a "privatio naturae," it was a "depravatio naturae," not a mere loss of a higher goodness, but a positive inclination towards evil, and it was inherited from Adam by physical transmission. It is doubtful whether Paul meant this. His language is more consonant with a belief that Adam's fall introduced a new power into the world, the power of sin, a power which in Paul's vivid language becomes almost itself personalized.

There was no formalized attempt to give an account of original sin before Augustine, but certain trends were becoming clear. One was the distinction between the traducianists, who held that the soul was handed on from the parents, a view common in the West, and the creationists in the East (though their view was shared by Hilary and Jerome) who held that it was a fresh creation. On the former view some transmission of what Tertullian termed a "vitium originis" is readily intelligible; on the latter view, the only transmission could be physical. It is a little curious that Augustine, who himself accepts the implications of traducianism, appears to discern original sin in the physical act of concupiscence, as we shall see. Origen, with his theory of the pre-existence of souls, is independent of either theory, for he regards tendencies which exist at the moment of birth as the direct consequence of the former existence.

[1] Clem. Al., *Protr.*, xi, 111, cf. Orig., *Comm.*, in Rom. v. 14.

[2] Aug., *De Corrept. et Grat.*, 10.

A certain amount of the Pelagian controversy turned on the language of the Bible about the fall of Adam and its results for posterity, but surprisingly little upon Augustine's deductions from it. For it will be clear that although Augustine might plead ignorance upon the origin of souls—"Argue de origine animarum cunctationem meam, quia non audeo docere vel affirmare quod nescio"[1]—he is in fact involved in some sort of traducianism, whereas Pelagius, ironically like Jerome, is an impenitent creationist. The one believes in the transmission of the soul from the parents, the other in the soul as a fresh creation and "tabula rasa." "Nemo enim corruptus nascitur, nec ante legitimi temporis spatium quispiam corruptione violatur."[2] But when Augustine is questioned as to the precise nature of this physical transmission he uses language which suggests that original sin is revealed in the act of concupiscence, in the fact that man's physical response to sexual stimulation seems not to be under the control of his will. It is perhaps here more than anywhere that a modern critic would feel inclined to press hard upon Augustine. It is indeed more than a little curious that Augustine accuses Manicheism of undermining the sense of personal moral responsibility by its doctrine of eternal substantial evil. By the ironies of time it is this identical accusation which modern scholars, like Harnack and Ottley, bring against his own doctrine of original sin and human depravity. As Julian of Eclanum saw in his own time, he never completely threw off his Manichean past. Disavow it though he might, residuary elements remain.

At the same time, it follows directly from Pelagius' disavowal of original sin that he does not hold what one might call a cosmic doctrine of the atonement. If mankind's sin is, so to speak, not solid but atomic, then there can be no single and solid act of redemption for mankind *en bloc*. Pelagius' views, it has been said, deny the necessity of the Cross: they make the Cross of Christ of none effect. It is undoubtedly true that Pelagius' theology is defective at this point. The Cross is not central to his thinking. He was of that temperament which sees in Jesus the example of human perfection, rather than God

[1] Aug., *De Corrept. et Grat.*, 10; *Op. Imp.*, iv, 104.
[2] Pel., *De Cast.*, iii, 5.

confronting Sin. It is the moral teaching of Jesus, and the pattern of humility and love which He presented, that show us the way of life. As we have seen in the commentary on the epistles, his interpretation of the Cross itself is in these terms: the Cross is an example of how to conquer and a finger-post pointing the road to victory.[1] But though we may feel that there is a false emphasis and that Pelagius' just and fruitful concern with the way of righteousness and love has led him to neglect other truths of Christian thinking, he had a rejoinder to make to such accusations. For the emphasis which he gave was designed to counterbalance contemporary neglect of the ethical implications of Christianity. But he would rebut any suggestion that his view inevitably led to a denigration of the place of the Cross. For he would say, as he did say, that he agreed that all had fallen short and were in need of redemption (the alleged sinlessness of some patriarchs is not an integral part of his thinking). And if it were argued that this was, according to his theories, "accidentally," and not of necessity, he could reply that the same was true of the Fall of Adam in orthodox theology, and that in any case we should deal in actualities not in abstract speculations. What matters is that here you and I stand, sinners, in need of redemption and the grace of God. What need to question further?

THE POSSIBILITY OF SINLESSNESS

Pelagius then is not concerned with these theoretical implications. He is concerned with answering the question "What is to prevent my acting righteously here and now?" His reply is "Nothing, except my own most grievous fault."

The possibility of sinlessness brought up a number of questions which may for convenience be treated independently of one another.

(1) Some portion of the dispute turned upon whether in fact sinlessness is imputed to patriarchs, prophets and saints of scripture. Pelagius, while insisting that a negative answer might be given without it affecting his general position, suggested that such righteousness is in fact imputed to a long list of them—"Abel, Enoch, Melchisedech, Abraham, Isaac,

[1] Pel., *Comm.*, in Col. ii. 15; 1 Cor. i. 18, ff, Rom. v. 16–9.

Jacob, Jesu Nave, Phinees, Samuel, Nathan, Elias, Joseph, Elisaeus, Michaeus, Daniel, Ananias, Azarias, Misael, Ezeckiel, Mardochaeus, Simeon, Joseph cui desponsata erat virgo Maria, Joannes." Among women he adduces Deborah, Anna mother of Samuel, Judith, Esther, Anna daughter of Phanuel, Elizabeth, and Mary the mother of Jesus.[1] Augustine's answer is to deny that the righteousness thus imputed was sinlessness, for John and Paul alike assert the sinfulness of all men.[2] But he is prepared to suspend judgment over Mary. If, as he implies elsewhere, it is in the act of sexual union that original sin is revealed, and is transmitted, and if the dogma of the immaculate conception of Mary as well as of Jesus be accepted, then the position is defensible, though it is mixed up with hopelessly antiquated theories of the part played by father and mother in shaping the heredity of the child. If there be any transmission of personality through the mother, the dogmas of immaculate conception do not evade the difficulty. But if either the equation of original sin with concupiscence, or the immaculate conception be not accepted, then Augustine's admission of even a theoretical possibility of the sinlessness of Mary destroys his case—unless he would claim a special miraculous dispensation in this single instance.

(2) It has already been frequently asserted, but because it is so frequently misunderstood, can hardly be said too often, that Pelagius' denial of original sin and his asseveration of the possibility of sinlessness did not involve him necessarily in maintaining that any individual had in fact achieved such sinless living. Because he saw the universality of sin and at the same time attributed it to individual failures his view of human nature was gloomier than that of his opponents, and because he did not regard sin as inevitable he took it more, not less, seriously than those who stood against him. This is why he speaks of the fact that it is possible for man to live without sin as "Dura haec revera et amara peccantibus vox."[3] As we have seen, he spoke of himself with humility, and the gibes of his opponents that he was claiming for himself an actual

---

[1] Aug., *De Nat. et Grat.*, xxxvi, 42, cf. the catalogue in Pel., *Ep. ad Dem.*
[2] 1 John i. 6; Rom. v. 12.
[3] Pel., *De poss. non pecc.*, iii, 1.

freedom from sin were quite unfounded and unfair.[1] "Sed ego non meae nescius conscientiae, multa in me esse, quae sint reprehensione digna, cognosco."[2]   And some of his finest and most passionate writing went into the description of mankind's sorry plight.

(3) The grounds on which the possibility of sinlessness are maintained are precisely what we should expect from a moralist like Pelagius.   In the Old and the New Testaments alike moral commandments are laid upon us unquestionably and absolutely.   We are to be holy as God is holy,[3] perfect as He is perfect,[4] without spot or blemish.[5]   If these commands are impossible of fulfilment, why are they enjoined upon us?[6] Chrysostom wrote "Let us not therefore infer this 'The injunction is hard' but let us consider also the reward, and think whom we are like, if we duly perform it, and to whom equal if we wander from it."   "Let us not therefore suppose His injunctions impossible.   Nay, for besides their expediency they are very easy, if we are sober-minded."[7]   Pelagius uses words very similar, but of greater vehemence : "We contradict the Lord to his face when we say : 'It is hard, it is difficult; we cannot, we are men; we are encompassed with fragile flesh.'   O blind madness!   O unholy audacity!   We charge the God of all knowledge with a two-fold ignorance, that He does not seem to know what He has made nor what He has commanded, as though, forgetting the human weakness of which He is Himself the author, He imposed laws upon man which he cannot endure."[8]   Reinhold Niebuhr's comment upon these words is interesting.   "There is a certain plausibility in the logic of these words, but unfortunately, the facts of human history and the experience of every soul contradict it."[9]   The comment is in the same spirit as that which, in Niebuhr's Gifford Lectures, dismisses F. R. Tennant (whose views upon the very theme of those lectures, whether acceptable or not, were among the most significant and substantial recent pronouncements, and surely merited full discussion) in a

[1] E.g. Jer., *Dial.*, ii, 23–4, Oros., *Apol.*, 16.
[2] Pel., *De poss. non pecc.*, ii, 1.   [3] Lev. xix. 2.   [4] Matt. v. 48.
[5] Phil. ii. 14–15; Col. i. 21–2.   [6] Pel., *De poss. non pecc.*, iv, 2.
[7] Chrys., *Hom.*, 18 in Matt. v.   [8] Pel., *Ep. ad Dem.*
[9] *Interpretation of Christian Ethics*, p. 128.

single sentence as "a modern Pelagian."[1]   The tendentious
word "plausibility" is to be observed.   A more straightforward
comment would be "The words are logically cogent.   But we
are in a tension.   Jesus certainly does lay upon us ethical
absolutes.   But we find ourselves unable to fulfil them."   To
this Pelagius would make answer "Certainly.   I wholly agree.
But do you blame anyone but yourself for that?"[2]   No adequate answer has yet been found.

(4) Pelagius is less happy when he argues that to impute
"depravatio" to human nature is to impugn the perfection of
the Creation and thus of the Creator.   That there is sin, evil
and imperfection in the world, and that this is not the direct
responsibility of God is common ground between Augustine
and himself.   But Augustine's orthodox conception of human
nature as created perfect but fallen fully meets his objection,
unless he is prepared to go further and criticize the whole
conception of the "lump" of human nature.   This he should
logically have done, but there is no evidence that he in fact did
so directly.

The Person of Jesus

It is surprising how little reference is made in the whole
controversy to the personal life of Jesus.   It might come to
the fore at two places.   One of the subsidiary questions turned
on whether death did in fact enter the world as a punishment for
Adam's sin.   It is expressed in the indictment of Caelestius at
Carthage as the two propositions "That Adam was created
mortal, and would have died even if he had not sinned" and
"That the race of man as a whole does not die by the death or
fall of Adam, neither does the race of man as a whole rise again
by the resurrection of Christ."   Now, Pelagius makes the
point that in Christ, who is sinless, death does not appear as the
punishment of sin.[3]   Augustine ignores the point in his answer
that Christ died by His own power, for in so saying he admits
Pelagius' case that death is not in fact universally the punishment for sin, for there is one example to the contrary.

More serious, because involving the very centre of the

---

[1] *Nature and Destiny of Man*, p. 262.   [2] Cf. *De Perf. Iust.*, vii, 16.
[3] Aug., *De Nat. et Grat.*, xxiv, 26.

Christian religion, is the question, legitimately to be asked of and by people who take the Incarnation seriously, whether the fact that Jesus' sinless life as Perfect Man is not itself a testimony to the fact that such a life is possible for any man. The Pelagians do not seem to have presented the argument, and Jesus is not among Pelagius' examples of sinlessness. But in the "libellus fidei" directed to Innocent, he sees reason to anathematize those who declare that by the Incarnation Jesus limited His moral capacity. Jerome, against whom this is perhaps directed, anticipates the point, and meets it by arguing the imperfections under which Jesus stood.[1] He does not go to the extent of suggesting that these were moral imperfections, and much of the argument of the Dialogue suffers from a defective understanding of the distinction between ethical and non-ethical qualities. But it serves to bring the matter to the surface. Augustine would no doubt meet it by saying that the virgin birth freed Jesus from the inherited taint of original sin. In general there is a tendency to treat Jesus as unique in such a way that no deductions may be drawn from His life bearing on the wider life of the rest of mankind. But this is in effect to deny the Incarnation. Anxiety to preserve the absolute uniqueness of the truth leads to a denial of the truth itself. "We have not a high priest who cannot be touched with a feeling for our infirmities; but one who was in all points tempted as we are, yet without sin."[2] To deny the right to judge Jesus as man is to deny this; to deny this is to deny what Christianity has always asserted as its central truth. To accept Jesus as man is to accept the possibility of human sinlessness, and to walk with Pelagius.

Failure to face this single fact has marred more than one modern attempt to reinterpret the doctrine of original sin against Pelagius. One example will suffice. William Temple put forward the idea that original sin is represented by the fact that the child is from its birth unavoidably self-centred. It cries because it is hungry, or thirsty, or uncomfortable, or lonely; it demands food or drink or comfort or motherly love for itself. This is an inescapable fact of human existence, and in putting self at the centre, the child fails to put God at the

[1] Jer., *Dial.*, ii, 11, 14-7.　　[2] Hebr. iv. 15.

centre. This is estrangement and sin. Temple's view, as usual, combines a fresh and acute insight with a clear and cogent exposition. But it ignores the equally irreducible fact that the same must have been true of Jesus, and to attribute sin (in this sense) to all mankind is to attribute sin (in this sense) to Him.

GRACE AND FREEWILL

But from where does the power to do good come? Jesus Himself in St. John's Gospel says "I can of Myself do nothing."[1] "The Son can do nothing of Himself."[2] Paul makes his plea "By the grace of God I am what I am : and His grace which was bestowed upon me was not found vain : but I laboured more abundantly than they all : yet not I, but the grace of God which was with me."[3] "God works in you both to will and to do."[4] "It is not of him that wills nor of him that runs but of God that has mercy."[5] And Augustine comments "O blessed Paul, O mighty preacher of grace, let me speak fearlessly . . . : your merits receive their crown of reward, but your merits are gifts from God."[6] So again "Even if men do good things which pertain to God's service, it is He Himself that brings it about that they do what He commanded."[7] And the implication of his famous prayer "Da quod iubes et iube quod vis"[8] is the same. Similar testimony is found throughout the history of the Church. Anselm writes "What a man has not from himself, but from God, he ought to regard as not so much his own as God's. For no one has from himself the truth which he teaches, or a righteous will, but from God,"[9] and he too uses in a prayer the words "Whatsoever our heart rightly wills, it is Thy gift." Thomas à Kempis portrays Christ as saying "They glory not of their own merits, for they ascribe no goodness to themselves but all to Me."[10] We have already looked at the tenth article of the Church of England : "We have no power to do good works, pleasant and acceptable to God,

---

[1] John v. 30. [2] *Ib.*, v. 19. [3] 1 Cor. xv. 10.
[4] Phil. ii. 13. [5] Rom. ix. 16.
[6] Aug., *De Gest. Pel.*, xiv, 35. This and several other references in this paragraph I owe to D. M. Baillie's admirable book *God was in Christ*, though it should be said that his version of this particular passage is a little peculiar.
[7] Id. *De Praedest. Sanct.*, 19. [8] Id. *Conf.*, x, 29.
[9] Anselm, *Cur Deus Homo*, i, 9. [10] à Kempis, *Imitatio Christi*, iv, 58.

without the grace of God by Christ preventing us, that we may have a good will, and working with us, when we have that good will." The Westminster Confession speaks to similar effect : "Their ability to do good works is not at all of themselves but wholly from the Spirit of Christ. And that they may be enabled thereunto, besides the graces they have already received, there is required an actual influence of the same Holy Spirit to work in them to will and to do of his good pleasure."[1] A recent litany contains the words "For the desire and power to help others, and for every hope and aspiration which lead us on toward better things, we praise Thee, O God." Harriet Auber's hymn, quoted earlier, expresses the same sentiment, that

> Every virtue we possess,
> And every victory won,
> And every thought of holiness
> Are His alone.[4]

The scholars, Hoskyns and Davey, deeply imbued with the New Testament and the Johannine understanding of Jesus, write that goodness is not a human achievement : it comes from God. "No New Testament thinker could think of Jesus in Pelagian terms."[3]

These are weighty witnesses, whether taken individually, or, so to say, in the lump. But there is another side to our experience, of equal validity, and that is our knowledge of our own freewill. It is there that Augustine lapses alike from perfect logic and from common human experience. Augustine declared that the will was free but that it was not always good. "Semper est autem in nobis voluntas libera, sed non semper est bona. Aut enim a iustitia libera est quando servit peccato, et tunc est mala : aut a peccato libera est quando servit iustitiae et tunc est bona."[4] This is mere verbal juggling, and confuses two separate and distinct meanings of the word "free." Further, he pours ridicule upon the "balance" theory of the Pelagians : "Libra tua quam conaris ex utraque parte per

---

[1] *Westminster Confession*, xvi, 3.
[2] Harriet Auber, *Hymn on the Holy Spirit*.
[3] Hoskyns and Davey, *The Riddle of the New Testament*, p. 255.
[4] Aug., *De Grat. et Lib. Arb.*, 15.

aequalia momenta suspendere, ut voluntas quantum est ad malum, tantum etiam sit ad bonum libera."[1] Yet this is exactly what he himself says of Adam: "Posset enim perseverare si vellet: quod ut nollet de libero descendit arbitrio, quod tunc ita liberum erat ut bene velle posset et male."[2] He does not escape the difficulty by making a distinction in the concept of grace. "Prima est enim qua fit ut habeat homo iustitiam si velit; secunda ergo plus potest qua etiam fit ut velit." If this be held, then the dispute becomes a dispute of names not ideas, for the first is what Pelagius means by free will. But even so the sway of grace is not unchallenged, for the experience of falling away after baptism is unquestioned, and free will, in the normal sense, has to reappear to account for this. Hence in the treatise "De dono perseverantiae" and elsewhere, it almost seems as if Augustine places perseverance, implicitly attributed to man's free will, above grace, and makes it the means of salvation. Augustine's whole treatment of free will is, in short, confused. It is bound to be if he is going to attempt to reconcile predestination and free will in any other way than the Stoics, who claimed that man was simply free to assent or otherwise to the predetermined course of events.

Now the fulcrum upon which the controversy with Pelagius turned was the meaning of grace. Pelagius and Augustine were agreed that we are what we are by grace of God. But Pelagius was speaking of "general grace" and Augustine of "special grace." Special grace came from the sacrifice of Jesus upon the Cross. It was mediated through baptism *ex opere operato*. Baptism administered *in articulo mortis* could thus guarantee salvation, and in every case brought about the condition in which good works could be done meritoriously, but for the unbaptized who were living outside the fold of grace there was no merit attaching to good works. This view seems decidedly alien from the spirit of Jesus, as expressed towards the end of the Sermon on the Mount,[3] or in the parable of the Good Samaritan, or that of the Sheep and the Goats. Pelagius asserted that the general grace of God in the endowment of human nature enabled us, if we were willing, to perform His

---

[1] Aug., *Op. Imp.*, iii, 117. [2] Id. *De Corrept. et Grat.*, 11.
[3] Matt. vii. 21–3.

will. It is sometimes said that this theological difference reflects a psychological difference between those whom it is fashionable to call the "once-born" and the "twice-born." There are those whose growth in the Christian life is gradual and steady. They are brought up in Christian homes, surrounded by Christian love, and continually assimilate themselves to their environment. Others, among whom Paul and Augustine are certainly to be numbered, are converted in a moment of cataclysmic decision. They can point, as the others cannot, to the very day and hour when they became Christian, when God called them.[1] Sometimes this distinction is used in defence of the position that there are two ways to God, equally valid, and which we tread is a matter of personal need. Sometimes it implies that the once-born are "second-class" Christians, who do not know the depths of Christian experience, and who are swollen with a false conceit of their own righteousness, instead of God's manifold and great mercies. But to explain away the Pelagian controversy in these terms is to oversimplify, and to ignore psychological realities. For Pelagius' youth was not easy, it was stormy, and we have already seen the seriousness with which he regarded the sin in his own life and all around him.

We have already examined Pelagius' mature statement of his own position, and it remains briefly to restate it. In any course of action there are three elements, "posse," "velle" and "esse." The first comes from God, the second from man, the finished work is the product of the co-operation between God and man. That a man possesses the possibility of willing and effecting any good work comes from God alone. This faculty does not depend upon the others, but the others do depend upon this. Thus to speak of the possibility of sinlessness is to praise not man, but God, from whom alone this possibility comes. But God goes further. Just as the Father went to meet the Prodigal Son, so He comes to meet us. He sets before us enlightenment, inspiration, example and encouragement. He sustains us in the action of fulfilling His will. From this last it may be seen, as one so unsympathetic to the Pelagians as Mozley realized, that the charge that Pelagius confined the

[1] For a very interesting discussion of these issues see A. D. Nock, *Conversion*.

sphere of grace to the initial endowment of human nature cannot be sustained. Julian described the operations of grace as sanctifying, restraining, inciting, and illuminating the human soul. Pelagius anathematized those who denied the necessity of the assistance of God's grace in every single action. In other words grace meant the initial endowment together with what Augustine called "co-operating" grace. What he could not accept was prevenient grace in Augustine's sense, an irresistible power, independent of the will, which forced the will.

The truth is that we are here face to face with one of those paradoxes of Christianity the grasp of which was G. K. Chesterton's major contribution to contemporary Christian thinking. The freedom of our will is an inescapable fact of experience. Even in the most holy and awesome moment of the Christian life, the moment when God calls to us, it is we who have to make answer. We have to say "Speak for Thy servant hears."[1] We have to say "Here am I; send me."[2] And we can remonstrate with God, as Jeremiah remonstrated,[3] and we may even reject the call and go away sorrowful because of great possessions which we prize too highly.[4] A friend told Holman Hunt that his familiar picture "The Light of the World" was unfinished, for the door outside which Jesus stood had no handle. The painter replied "That door is the door to the human heart: it opens from the inside only." In the call of the Christian, in every response to God, there is no constraint, however great the divine imperative. But, recognizing that, when the event is now passed, our impulse is, and is rightly, to give all the praise to God. Light shines from us to men that they may praise not us, but our Father in Heaven.[5] The same experience is found in those who know that they must freely turn to God in penitence, and yet know that the penitence itself comes from God.

[1] 1 Sam. iii, 10.
[2] Isa. vi. 8.
[3] Jer. i. 6, cf. xx.
[4] Matt. xix. 22; Mk. x. 22.
[5] Matt. v. 16.

> Ah, Lord! if Thou art in that sigh,
> Then hear Thyself within me pray;
> Hear in my heart Thy Spirit's cry,
> Mark what my labouring soul would say;
> Answer the deep unuttered groan,
> And show that Thou and I are one."[1]

There is no logical means of effecting a complete reconciliation between these two facts of experience. But any view of the Christian life which does not have room for both of them is in some measure inadequate.

There is a sense in which it is true to say that the divergence between Augustine and Pelagius is due to a difference of emphasis within the totality of this picture. Thus Augustine lays his stress upon the divine initiative, Pelagius upon the human response. In any real meeting of God and man there must be both. Augustine won in part because the Church, seeing how God is greater than man, and the divine initiative greater than the human response, felt that his emphasis was right. But as Augustine formulated his full theory of predestination he left no room for human freedom. Pelagius' emphasis was not objective; it did not arise from any denial of the initiative or power of God. Indeed Pelagius in some ways made more of the power of God than Augustine, for he saw in Augustine's denial of the possibility of sinlessness a derogation from God's power. Pelagius was accepting as common ground with Augustine the initiative of God. But upon that common ground he wished also to assert man's free response. This he did by his division of any action into "posse," "velle" and "esse." It is hard to see that he was wrong.

THE RELATIONSHIP BETWEEN GOD AND MAN

On the relationship between God and man three things should be said. First, as the last section should have made clear, that in any encounter between man and God there is a two-way movement. No matter how great the divine initiative it stops short of constraint. There must be a free human response. It was with this response that Pelagius was concerned. Not because he ignored or neglected the other, but because he was a moralist not a theologian, and his aim was

[1] Charles Wesley, *Jesus if still the same Thou art.* Based on Romans, vii.

practical not theoretical. He was driven into the theoretical considerations, partly because he felt the prevalent theology of Augustine laid insufficient stress upon the human response even to the point of denying it any place at all, and partly from the opposition which his presentation of his exhortations received at the hands of the orthodox.

Secondly Pelagius is weak in his understanding of the Holy Spirit. This follows from the last point. Augustine with his strong central stress upon God's activity, sees that man can only find fulness of living if God acts in and through him. Love, for example, is spread in our hearts by the active operation of the Holy Spirit.[1] Pelagius rightly says that the test of a life thus inspired by God, and directed by His Spirit, is in its fruits, but we have seen from the commentaries that he inclines almost to suggest that if we of our own resources live a life of long-suffering, meekness, patience and love, then that is identical with having the Spirit living in us. He could have preserved the truth he did not wish to lose better by saying that we have two responsibilities upon us, to open our hearts to the Spirit, and to obey His directions in our practical living.

But if here Pelagius failed to do justice to the riches of Christian experience, in his understanding of the kindling power of the love of God he reached the heights. Augustine was well aware how one human heart takes fire from another. "Namque ex amante alio accenditur alius." But he is so deeply impressed with the transcendent majesty of God that he does not see the source of that fire in God's love for man. For Augustine such words as "amor," "dilectio," "caritas Dei," regularly mean man's love for God, and it causes him no little puzzlement to find in scripture references to God's love for man. Because love springs from need, and God cannot need man. He is reduced to supposing that it is because of the use to which God puts us that He may be said to love us. "Otherwise I am at a loss to discover in what way He can love us."[2] But it never became an effective part of his thinking, and it is particularly striking that in his commentary upon St. John's Gospel, he has literally no comment upon iii. 16, "God so

[1] Aug., *De Spir. et Lit.*, xxxiii, 57.
[2] Aug., *De Doct. Chr.*, i, 34.

loved the world," and in the epistles on 1 John iv. 8 ff. "God is love," he has nothing to say apposite. Of a free love springing from and.expressing the very nature of God he seems to have had no conception. And it is just here that his doctrine of grace seems intolerably harsh. Augustine is overwhelmingly conscious of the immeasurable mercy of God towards those sinners whom He freely pardons. He cannot treat the whole doctrine with objectivity; he is dominated by what it means to himself. He judges, and can only judge, from inside the process, not outside it. But the great bounty of the doctrine of election cannot shut out from us that with it goes an uncompromising doctrine of rejection. And the harshness of Augustine's outlook at this point is due to the fact that in his philosophy grace has its origin in the arbitrary will of God, and not in His love. Pelagius has a far juster awareness that our love springs from the love that is the nature of God, and that we love Him because He first loved us.

THE LAW AND THE GOSPEL

One of the secondary issues was whether the law and the gospel have the same power in bringing man to God. This was an early assertion of the Pelagians, but one which they later abandoned. It was natural to expect some such assertion to be made in the extremity of the first challenge to orthodoxy. If God's grace was revealed through teaching and example, then the teaching of the Law and example of its adherents must be a means to righteousness. Further if sinlessness was actually found in the Old Testament, there must be the means to that sinlessness. The clause formed part of the indictment of Caelestius at Carthage, and Pelagius at Diospolis. On the latter occasion Pelagius disavowed it, anathematized those who held it, and explained his position to be simply that the Law assisted men to virtue.

INFANT BAPTISM

In a recent work on Augustine, Professor Burleigh writes "The Pelagian controversy actually has much less to do with "merit" than with the supernatural effects of baptism."[1] This

---

[1] J. H. S. Burleigh, *The City of God*, pp. 181–2.

is not in fact true. The discussion of baptism, though recurrent relates principally to the views of Caelestius, and to the early stages of the dispute, and the effect of baptism was common ground between the orthodox party and the Pelagians : it was agreed that baptism blotted out sin. They were not agreed that in the newly-born infant there was any sin to be blotted out.

The Pelagians reconciled their views with current Church practice, which they accepted, in two ways. In the first place, they suggested that from the moment of birth the infant is capable of sinning, and therefore, by the time the baptism was administered, in fact stood in need of it. In this way they were able sincerely to claim that they acknowledged one baptism for the remission of sins, and to assert their orthodoxy in Church practice without need to inquire more deeply into the precise grounds for that orthodoxy.

Secondly, they suggested that though unbaptized infants were not damned, baptism led to a higher sanctification. They made a distinction between salvation or eternal life, and the kingdom of heaven; the latter was the peculiar salvation of the Christian, and baptism was the gateway thereto. This is clearly put later by Julian : "We do not baptize for the purpose of freeing from the claim of the devil, but that those who are the work of God may become His children, as pledges of His love, that those who have come forth from God's tuition may be still further advanced by His mysteries, and that those who bear the work of nature may attain to the gifts of grace, and that their Lord, who has made them good by creation, may make them better by renovation and adoption."[1] Baptism, in other words, is the instrument not of justification but of sanctification. Ince calls this distinction between the lower salvation and the higher entry into the kingdom of heaven "untenable."[2] He fails to notice that Augustine and orthodox Catholicism make a parallel distinction, only in the realm of damnation. There is a distinction of punishment. "The mildest punishment," writes Augustine, "indeed will be theirs who have added no sin besides original sin."[3] So too, Pope Gregory XIII, more

---

[1] Aug., *Op. Imp.*, v, 9.
[2] Art. Pelagius in Smith's *Dict. of Chr. Biog.*   [3] Aug., *Enchir. de Fid.*, 93.

recently: "Illorum autem animas qui in actuali mortali peccato, vel solo originali decedunt, mox in infernum descendere, poenis tamen disparibus puniendas."[1] And, more exactly, the penalty of original sin is exclusion from the full glory of the Beatific Vision, and no more. "Poena originalis peccati est carentia visionis Dei, actualis vero poena peccati est gehennae perpetuae cruciatus."[2]

One further fact in the consideration of baptism has already been mentioned. To Augustine baptism was the necessary precondition of merit attaching to good works. To Pelagius, given the same action and the same goodwill, the merit was independent of any sacramental administrations. But the Pelagians had a very pertinent challenge to the orthodox view in the question "If baptism effaces original sin, why are the children of baptized parents born into original sin?" This was treated as a quibble and never adequately answered. It is in fact a substantial criticism of the whole system.

A modern nonconformist is apt to find much of this whole discussion sterile and irrelevant. He sees the logic of Augustine's position, with its inevitable corollary of the damnation of unbaptized infants, and admires its consistency. But he finds it repulsive and unacceptable. Yet if you once accept the existence of original sin as a punishable fact of human experience—and if original sin makes no difference to our ultimate destiny it is not easy to see what it means—it involves accepting the damnation of those who are not by some means redeemed from it. To reject the damnation of unbaptized infants is to go a long way towards accepting the part of Pelagius' case that is really significant.

Death

We have already mentioned that one question was whether death did in fact enter the world as a punishment for Adam's sin. Although two of the original seven charges at Carthage centred upon this it was in fact a subsidiary question and none of the great issues of the controversy turned upon it.

Here it is enough to note that we are in this face to face with

---

[1] Greg., XIII, *Professio Fidei Graecis Praescripta.*

[2] Inn. III, *Decr.*, iii, 42, 3, cf. Thos. Aq. *Summa*, III, i, 4.

N

one of the great unsolved mysteries of life, the problem of pain and death. Orthodoxy has always sought to make the problems of sin and suffering one and the same, and a great deal of mental confusion has resulted from the use of the single word "evil" to cover both sin and suffering. In the two propositions "sin is evil" and "suffering is evil," the word has a different sense, and much of the talk about the necessity of choosing the lesser of two evils, and hence the impossibility of Christian perfectionism, errs at this point. The problems may be cognate but they are not identical, and it would appear that Jesus insisted on separating them, as opposed to the Pharisees who insisted on linking them.[1]

Certainly the position of Paulinus and Augustine was that death entered the world as a punishment for Adam's sin. The Pelagians admitted that death entered the world through Adam, in that he was the first to die, but not that that death was connected with the Fall, nor that the Fall was the cause of our own mortality.

This is a problem which neither orthodoxy nor heterodoxy has successfully solved. Certainly no crude equation of sin and suffering will meet the facts. Perhaps a solution may be sought through the words of Romans viii. "The world of creation cannot as yet see Reality, not because it chooses to be blind, but because in God's purpose it has been so limited—yet it has been given hope. And the hope is that in the end the whole of created life will be rescued from the tyranny of change and decay, and have its share in that magnificent liberty which can only belong to the children of God! It is plain to anyone with eyes to see that at the present time all created life groans in a sort of universal travail."[2] The most that we can say is that external imperfection and limitation is the necessary condition of free moral obedience. It is in the valley of the shadow of death that we learn not to fear evil. As J. S. Whale has said, Christianity cannot explain the origin of evil (in either sense) : it can teach us to face it and to conquer it.[3] But one wishes at this point that we had the positive guidance of Pelagius, and not what is in fact a mere negation.

---

[1] John ix. 1–3, but cf. Mark ii. 1–12.   [2] Rom. viii. 20–2 (tr. J. B. Phillips).
[3] J. S. Whale, *The Christian Answer to the problem of Evil.*

PRAYER

More important, and surprisingly neglected in most accounts of the controversy, is the subject of prayer. It was with a prayer of Augustine's that the first record of dissension is concerned. Pelagius reacted strongly, almost violently, from the words "Da quod iubes, et iube quod vis," partly, as we have seen, because they minimized the moral effort needed on the side of man, but partly also because they implied that we were asking God for what He had already granted to us. It was in a similar spirit that some of the Pelagians at Rome objected to the prayer "Lead us not into temptation." It was unthinkable that God would ever lead us into moral temptation, and improper in its implications to ask Him not to. Yet the words were dominical and therefore authoritative. Some other explanation must be found, and it was found in interpreting the words, rather forcedly, of physical peril, traffic-accidents, falling in with robbers and the like.[1]

The doubts of the Pelagians on these points are not without reason, but Augustine saw further. If it be wrong to pray to God for that which He has already placed within our powers, and if in the initial endowment of our human nature He has already placed within our powers the possibility of sinlessness, then there is no further need of prayer. So the synod at Carthage in 416 claimed that Pelagius' exaltation of freewill virtually did away with the need for grace and recourse to prayer, the convocation at Milevum saw the denial of prayer as one of the two great stumbling-blocks of the Pelagian position, and the canons of Carthage dealt in some detail with the true nature, meaning and purpose of prayer.

Yet Pelagius had his answer, which appeared in the treatise on freewill. For in the first place we have actually sinned, and therefore stand in need of the grace of God for which we may pray. And secondly God goes beyond the initial endowment of human nature. He co-operates with us—as he later said, not merely in every act but at every moment. He guides us and enlightens us, and for this gift of illumination we may properly pray. So it comes about that in his very praise of

[1] Aug., *Serm. Fr.*, i, 1.

the virtues of Demetrias, Pelagius lays upon her the duty of prayer.[1]

The fact is that Augustine, whose own prayers were so passionately personal, was in theorizing about prayer almost inclined to turn prayer, as he was almost inclined to turn the action of grace, into something purely mechanical. It is not possible to make of prayer a necessary or a limited relationship. Prayer is a free relationship between persons; it is converse with God. Even Pelagius did not wholly see this, when he sought to define the function of prayer as "illumination." But he was groping towards the truth.

Conclusion

John Wesley once stated that Pelagius was wrongly called a heretic, and that his so-called heresy was no more than holding that Christians may, by God's grace, "go on to perfection" and so fulfil the law of Christ. If a heretic is one who emphasizes one truth to the exclusion of others, it would at any rate appear that he was no more a heretic than Augustine. His fault was in exaggerated emphasis, but in the final form his philosophy took, after necessary and proper modifications as a result of criticism, it is not certain that any statement of his is totally irreconcilable with the Christian faith or indefensible in terms of the New Testament. It is by no means so clear that the same may be said of Augustine.

To this three things must be added. First, much that has been written about Pelagius is a loose expression of a general impression and is not based upon a detailed examination of his views. J. B. Mozley was one of the foremost English scholars in this particular period of Church History and its underlying theology. But when he wrote "The philosophical fault of Pelagianism was that it went upon ideas without considering facts" he did not realize that Pelagius went further than Augustine in his sombre estimate of the actual facts of human sin, and added to that the fact of self-knowledge in terms of his own personal responsibility for the sin in his own life, whereas the theorizing of Augustine left no room for this last fact.

[1] Pel., *Ep. ad Dem.*, 9–10.

When Niebuhr uses the word "Pelagian" as enough to dismiss a theory, however "plausible," without further examination, he is going upon ideas and refusing to face the facts. It was Pelagius who was always calling his critics to face the facts, alike of scriptural teaching and human experience. When they did this, he modified his view accordingly. Dean Church wrote "The fact of what is meant by original sin is as mysterious and inexplicable as the origin of evil, but it is obviously as much a fact. There is a fault and vice in the race, which, given time, as surely develops into actual sin as our physical constitution, given at birth, does into sickness and physical death." This is a typical piece of confused thinking. The obvious fact is that of universal sin; the rest is not obvious fact, but theoretical speculation. Pelagius would add a second fact in knowledge of guilt. Even Harnack, a far acuter critic, gave as his conclusion "Pelagian doctrine in its deepest roots is godless." But if to deny original sin as contrary to the goodness of God, and to maintain the need for human initiative in turning to the outstretched hand of God, and exercise of those moral faculties which we should not have were they not given us by God, in accordance with the pattern of life He has given to us, if this be godlessness, then terms have lost their meaning. There are two points at which Pelagius' theology may be justly criticized, the absence of any clear doctrine of the Atonement (I do not here suggest what doctrine might be acceptable, but only repeat that the Cross is not central to his thinking), and the weakness of his effective belief in the Holy Spirit. These are rarely mentioned. Instead attention is focussed upon his anthropology. Here his extremer statements were modified in face of justifiable criticism from Augustine and others. His final position seems to me at least to be sounder and to reflect the facts of experience more fairly than that of his critics.

The second point is this. The only cogent and effective answer ever given to Pelagius was given by Augustine and those who went all the way with him. And that involved the doctrines of total depravity (not of course in the sense of utter extinction of the light of God, but in the sense of a depravity from which no part of the human race is free) and arbitrary election; together with these went predestination, belief in the physical inheritance of the original taint through man's sexual nature, and the damnation of the unbaptized. More moderate formulations such as those of Orange or those of Trent do not really meet Pelagius' arguments. Augustine does, but at what a cost!

Thirdly, there is in all this something of historical accident. The semi-Pelagianism of John Cassian and his successors, because it did not actually deny inherited corruption of a sort, has not been completely laid outside the bounds of Catholic orthodoxy. Ironically, it was one of the school, Vincent of Lerins, who coined the famous phrase "quod ubique, quod semper, quod ab omnibus." The Council of Orange says practically nothing about the predestination which Augustine thought so important. The Council of Trent spoke of the results of the Fall simply as "the loss of holiness and righteousness." Augustine would have fought tooth and nail against all three. All conflicted with the majesty of his conception of God's purpose. And, as a matter of fact, though there are occasional Augustinians among the Catholic leaders, Leo I, Gregory I, or the Venerable Bede, Augustinianism never asserted itself as Catholic orthodoxy, except under the impact of the man's own personality, and it was the heretics Luther and Calvin, not the orthodox Catholics, who were the real heirs of Augustine.

The real issue was original sin. In the battle of texts honours are fairly even: there certainly appear to be conflicting views within the body of scripture. On three points Pelagius remains to be answered, first, the definition of sin and the nature of our moral responsibility, second, the nature of its physical transmission, third, the reconciliation of a belief in universal sin with the full humanity and yet the perfect sinlessness of Jesus.

Principal Sources

Primary : Augustine, Pelagius.

Secondary : G. de Plinval, *Pélage*; N. P. Williams, *The Ideas of the Fall and of Original Sin*; J. B. Mozley, *Augustinian Doctrine of Predestination*; F. R. Tennant, *Original Sin*; id., *Origin and Propagation of Sin*;

id., *Concept of Sin*; J. Oman, *Grace and Personality*; C. C. J. Webb, *Problems in the Relations of God and Man*; R. C. Moberly, *Atonement and Personality*; E. J. Bicknell, *Theological Introduction to the Thirty-Nine Articles of the Church of England*; H. D. Lewis, *Morals and the New Theology*; Arts. in Smith & Wace, *Dictionary of Christian Biography*; Hastings, *Dictionary of the Bible.*

APPENDIX I

THE WRITINGS OF PELAGIUS

The list that follows is based on de Plinval, *Pélage*, c.i. :—

1. Epistola exhortatoria. "Qui Aethiopem invitat" (P.L., 30, xxxii, 239–242).

2. Epistola de vera paenitentia. "Ad te surgo hominem" (P.L., 30, xxxiii, 242–245).

3. Epistola ad virginem devotam. "Audi filia" (P.L., 17, 579–598).

4. Epistola de contemnenda hereditate. "Cuncti mei sensus" (P.L., 30, ii, 45–50).

5. Tractatus de vera circumcisione. "Superiore epistola" (P.L., 30, xix, 188–210).

6. Liber de induratione cordis Pharaonis. "Perfectorum est" (ed. de Plinval : Fribourg, 1947).

7. Expositiones xiii epistularum Pauli. "Primum queritur" (ed. Souter, *Texts and Studies*, IX : Cambridge, 1926).

8. Liber de vita christiana. "Et ego peccator ultimus" (P.L., 40, 1031–1036; cf. 50, 380 ff.).

9. Tractatus de divitiis. "Mirarer quorumdam" (Caspari, 25–67).

10. Epistola de malis doctoribus et operibus fidei et de iudicio futuro. "Quantam de purissimae" (Caspari, 67–73).

11. Tractatus de divina lege. "Praesumptionem meam" (P.L., 30, iv, 55–60).

12. Tractatus de virginitate. "Quantam in caelestibus" (P.L., 30, xiii, 163–175 = C.S.E.L., i, 224–250).

13. Epistola de castitate. "Quamquam illius Christianitatis" (Caspari, 122–187).

14. Epistola ad iuvenem. "Humanae referunt litterae" (Caspari, 14–21).

15. Tractatus de possibilitate non peccandi. "Qualiter religionis" (Caspari, 114–119).

16. Consolatio. "Si Deus ac dominus noster" (P.L., 30, iv, 55–60).

17. Epistola ad Claudiam. "Lectis epistolis" (P.L., 20, 223–227 = C.S.E.L., i, 219–223).

18. Epistola ad Oceanum de ferendis opprobriis. "Diversorum opprobria" (P.L., 30, xii, 282–288).

19. Epistola ad Marcellam. "Magnam humilitati" (P.L., 30, iii, 50–55 = C.S.E.L., xxix, 429–436).

20. Epistola ad Caelantiam. "Vetus scripturae" (P.L., 22, 1204–1212 = C.S.E.L., xxix, 436–459; lvi, 329–356).

21. Epistola ad Demetriadem. "Si summo ingenio" (P.L., 30, i, 15–45).

22. Libellus fidei. "Credimus in Deum" (P.L., 45, 1716 = Mansi, iv, 355).

To this list may be added extracts and fragments as follows :—

23. Liber eclogarum
    apud Jerome, Dialogus adversus Pelagianos, I (P.L., 23, 495–510).

24. Tractatus de natura
    apud Augustine, De natura et gratia (P.L., 44, 247–290 = C.S.E.L., lx, 231–299 = Bright, Select Anti-Pelagian Treatises of St. Augustine, 59–117).

25. Tractatus de Trinitate
    fragmenta (Martini, Antonianum, xiii, 318–335 : Rome, 1938).
    fragmenta (Souter, P.B.A., ii, 435 : London, 1905).

26. Tractatus de libero arbitrio
    apud Augustine, De gratia Christi : de peccato originali (C.S.E.L., xlii, 123–206 = Bright, op. cit., 202–270).
    fragmenta (MS., Paris, 653; Souter, P.B.A., ii., 437–438 : London, 1905; J.T.S., xii, 32–35 : London, 1910–11).

27. Epistolae ad Livaniam
    apud Jerome, Dialogus adversus Pelagianos, III, 16 (P.L., 23).
    apud Mercator, Commonitorium Caelesti, IV, 3 (Mansi, iv, 296).
    fragmenta (MS., Vienna, 954 theol., Révue bénédictine, xxxiv, 265–275 : 1922).

28. Expositio Cantici Canticorum
    apud Bede (P.L., 91, 1066–1077).

29. Tractatus de bono constantiae
    apud Bede (P.L., 91, 1066–1077).

P.L.   Patrologium Latinum (Migne).
C.S.E.L.   Corpus Scriptorum Ecclesiasticorum Latinorum.
Mansi.   Sacrorum Conciliorum nova et amplissima collectio (Florence, 1759).
Caspari.   Briefe, Abhandlungen und Predigten aus den zwei letzten Jahrhunderten des Kirchlichen Altertums und dem Anfang des Mittelalters (Christiania, 1890).
P.B.A.   Proceedings of the British Academy.
J.T.S.   Journal of Theological Studies.

APPENDIX II

BIBLIOGRAPHY

This contains all the articles of direct relevance published during this century with which I am acquainted, together with a selection of earlier works, and of more recent works whose scope is somewhat wider. There are useful bibliographies under Loofs' two articles, and Gilson's book gives a valuable bibliography for Augustine. Because it is easy to get lost in a list of this kind, I have asterized one or two of the more important publications.

BAER, J: De operibus Fastidii britannorum episcopi (*Dissertatio inauguralis*), Nuremberg, 1902.

BALLERINI: Observationes (*P.L.*, 56, 1006–1042).

BARMBY, J.: Innocentius I (Smith & Wace: *Dictionary of Christian Biography*), 1887.

BARMBY, J.: Zosimus (Smith & Wace: *Dictionary of Christian Biography*), 1887.

BARONIUS: *Annales Ecclesiastici*, Antwerp, 1956.

*BRIGHT, W.: *Select Anti-Pelagian Treatises of St. Augustine*, Oxford, 1880.

BRUCKNER, A.: *Julian von Eclanum, sein Leben und seine Lehre*, Leipzig, 1897.

BRUCKNER, A.: *Quellen zur Geschichte des Pelagianisches Streites*, Tübingen, 1906.

BRUCKNER, A.: *Die vier Bücher Julians von Eclanum am Turbantius*, Berlin, 1910.

BURY, J. B.: The Origin of Pelagius (*Hermathena*, xiii, 26–35), 1905.

*CASPARI, C.P.: *Briefe, Abhandlungen und Predigten aus den zwei letzten Jahrhunderten des Kirchlichen Altertums und dem Anfang des Mittelaltars*, Christiania, 1902.

DAVIDS, T. W.: Julianus of Eclanum (Smith & Wace: *Dictionary of Christian Biography*), 1887.

DE BRUYNE, D.: Le Prologue Inédit de Pélage à la Première Lettre aux Corinthiens (*Revue Bénédictine*, xxiv, 257–263), 1907.

DE BRUYNE, D.: Etude sur les Origines de notre Texte Latin de Saint Paul (*Revue Biblique*, xii, 358–392), 1915.

DE PLINVAL, G.: Recherches sur l'oeuvre littéraire de Pélage (*Revue de Philologie*, lx, 10–42), 1934.

DE PLINVAL, G.: Le problème de Pélage sous son dernier état (*Revue d'Histoire Ecclésiastique*, xxxv, 5–21), 1939.

*DE PLINVAL, G.: *Pélage, ses écrits, sa vie et sa réforme*, Lausanne, 1943.

*De Plinval, G. : *Essai sur le style et la langue de Pélage*, Fribourg, 1947.

De Pressensé, E. : Augustinus (Smith & Wace : Dictionary of Christian Biography), 1887.

De Tillemont : *Mémoires pour servir a l'Histoire ecclésiastique des six premiers siécles*, xiii, 212 ff., Paris, 1702.

*Dill, S. : *Roman Society in the Last Century of the Western Empire*, London, 1898.

*Dinkler, E. : Pelagius (Pauly-Wissowa : *Real-Encyclopädie der classischen Altertumwissenschaft*), 1936.

*Duchesne, L. : *Histoire Ancienne de l'Eglise*, III, Paris, 1910.

Freemantle, W. H. : Hieronymus (Smith & Wace : *Dictionary of Christian Biography*), 1887.

Gammack, J. : Coelestius (Smith & Wace : *Dictionary of Christian Biography*), 1887.

*Garnier, J. : VII Dissertationes (*P.L.*, 48), First published Paris, 1673.

*Gilson, E. : *Introduction à l'étude de Saint Augustine*, Paris, 1929.

Haddan and Stubbs : *Councils and Ecclesiastical Documents relating to Great Britain and Ireland*, I, Oxford, 1869.

*Harnack, A. : *Lehrbuch der Dogmengeschichte*, iii, 4, Tubingen, 1910.

Haslehurst : *The Works of Fastidius*, London, 1927.

Hedde and Amann : Pélagianisme (Vacant-Mangenot-Amann : *Dictionnaire de Théologie catholique*, xii, 675–715), 1933.

Heffle-Leclercq : *Histoire des Conciles*, II, i, 118, Paris, 1908.

Holl : Augustins Innere Entwicklung (*Gesammelte Aufsätze*, III), Berlin, 1928.

Jacobi, J. L. : *Die Lehre des Pelagius*, Leipzig, 1842.

Jansen : *Augustinus*.

*Kidd, B. J. : *History of the Christian Church to A.D. 461*, III, Oxford, 1922.

Kirmer, I. : *Das Eigentum des Fastidius im pelagianischen Schrifttum*, St. Ottelier, 1938.

Klasen, F. : *Die Innere Entwickelung des Pelagianismus*, Freiburg, 1882.

Koch, H. : Pelagio e la lettera agli Ebrei (*Religio*, xi, 21–30), 1935.

Loofs, F. : *Leitfaden zum Studium der Dogmengeschichte 4te Aufl.*, Halle, 1906.

*Loofs, F. : Pelagius, gest. nach 418, und der pelagianische Streit Hauck : *Realencyklopädie fur protestantische Theologie und Kirche*, xv, 747–774), 1904.

*Loofs, F. : Pelagius, gest. nach 418, und der pelagianische Streit (Hauck : *Realencyklopädie fur protestantische Theologie und Kirche*, xxiv, 310–2), 1913.

Madoz, J. : La herencia literaria del presbitero Eutropio (*Estudios Ecclesiasticos*, 27–54), 1942.

Mangenot, E. : Saint Jérome ou Pélage-éditeur des Épîtres de St. Paul dans la Vulgate (*Revue du Clergé français*), 1916.

Marrou, H. I. S. : *Augustin et la Fin de la Culture antique*, Paris, 1938.

Martini, C. : Quattuor fragmenta Pelagio restituenda (*Antonianum*, xiii), 1938.

Mercati, G. : Some New Fragments of Pelagius (*J.T.S.*, viii, 526–535), 1905–06.

*Merlin, P. : Véritable Clef des Ouvrages de S. Augustin contre les Pélagiens, prouveé par l'état même des questions et des controverses qui sont traitées dans les ouvrages du Saint Docteur (*Mémoires de Trévoux*), Dec, 1736.

Montgomery : *Saint Augustine : Aspects of his Life and Thought*, London, 1914.

Morin, G. : Jean Diacre et la Pseudo-Jérôme sur les Épîtres de S. Paul (*Revue Benedictine*, xxvii, 113–117), 1910.

Morin, G. : *Études, Textes, Découvertes : Contributions à la Littérature et à l'Histoire des douze premiers siècles*, I, Paris, 1913.

*Mozley, J. B. : *Augustinian Doctrine of Predestination*, London, 1878.

Norisius : *Historia Pelagiana*, Padua, 1673.

Ottley : *Studies in the Confessions of St. Augustine*, London, 1919.

Phereponus, J. : *Appendix Augustiniana*, Antwerp, 1703.

Portalie, E. : Augustin (Vacant-Mangenot : *Dictionnaire de Théologie Catholique*, i, 2460–2461).

Quesnel, P. : Dissertatio XIII (*P.L.*, lvi, 959–1006), First published Paris, 1675.

Riggenbach, E. : *Unbeachtet gebliebene Fragmente des Pelagius-Kommentars*, Gutersloh, 1905.

Riggenbach, E. : *Die ältesten lateinischen Kommentare zum Hebräerbrief*, Leipzig, 1907.

Riggenbach, E. : Eine wichtige Entdeckung für die Pelagius-forschung (*Theologisches Literaturblatt*, xxviii, 73–75), 1907.

RIGGENBACH, E.: Neues über Pelagius (*Theologisches Literaturblatt*, xxviii, 425), 1907.

SCHOLTZ : *Glaube und Unglaube in der Weltgeschichte*, Leipzig, 1911.

SEECK : *Geschichte des Untergangs der antiken Welt*, Berlin, 1909–13.

SMITH, A. J.: The Latin Sources of the Commentary of Pelagius on the Epistle of St. Paul to the Romans (*J.T.S.*, xix, 162–230; xx, 55–65, 127–177), 1917–19).

SOUTER, A.: The Commentary of Pelagius on the Epistles of St. Paul (*Expositor*, i, 455–467), 1907.

SOUTER, A.: Prolegomena to the Commentary of Pelagius on the Epistles of St. Paul (*J.T.S.*, vii, 568–575), 1905–06.

SOUTER, A.: The Commentary of Pelagius on the Epistles of Paul : the Problem of its Restoration (*P.B.A.*, ii, 409–439), 1905–06.

SOUTER, A.: The Relation of the Roman Fragments to the Commentary in the Karlsruhe MS. (*J.T.S.*, viii, 535–536), 1906–07.

SOUTER, A.: Another New Fragment of Pelagius (*J.T.S.*, xii, 32–35), 1910–11.

SOUTER, A.: Freiburg Fragments of an MS. of the Pelagian Commentary on the Epistles of St. Paul (*J.T.S.*, xiii, 515–519), 1911–12.

SOUTER, A.: New Manuscripts of Pelagius (*Theologische Literaturzeitung*, xxxviii, 442), 1913.

SOUTER, A.: Pelagius and the Pauline Text in the Book of Armagh *J.T.S.*, xvi, 105), 1914–15.

*SOUTER, A.: Pelagius' Doctrine in Relation to his early life. (*Expositor*, i, 180–182), 1915.

SOUTER, A.: The Character and History of Pelagius' Commentary on the Epistles of St. Paul (*P.B.A.*, vii, 261–296), 1915–16.

SOUTER, A.: Pelagius' Text of Romans v. 12, with Comment (*Expository Times*, xxviii, 42–43), 1916–17.

SOUTER, A.: The Earliest Surviving Book of a British Author (*Contemporary Review*, cxv, 76–82), 1919.

*SOUTER, A.: Pelagius' Expositions of Thirteen Epistles of St. Paul (*Texts and Studies*, IX), Cambridge, 1922–31.

STERN, L. C., *Epistolae Beati Pauli glosatae glosa interlineali*, Halle, 1910.

*TROELTSCH : *Augustin : Die Christliche Antike und das Mittelaltar*, 1915.

TURNER, C. H.: Pelagius' Commentary on the Pauline Epistles and its History (*J.T.S.*, iv, 132–141), 1902–03.

USSERIUS : *Britannicarum Ecclesiarum antiquitates*, Dublin, 1639.

Vaccari : *Un commento a Giobbe di Giulano di Eclana*, Rome, 1915.

Von Schubert, H. : Die sogenannte Praedestinatus, ein Betrag zur Geschichte des Pelagianismus (*Text. und Untersuch.*, xxiv, 4), Leipzig, 1903.

*Vossius, G. J. : *Historiae de controversiis quas Pelagius eiusque reliquiae moverunt. libri* vii, Leiden, 1618.

*Wiggers, G. F. : *Darstellung des Augustinismus und Pelagianismus*, 1821–33.

Worter, F. : *Der Pelagianismus*, Freiburg, 1874.

Zimmer, H. : *Pelagius in Irland*, Berlin, 1901.

GENERAL INDEX

ELLERTON, JOHN, *Behold us, Lord*, 26
EPHESUS, council of, 115
EPIPHANIUS, associate of Jerome, 76
EULOGIUS, metropolitan of Caesarea, called synod of Diospolis, 86
EUSTOCHIUM, 74–5, 98
EUTROPIUS, bishop, document sent to Augustine, 62, 81, 160
EXAMPLE, Pelagius' views, 128–31

FAITH, problem of defining true Faith, 22–4, freewill the 'via media' to, 57, in Christ needless if no original sin, 69, demand that Pelagius should give profession of, 94, issues of Pelagianism outside central dogmas of, 104, Pelagius' views, 127–8, 154–8
FREEWILL, natural gift of God, 57, Pelagius' comment in letter to Demetrias, 59–60, makes freedom from sin possible, 67, comes together with grace in work of salvation, 79–80, Pelagius' views at synod of Diospolis, 87, exaltation of, by Pelagius and Caelestius, 93, treatise by Pelagius, 95, Pelagius' letter to Innocent, 99, Pelagius' theology, 137–41, controversy, 170–5
GRACE, forgiveness for backslider, 24, Augustine's views, 54–5, necessity of, 57, need for, 61, means to life without sin, 65–6, live without sin otherwise than by, 70, includes endowment of human nature, 70, comes together with freewill in work of salvation, 79–80, Pelagius' views at synod of Jerusalem, 84, Orosius' views at synod of Jerusalem, 84, Pelagius' views at synod of Diospolis, 88, importance to Augustine, 90, 'De Natura' denies necessity, 95, Pelagius admits necessity for salvation, 96, Pelagius' letter to Innocent, 99, Augustine's position, 100, Caelestius' position, 102, canons of Carthage, 111, Pelagius' belief in, 114, Pelagius' theology, 132–5, controversy, 170–5

HADDAN, *Remains*, 35–6
HARNACK, 164, 183
HEROS, bishop of Arles, behaviour in siege, 86, opposition to Pelagius, 90, letter to synod, 93, meeting with Caelestius, 101, denounced by Zosimus, 104–6
HILARY, toleration, 17, name used for buildings in Britain, 35, felicitates British church, 37, letter from Sicily, 61, concern about riches, 147
HOLY SPIRIT, loss of effective belief in, 21, Pelagius' views, 133–4, 176, Augustine's views, 176
HONORIUS, emperor, intervenes in Rome controversy, 110
HOSKYNS and DAVEY, *The Riddle of the New Testament*, 171
HUNT, HOLMAN, 174
HYPOSTASIANISM, 23

INNOCENT I, bishop of Rome, letters to John and Jerome, 80, appeal to his arbitration, 85, letter from synod of Carthage, 93, called local synod of Rome, 95, death, 95

JAMES, persuaded by Pelagius to renounce worldly riches, 46, 72, 147, encounter with Augustine, 66–71, remained layman, 146
JEROME, attitude to moral atmosphere of Empire, 7–11, attitude to wealth of clergy, 11, views of culture of age, 14, view of corruption of clergy, 19, views of monasticism, 26, meeting with Pelagius in Rome, 45, friend of Pelagius, 46, 72, letter to Demetrias, 59, one of great Church leaders, 73, birth and origins, 73, education and travel, 73–4, in Rome, 74, follower of Origen, 74, temper in controversy, 74, in Palestine, 75, scholastic writings, 75, liaison with Augustine, 75, controversies, 75, turns against Origen, 76, turns against Rufinus, 76, controversy with Pelagius, 77–81, escape in raid on monastery, 80, letter from Innocent, 80, view of synod of Diospolis, 89, letter to Augustine, 93, Pelagius' writing attributed to him, 116, takes priestly orders, 144, view of sinlessness of Jesus, 169

OROSIUS, fears of Jerome's heresy, 76, bitter opponent of Pelagius, 81, birth and origins, 81, opponent of heresy of Origen, 81, journey to Augustine, 81, journey to Jerome, 82, summoned to synod of Jerusalem, 82, meeting with Pelagius, 82, at synod of Jerusalem, 82-5, leaves Palestine for Carthage, 93, surprise at admission of layman to synod, 144

ORTHODOXY, Ambrose's victory over Arian Empress, 18, expression in Hypostasianism, 23, attitude to sex, 24, of church in Britain, 37, Pelagius dangerous enemy of, 42, of Augustine, 54, document circulating in Sicily, 62, suspicion of Jerome's, 74, Augustine as champion, 83, Pelagius' concern for, 91, Pelagius' statement of his position, 96-7, Caelestius protests his, 102, Pelagius' declared, 106, canons of Carthage, 111, Pelagius', 116-8, making problems of sin and suffering the same, 180

PALESTINE, Pelagius' visits to, 44-5, 50, 72, events in, ch. VI passim, Jerome in, 75, Orosius' visit to, 82, Pelagius in, 95-100, Caelestius' visit, 101-2, Pelagius leaves for Egypt, 114

PAMMACHIUS, friendship with Pelagius and Jerome, 45, 72, introduced Pelagius and Rufinus, 47

PATRICK, 35-6

PAULINUS, deacon of Milan, accuses Caelestius of heresy, 50-2, letter from Zosimus, 108, views of death, 180

PAULINUS of Nola, friend of Pelagius, 45, 47, 72, letter from Augustine, 100

PAULINUS, bishop of Sicily, document sent to Augustine, 62, 81, 160

PAX ROMANA, 2, 17

PELAGIANISM, Augustine's study of issues, 54-5, Marcellinus harried by Pelagians, 55, spreading in Carthage, 57, rife in Sicily, 61, Augustine's sermons against, 57-8, becoming systematized, 70, John's part in controversy, 76, Jerome's treatise against, 79, Orosius' arguments against, 85, views still spreading, 94, adherents at Nola, 100, general condemnation following Zosimus' judgment, 113-5, shadow of, 132-43, Ch. X passim

PELAGIUS, only known writer in early British Church, 35, called Brito, 39, origins, 39-41, birth, 41, education, 41-3, occupation, 43, in Rome, beginning of controversy, 44, appearance and character, 45-6, in Rome, 384-409, 47-8, most substantial works written, 47, joined by Caelestius, 48, in Sicily and Carthage, 49-50, emphasis on Christian living, 46, 50, 91, 146, in Palestine, 50, correspondence with Augustine, 58, letter to Demetrias, 59, intellectual argument subservient to righteous living, 70, living in Palestine, 72, wealthy and influential friends, 72, Rufinus incarnate to Jerome, 76, critic of Jerome's writings against Jovinian, 77, attempt at reconciliation with Jerome, 78, grew in esteem of some Jerusalem Christians, 80, meeting with Orosius, 82, summoned to synod of Jerusalem, 83, summoned to synod of Diospolis, 87, acquitted at Diospolis, 89, condemnation at Carthage, 93, letter to Innocent, 99, Zosimus declares his creed orthodox, 106, banished from Rome, 111, excommunicated, 113, longed for reconciliation with Augustine, 114, in Egypt, 114, commentary on Song of Songs, 114, lay vocation, 144-6

PELAGIUS, monk, referred to by Chrysostom, 44-5, critic of Jerome's writings, 77

PELAGIUS of TARENTUM, 39

PELAGIUS' THEOLOGICAL VIEWS, derivation from Origen, 44, heretical opinions imbied from Rufinus, 44, correspondence with Theodore of Mopsuestia, 44, Augustine's fundamental criticism, 69, following Christ's example, not receiving grace, 69, statement of position, 96-7, concern with moral exhortation, 118-9, Ch. VIII passim, force of example, 128-31, place of Cross, 164, absence of doctrine of Atonement, 183, Augustine's answer, 183-4

PHILOSOPHY, state of, in Empire, 14, Pelagius' knowledge of, 42

PLATO, Platonic Idea, 22, Theory of Ideas, 42, influence on Augustine, 53, influence on Pelagius, 130, *Republic* and *Gorgias*, 153

INDEX OF ANCIENT AUTHORITIES

INDEX OF SCRIPTURAL PASSAGES

(The references are to the Biblical passages and to
Pelagius' Commentaries on them.)